Death, Deeds, and Descendants
Inheritance in Modern America

SOCIAL INSTITUTIONS AND SOCIAL CHANGE
An Aldine de Gruyter Series of Texts and Monographs
EDITED BY
Michael Useem • James D. Wright

Mary Ellen Colten and Susan Gore (eds.), **Adolescent Stress: Causes and Consequences**

Clignet, Remi, **Death, Deeds, and Descendants: Inheritance in Modern America**

Rand D. Conger and Glen H. Elder, Jr., **Families in a Changing Society: Hard Times in Rural America**

Paul Diesing, **Science and Ideology in the Policy Sciences**

G. William Domhoff, **The Power Elite and the State: How Policy is Made in America**

Paula S. England, **Comparable Worth**

Paula S. England and George Farkas, **Households, Employment, and Gender: A Social, Economic, and Demographic View**

F. G. Gosling (ed.), **Risk and Responsibility**

Richard F. Hamilton and James D. Wright, **The State of the Masses**

Gary Kleck, **Point Blank: Guns and Violence in America**

James R. Kluegel and Eliot R. Smith, **Beliefs About Inequality: Americans' Views of What Is and What Ought to Be**

David Knoke, **Organizing for Collective Action: The Political Economies of Associations**

Dean Knudsen and JoAnn L. Miller (eds.), **Abused and Battered: Social and Legal Responses to Family Violence**

Robert C. Liebman and Robert Wuthnow (eds.), **The New Christian Right: Mobilization and Legitimation**

Theodore R. Marmor, **The Politics of Medicare** (*Second Edition*)

Clark McPhail, **The Myth of the Madding Crowd**

Clark McPhail, **Acting Together: The Organization of Crowds**

John Mirowsky and Catherine E. Ross, **Social Causes of Psychological Distress**

Carolyn C. and Robert Perrucci, Dena B. and Harry R. Targ, **Plant Closings: International Context and Social Costs**

Robert Perrucci and Harry R. Potter (eds.), **Networks of Power: Organizational Actors at the National, Corporate, and Community Levels**

David Popenoe, **Disturbing the Nest: Family Change and Decline in Modern Societies**

James T. Richardson, Joel Best, and David G. Bromley (eds.), **The Satanism Scare**

Bernard C. Rosen, **The Industrial Connection: Achievement and the Family in Developing Societies**

Alice S. Rossi and Peter H. Rossi, **Of Human Bonding: Parent-Child Relations Across the Life Course**

Roberta G. Simmons and Dale A. Blyth, **Moving into Adolescence: The Impact of Pubertal Change and School Context**

David G. Smith, **Paying for Medicare: The Politics of Reform**

Walter L. Wallace, **Principles of Scientific Sociology**

Martin King Whyte, **Dating, Mating, and Marriage**

James D. Wright, **Address Unknown: The Homeless in America**

James D. Wright and Peter H. Rossi, **Armed and Considered Dangerous: A Survey of Felons and Their Firearms**

James D. Wright, Peter H. Rossi, and Kathleen Daly, **Under the Gun: Weapons, Crime, and Violence in America**

Death, Deeds, and Descendants
Inheritance in Modern America

Remi Clignet

Aldine de Gruyter
New York

About the Author

Remi Clignet is Professor of Sociology at the University of Maryland, and is currently associated with ORSTOM, a French research institute dealing with problems of economic development. Dr. Clignet is the author of five books concerned with various facets of economic and cultural capital. His goal is to use the experience he has acquired writing this book to evaluate the impact of inheritance on the economic changes of Third World countries.

Copyright © 1992 Walter de Gruyter, Inc., New York
All rights reserved. No part of this publication may be reproduced or transmitted in any form or by any means, electronic or mechanical, including photocopy, recording, or any information storage and retrieval system, without permission in writing from the publishers.

ALDINE DE GRUYTER
A division of Walter de Gruyter, Inc.
200 Saw Mill River Road
Hawthorne, New York 10532

The paper used in this publication meets the minimum requirements of American National Standard for Information Sciences—Permanence of Paper for Printed Library Materials, ANSI Z39.48–1984.

Library of Congress Cataloging-in-Publication Data
Clignet, Remi.
   Death, deeds, and descendants : inheritance in modern America / Remi Clignet.
     p. cm. — (Social institutions and social change)
   Includes bibliographical references and index.
   ISBN 0-202-30398-5
   1. Family—United States.   2. Inheritance and succession—Social aspects—United States.   3. Wealth—Social aspects—United States. 4. Property—Social aspects—United States.   I. Title. II. Series.
HQ536.C55   1992
306.85'0973—dc20   91-40035
                                                                                               CIP

Manufactured in the United States of America
10 9 8 7 6 5 4 3 2 1

Contents

Preface ix

1 Challenges of a Study of American Inheritance 1

    Liberty and Equality in Inheritance: The Views of the French Revolution Model 10
    The American Historical Experience of Inheritance 13
    Romantic Motives versus Rational Efficiency 15
    Property and Inheritance 20
    The Outline of the Book 25

2 Inheritance and Reproduction 29

    Reproduction: The Historical Background of the Term 30
    Inheritance and Reproduction: The Challenge 32
    The Conscious or Unconscious Nature of Reproduction 33
    The Three Components of Reproduction: What Endures? 35
    The Specificity of Reproduction in American Society: The Evidence 41
    Determinants of Reproduction 44
    The Limits of the Notion of Reproduction 53
    Summary and Conclusions 57

3 The Burden of Proof in the Study of Heirship 59

    The Representativeness of Samples 60
    The Choice of a Sample of Estate Tax Returns 63

The Overall Demographic and Socioeconomic Profile of the Sample	71
The Validity of the Data	75
Conclusions	79

4 On the Variety of American Wealth — 81

The Relevance of the Theory of Segmented Labor Markets	81
On Patterns of Capital Formation	83
On the Distinct Forms of American Wealth	90
The Variability in the Composition of Estates in 1920 and 1944	99
The Composition of the Estate: An Overall Picture	102
The Diversity of the Composition of Estates	104
Conclusions	119
The Materialist Logic of Wealth Accumulation	119

5 Testacy and the Limits of Free Wills — 123

Death and Time	124
What Is Known about Testacy in the United States	126
The Role of Testacy in 1920 and 1944	133
Joint Property	134
The Role of Gifts *Inter Vivos*	135
The Incidence of Wills	137
Time Interval between Testacy and Death	140
The Incidence of Trusts	142
Testacy and the Control of Time	143
Instruments of Transfers as Instruments of Ordering Things and People	144
Conclusions	153

6 Bequests and Inequality between and within Families — 155

The Testators' Dilemmas	156
The Evidence	165

Determinants of Inequality	169
An Assessment of Inequalities among the 1920 and 1944 Decedents	170
The Variety of Forms of Inequality	177
Conclusions	186

7 Inheritance of Yesterday, Inheritance of Today 189

Inheritance and Reproduction: The Overall View	191
Mechanical and Interpretive Forms of Inheritance	193
The Relativity of the Results	203
Policy Implications	206

Notes 209

References 221

Index 232

Preface

As this book is the last work (albeit the only one of its kind) I have written in and on the United States, it represents a parting gift. In more than one way, it sums up the wisdom I have acquired teaching and doing research in American universities, wisdom that I would like to pass down to new social scientists.

Beyond or behind the melodic line of the argument, the wisdom I am referring to comprises four distinct legacies. First, the fact of the matter is that, willy-nilly, American social scientists act as if the world was a free marketplace sheltered from any institutional constraint. Take any textbook of sociology of education and count the number of analyses concerning the impact of federal courts on school revenues, on integration, or on student newspapers. There are very few. Take any textbook of industrial sociology and count the number of analyses concerning the impact of collective bargaining agreements, discussions of arbitration boards, or regulations of federal agencies on the daily lives of workers in the plant. There are very few. Take any textbook of sociology of the arts and count the number of analyses concerning the impact of censorship or of property rights on the life of artistic communities. There are none. Take finally any textbook of sociology of the family and count the number of analyses concerning the impact of courts on the incidence of divorce and of abortion. Again, the score is close to zero. The point is that sociologists act as if the legal aspects of social phenomena were trivial. This stance represents either a form of wishful thinking, or a strange blindness to institutional mechanisms. In either case, social scientists forget that the practices of all social actors depart consciously or unconsciously from the norms of the major groups to which they belong, and a fortiori from the institutional rules of the state or of the federal government. How is it possible to disregard such a source of significant variations in social interaction? My plea, then, is that we sociologists must pay more attention to the legal aspects of American social life.

Second, American familial life is richer and more diversified than what sociologists induce us to believe. Nothing is written on the differential status of sons-in-law and daughters-in-law. Very little (and whatever there is reads like a plea rather than a dispassionate speech) is written on the particular kind of stepchildren, who have one "natural" parent and another, "social," born with the remarrying of the first one. Against all the revolutions that have undermined American familial life, there are some signs that so called "archaic" forms of familial life are undergoing a renascence: for example, bonds between maternal grandparents and their grandchildren are richer and more interesting than what many observers induce us to believe. There are other signs that such matrilineal loyalties are not necessarily dead, or that their decline is not irreversible. My plea, then, is that we sociologists must identify forms of familial life that are seemingly submerged and assess the conditions under which they can be revived.

Third, the stress placed on familial structures and modes of interaction is not an end in itself. Even though family size declines, both matrimonial mobility and the structural as well as the ideological forces at work in society at large render increasingly problematic the definition of intergenerational loyalties. Correspondingly, what goes on between relatives is an increasingly important determinant of the social rank occupied by each of them in the larger society. My plea, then, is that we sociologists must remember that stratifications within and across families are linked.

Fourth and last, it seems increasingly misleading to act as if social science research was placed out of historical time. It is not. Sociology will enhance our understanding of social life as soon as it treats time, dynamics, evolution, and revolution as the most significant enigmas of current societies. My plea, then, is that we sociologists devote more attention to the meaning of time.

I thank Marshall Shumsky, Kenneth Kammayer, Edward Dager, Mark, Rachel, and Adam Schwartz, Jean Marc Philibert, and Sheldon Gittelman, who were kind enough to read parts of the text and to encourage me to go on. Whatever merits the book may have, I owe to them, even though I remain responsible for the "warts" and the shortcomings of the work. I also thank the Internal Revenue Service for having trusted my intuition at a time when it was not obvious to do so. Indeed, the material support I got has been sparse. I gratefully acknowledge a summer grant from the University of Maryland.

As it is, I would like to offer the manuscript to my "ancestors" in the field who have helped me, and more specifically to Jeff Rosenfeld, Sonya Salamon, and Malcolm Voyce, who gave me a number of leads on the literature, Judith Cates, who gave me a lot of background material with-

Preface

out even knowing me, Mike Alexander, Janet Mc Cubbin, and Marvin Schwartz, who helped me find my way through the maze of the appropriate IRS file, Alan Fertziger, who accepted gracefully to act as a sounding board, and Bruce Wiegand, who acted as my stage manager. My only hope is that individually and collectively, they feel that the text matches the support they gave me, in good as well as in bad times.

Remi Clignet

1
Challenges of a Study of American Inheritance

The myth of Horatio Alger is not only about going from rags to riches. Insofar as the myth is also about progress and the promises of the future, those who believe in it reject as despicable all material and symbolic transfers received from preceding generations, including inheritance.

Contempt for the marks of the symbolic and material continuity of familial groups is more accentuated during certain historical eras and in certain cultures than in others. It was a trademark of the French Revolution. It tends to be a recurrent leitmotiv of the American ethos. The United States is supposed to be the promised land for individuals who have lost a cherished political or religious freedom, or even their economic well-being. American cultural leaders keep inviting new immigrants to exorcize the demons of their pasts by erasing the effects of these losses and worshiping the unfolding of future seasons. When Margaret Mead noted that Americans are immigrants both in space and in time, she was suggesting that her fellow citizens often impute their failures to the traditions and the history of the countries from which they originate. Implicitly at least, a faith in the melting pot, in the shining future, and in the upward mobility that goes with Americanization justifies social amnesia. Implicitly, it calls also for the elimination of intergenerational transfers from the grammar of laudable or acceptable motives. It calls for a society without fathers.[1]

In their pragmatism, many American social scientists seek to justify the elimination of the father image from popular culture. More specifically, they try to find scientific reasons to do away with inheritance or—to use more technical jargon—with transfers *mortis causa*. On the right side of the political continuum, functionalist analysts such as Kingsley Davis and Wilbert Moore (1945) or Melvin Tumin (1967) assert implicitly that to be the beneficiary of bequests is incompatible with the work ethic and the notion of self-reliance, which are both at the very core of the American exceptionalist ideology. These writers believe in the merits of giving but certainly not of receiving. In their eyes, achievement requires delayed gratification, certainly not indulgence in unwarranted windfalls. For them, the success of the American experiment results from the fact that their fellow citizens are self-made persons who are independent of their pasts.

On the left side of the same political continuum, Samuel Bowles and Herbert Gintis (1986) view the money transferred by inheritance as both a symbol and an instrument of inequality and oppression. In their eyes, however, bequests or estates pertain only to big or old money. But in positing that intergenerational solidarity is only an obsolete leftover of some *ancien régime*, they eliminate altogether the need for any empirical exploration of the current forms taken by intergenerational solidarity.

Both functionalist and radical analysts concur that resources transferred *mortis causa* are sinful or illegitimate. The former see them as marking the unfair triumph of ascription over achievement; the latter view them as instruments of the privileges unfairly exerted by undeserving elites. Both would probably consider it desirable to confiscate individual bequests for the benefit of the larger community. Yet, the stress that both sets of analysts place on self-reliance, albeit for opposite reasons, leads them to reject any intervention of the capitalist state. For functionalists, this intervention could not but hinder and hamper individual achievement. For their radical counterparts, its effects would be illusory, since they view existing elites as constantly subverting the authority of the state. In short, the two positions engender a number of internal contradictions. Even though their respective champions see inheritance as socially dysfunctional, they do not believe that anything should be done about it. Indeed, they treat intergenerational relations as a nonproblem.

In contrast, I invite readers to withhold judgment, to assume temporarily that the material and symbolic transfers that constitute inheritance are neither good nor bad, that they are not only about big or old money, and that they are not only about enjoying a windfall, but also about being held liable for the debts incurred by decedents. The death of a relative forces survivors to take a variety of actions to close his or her books and, inter alia, to pay his or her debts. In this sense, inheritance is about the economics of love and hence about the economics of both giving and receiving. In view of the corresponding symbolic properties of inheritance, the purpose of this book is to identify in what sense patterns of the accumulation and distribution of wealth reflect the symbols specific to the decedents' major reference groups, notably, to their age, their gender, their occupation, and their national origin. It is also to ascertain the stability of the ensuing contrasts.

Herein lies the thrust of the argument: As I seek to undermine the dimensions of intergenerational continuity and to locate inheritance within the texture of American social and cultural fabric, I want to make four contributions to the existing literature. The first one concerns the impact of transfers *mortis causa* on social stratification and on the rank ordering of distinct families. The second concerns the symbolic quality of such transfers and the extent to which they mirror familial solidarities and hierarchies. The third underlines the role of transfers *mortis causa* as mechanisms of social and cultural stability, and highlights the need to introduce time dimensions in social analyses. The fourth and final contribution of the book is to explore what the benign neglect of sociologists for transfers *mortis causa* tells us about the social ambiguities of the discipline.

Inheritance and Social Stratification

The challenge is to ascertain the extent to which transfers *mortis causa* contribute to recurrent inequalities in the distribution of wealth across social groups. Even when and where this distribution proves to be stable, the origin of this stability remains still problematic: maybe material wealth is passed across generations and maybe some people are born with a silver spoon in their mouths; or maybe parents teach their children, generation after generation, how to seize opportunities and clear hurdles on their way to fortune. In the first case, the origin of the stability of inequalities is material; in the second, it is cultural, rooted either in the differential effectiveness of varying child-rearing practices that are all geared toward the same goal, or in the differential application of the same body of legal rules in favor of some groups at the expense of others.

Should we believe that inheritance is instrumental in perpetuating such inequalities, we need to explain the links between *inter-* and *intra-*family differences in wealth (Sheshinsky and Weiss 1982). The stability of the boundaries between social classes, and hence between families, may depend on the extent to which siblings get differing bequests and/or make different use of the corresponding windfalls. Stories of merry widows or prodigal sons who gobble up their shares of the familial war chest and condemn some or all of their dependents to downward mobility abound both in fiction and in the sociological literature.

But insofar as there are inter- and intrafamilial differences in the strategies concerning investments, what is their origin? The dynamics governing social stratification may be, at least in part, conditioned by the nature of the assets acquired by Americans. In the same way that there is a segmentation of labor markets, there should be a segmentation of various forms of capital. Differing types of assets involve differing risks and differing rewards over differing periods of time. Success in dealing with real estate, bonds, or stocks requires distinct modes of adaptation.

Yet, one can challenge this materialistic assumption by taking a cultural view of human phenomena to argue that differences in the returns to various types of capital or in the bequests generated by such assets are all ideological stories that the owners of distinct forms of capital, or at least the wealthiest of them, elaborate a posteriori in order to justify their investments, and their success.

Inheritance and Familial Bonds

The nature and the direction of transfers *mortis causa* reveal a great deal about the structure of familial networks and the distributions of loves and hatreds. In a synchronic perspective, the analysis of these transfers says as much about the relative emphasis placed on conjugal ties, or on relations between siblings, as on the stress placed on the bonds between ascendants and descendants. Analyses of the constraints imposed by public authorities on wills should also highlight disparities between formal and informal definitions of the family. Thus, courts intervene to remind spouses and parents of their obligations toward the relatives they no longer like. For instance, the first wives of diplomats who have remarried are entitled to their own share of the pensions to be disbursed to their husbands by the State Department (Weitzman 1985).

In a more diachronic perspective, the analysis also offers a sense of continuities and reversals in the evolution of familial obligations and feelings. For example, despite the American commitment to progress, successive generations of Irish- and German-American farmers still retain the rules of descent followed by their forebears in their countries of origin. But are American farmers exceptional on that score? What traditions are retained by the various national groups present in the United States? And for how long? As another example, despite or perhaps because of rising divorce rates, some maternal grandparents use the additional resources they derive from their newly acquired social security benefits for helping their grandchildren who suffer from their divorced mothers' downward mobility. In this sense, the more the outside world changes and becomes threatening, the more one hopes that the family remains a haven in a heartless world. Heirship practices and ideologies tell us a lot about the stability of the boundaries separating familial groups from one another. They tell us as much about the stability of interpersonal loves and hatreds.

Inheritance and Cultural Stability

To argue that inheritance reproduces social arrangements and contributes to the perpetuation of social hierarchies as well as of familial loyalties is to underline the stability of all human organizations. Regardless of the social system studied, the first challenge raised by the argument is to ascertain the speed, the direction, and the intensity of changes in the composition of individual investments, or in the number and the profile of the beneficiaries of bequests or gifts. The second challenge is to identify time lags between changes in the amount and type of wealth accumulated by individuals or by communities, and changes in the personal or collective ideological orientations concerning the definitions of the ideal assets to be acquired, of the timing as well as the amount of the bequests to be made, and of the profile of their beneficiaries (Ogburn 1955). In the United States as in Europe, the persistence of privileged classes may often be explained only by taking into account the slow pace with which ideological changes affect individual or collective practices (Mayer 1980). The final challenge is to determine whether the relationship between ideological and material changes is reversible. Do decedents abandon the heirship practices of their forebears whenever the "going gets rough" and restore them under more favorable circumstances? I will allude several times to the persistence of Irish and German heirship practices in the United States. Is this persistence continuous? Or have these peoples rediscovered their roots, and if so, when and how?

In sum, the purpose of this book is to assess the continuity that governs the links between familial bonds and the relations between social groups. People divorce, mourn their spouses, remarry, disinherit some of their children before forgiving them, and keep riding the merry-go-round of feelings. Analogous tensions between stability and change characterize social stratification. Exclusive reference to the poor or to the rich—the opposite ends of the social hierarchy—is not sufficient to explain disparities in individual socioeconomic trajectories. The fact of the matter is that, regardless of their positions on the social ladder, some people go up and down for reasons that have little to do with their surroundings. Both oppressors and oppressed vary in their abilities to take advantage of new opportunities at the right time or to recognize the seasons that call for saving rather than for spending. For this reason, to view, as I do, the basis of social or cultural reproduction as being as much endogenous as exogenous is to emphasize the need for diachronic studies of both stratification and familial loves or hatreds.

Inheritance and the Sociology of Knowledge

Inheritance triggers extreme reactions. Despite the belief of many Americans in the infinite opportunities that their land offers, many of them would like to believe that wealth is exclusively monopolized by the scions of already rich families, or that poverty breeds poverty.

While the myth of progress allows Americans to condemn the opposite extremes of the wealth continuum, it also enables them to adopt similarly polarized attitudes toward tradition. Many of them denounce the evils of any commitment to the past and equate heirlooms with obsolete rubbish. Others, however, are tempted to endow the past with sacred qualities they would like to purchase, and herein lies the success of genealogic studies in certain quarters, as if it were possible to buy a past that one has already lost.

This brief review of the ambivalence triggered by inheritance underlines the need to explore why the topic remains off limits to many social scientists.[2] Clearly, some methodological reasons account for the scarcity of studies concerning transfers *mortis causa*. Some of them pertain to the equivocations attached to the definition of appropriate samples. Should the exploration of inheritance be guided by the representativeness of death cohorts and hence of individuals who died the same year at a particular age? Should this exploration be rather guided by the size of estates? Independently of the difficulties of tracing the successive residences of decedents, should this exploration be guided by geographic considerations, notably by the sense of the differential opportunities and constraints that the legal or economic structures of each state offer to its citizens?

Of course, some of these difficulties also concern the equivocations attached to definitions of testacy. For instance, should formal wills and informal intentions reported in interviews carry the same weight in explaining heirship strategies? As another example, is the meaning of a will contingent on the date at which it has been written? And what can be done to interpret in a meaningful way the successive versions of the same will?

But these difficulties are not sufficient to explain the dearth of empirical studies about inheritance, a dearth that also results from the specific ideological orientations of many sociologists. In their eyes, it is socially acceptable to bequeath, but less so to inherit. Nor for them is acceptable the notion of average estate—estates are supposed to be large or trivial. Given these contradictions, the celebrated pragmatism of American culture operates within certain limits. To make wealth equally accessible and at least equally understandable by all would jeopardize the very scarcity that ensures the power and the fame of the "fortunate few." References to luck and black boxes rather than to inheritance may turn out to be useful instruments of social control. Thus, some analysts claim that Americans prefer the impersonal arbitrariness of lottery to the particularist passions of familial bonds (Green 1973). Indeed, to hide the fate of affluent people behind this mask of irrationality feeds the fantasies of the poor and induces them to try their hand at the wheel of fortune. If the "buck" is really in the hands of luck, nobody can be angry at the whims of the goddess of chance because nobody can do anything rational about them.[3] In other words, the perpetuation of the existing social order requires people to believe that this very order is irrational and is thus sheltered from research.[4]

At the psychological level, Americans are particularly prone to fear death. The decay that usually marks the end of life is at odds with the ideology of progress of the larger society. The underlying conflict triggers a flurry of contradictory reactions. As far as biological choices are concerned, for instance, some Americans reject *any* link between inheritance and heredity as being inimical to the ideological project of the country.[5] In their eyes, all human behaviors can be explained and improved by the immediate environment. Conversely, other Americans overemphasize the weight of the biological past. For instance, some people believe in the merits of negative eugenics and of sterilizing individuals declared socially unacceptable. Others would like to believe that the creation of sperm banks will remove once and for all the weight of history, as if mixing the genes of Nobel Prize and of Oscar winners could produce only beautiful, intelligent, and moral children who would live in perfect harmony with one another.

As far as economic choices go, Americans are also sharply divided over the causes and consequences of inheritance (Brittain 1978; Chester 1982). Some economists assert that 80 percent of the present wealth is created by the current generation, but others prefer to believe that the same percentage has been transferred by previous generations. Such a dramatic split raises the question of whether analysts base their conclusions on distinct subparts of the same empirically testable reality or whether they fall prey to ideological phantasms that make them see the world through different lenses. But the split also seems to absolve practitioners from evaluating the variability of *who* transfers *what* to *whom* among the various groups that make up American society or across successive periods. By fiat, these researchers have decided that inheritance is monopolized by the wealthiest social groups, that poverty breeds poverty, and that transfers *mortis causa* are of no concern for the middle classes that still represent the largest segment of the American population.[6]

Further, as far as methodological choices are concerned, the effects of American ambivalences toward inheritance as a determinant of social status are exacerbated by the preeminent status of subjective individualism in the construction of social reality. Many researchers prefer to report the body of beliefs and attitudes concerning the relative fluidity of social boundaries, rather than documenting the objective forces that strengthen or weaken such boundaries.[7] In their eyes, social classes should be treated as subjective experiences rather than as objective indicators. Moreover, they assume that these experiences pertain to the perception that subjects have of other groups rather than to their own subjective identity (McNamee and Miller 1989). Since these researchers believe that one's status depends more on others than on oneself, they tend to see social class as exclusively determined by how people *perceive* the wealth or the poverty of the various members of a particular community (Tickamyer 1981).

The same stress on subjective individualism also explains why students of family law prefer to examine the professed preferences for distinct heirship practices, rather than assessing their variability.[8] Not only this, but concrete evaluations of the actual impact of transfers on current wealth are few and selective. For example, the exploration of the divergence between the egalitarian ideology of the Jacksonian era and the impact of bequests on accentuating the patterns of stratification existing at the time has not been replicated for subsequent periods. Yet, even if the base of individual power or status has shifted from property to skill and from the ownership of material capital to the possession of human capital, the role of the family as an agent of transfer still needs to be ascertained: in material as well as symbolic terms, what is the current overall contribution of parents to their children's education?

Finally, the stress on subjective individualism induces researchers to treat their subjects as isolated islands representing abstract social groups. They forget that individual choices are constantly inhibited by the prodding and nudging of significant others in the immediate environment. As an illustration, the decision to make a will is not made in vacuo. Rather, it depends on the knowledge that the lawyers or advisers we choose have of the relevant state laws. The "benign neglect" of social networks by many sociologists induces them to disregard arbitrarily the role of the immediate legal context in decision-making processes, including heirship strategies.

All these ambivalences contaminate the analyses of inheritance. To the extent that there is a literature about inheritance, it is concerned with the profile and the behavior of testators rather than of beneficiaries. As the development of capitalism continues to require the glorification of both property and money as indicators of success, public authorities feel it is desirable to minimize the constraints imposed upon those who earn a large income and those who have accumulated large and diversified wealth (Gouldner 1970). But at the very same time that capitalist ideology favors this form of liberty, it considers with disdain the beneficiaries of bequests, whom it views as parasites or at least as dilettantes whose presence threatens the ideology of the self-made person. For this very reason, testators sometimes claim that their children would resent bequests of money they have not earned and do not deserve to receive.[9]

The same ambivalence about the place occupied by individuals in the social structure leads students of social stratification to dismiss the role of money in the creation of status. They would like such a status to depend exclusively on educational and occupational attainments.[10] For the same reason, they prefer to rely on *income*, which offers recurrent measurements of individual deeds, rather than on *wealth*, the origin of which is more independent of our ephemeral fortunes and foibles. It is no wonder that Andy Warhol made headlines when he suggested that everyone is entitled to a moment of fame. Americans like to believe that the wheel of fortune never stops.

To conclude, solutions to the social problems caused by transfers *mortis causa* are frequently couched in global terms because the doctrines from which they are derived rest on scientific arguments that receive an exaggerated and completely unjustified credibility (Boudon 1986). To be sure, the existing literature foreshadows scientific explanations of inheritance since its authors seek to identify general and invariant responses as to whether transfers between the deceased and their survivors are socially desirable. Yet, following the egocentric modes of thinking of the child, these authors sidestep the notion that the statements they make about this desirability are relative, because they are conditioned by their own positions in the social structure (Piaget 1951).[11]

All these considerations underscore the need to explore concrete variations not only in the patterns of accumulation of wealth, but also in the nature of the instruments used by decedents to transfer their assets as well as in the form and the amount of the bequests they make. In contrast to the implicit or explicit stance of so many American social scientists who unreasonably act as if there were *no* conscious or unconscious intergenerational continuity, *no* deliberate patterns of reciprocal exchanges between parents and children, *nor* any involuntary mimicry of the former by the latter, I seek to show that social stratification depends on what goes on in the family. In this context, I would like to show how the ambivalences concerning inheritance reflect recurrent tensions between liberty and equality, between romantic and rational views of social life, and finally between private and public concern.

Liberty and Equality in Inheritance: The Views of the French Revolution Model

All societies have contradictory feelings about the past. While this past evokes the reassuring role of tradition and acts as a source of legitimacy, it also represents a force that impedes liberty, forbids entrepreneurship, and retards economic development. As a result, all societies are tempted to limit the impact of heirship. Indeed, the variety of sources of the hostility displayed toward the past or toward inheritance is matched by the variety of solutions adopted to limit the influence of the dead on their survivors.

At first glance, ambivalent feelings toward the past seem to synthesize the diverging effects of liberty and equality. Each generation is tempted to reject inheritance in order to be free of the chains of tradition. It may also do so because the pursuit of equality requires the race to riches to start anew with each generation. Alternatively, while the stress placed on liberty allows individuals to transfer whatever they want to whomever they want, the stress placed on equality implies an obligation to make uniform bequests or to transfer estates to the community as a whole.

Yet, actual syntheses of the contradictions between liberty and equality are often superficial and doomed to fail. Condemnations of behaviors or beliefs deemed questionable are always selective. The success of these condemnations depends on whether they are representative of questionable "others." For instance, American public opinion surveys of 1989 reported citizens to be skeptical of the morality of politicians *in general*, but to trust the senator or the representative of their own communities. In this sense, they are akin to the views of the French revolutionaries of 1789, who condemned only the modes of intergenerational transfers of the past or those of the groups they disliked. Implicitly or explicitly, these revolutionaries saw in such transfers the transmission of exorbitant economic or political privileges that they believed to be at odds with the ethical outlook of their own subcultures. Thus while they condemned the hereditary transmission of money or of power in the case of other social categories (the nobility and the clergy) or of other periods, they still favored transfers *within* their own familial groups.

Indeed, many orators of the French Revolution juxtaposed the rational benevolence of bourgeois fathers and the capricious blindness of princes and prelates. While these orators professed to be against tradition, they only intended to attack the "Red and the Black", those two targets of popular resentment. In being selective as to which aspects of tradition should be eliminated, they followed American political attitudes toward the British legacy. Some Americans have treated these antecedent roots as symbols of feudalism; others, have seen them as the cornerstones of any civilized political system (Miller 1965).

Even though French revolutionaries sought to conjure up the mutually exclusive properties of liberty and equality by marrying the initial letters of these two words on the facades of their public buildings, the famous law of August 4, 1789 that abolished privileges remained fraught with ambiguities. While such privileges symbolized the unequal distribution of power and wealth between the three estates, they were also sources of irritation for those enterprising "bourgeois" who wanted to enjoy a greater range of opportunities in their attempts to fulfill their own economic aspirations (Schama 1989).

References to the ambiguous results of the August 4, 1789 session of the French national assembly are not academic. Today as yesterday, few people like to be reminded that liberty and equality tend to be mutually exclusive.[12] Few people like to be reminded that, historically, liberty is most frequently associated with a weak state, equality with a strong centralized government whose function is to harness the power of monopolistic private interests in order to protect minorities.

When the French National Assembly began to discuss the new legal bases of family life, it became immediately apparent that the champions of the abolition of privileges and more generally of the legal system created by the *ancien régime* were dramatically divided among themselves as to the objectives of their votes and hence as to the differential value they attached to liberty and equality.

In the early days of April 1791, the French representative Saint Martin congratulated his colleagues of the assembly for having eliminated as obsolete the rule of primogeniture and all the other forms of inequality deriving from past customs. At the same time, he contrasted the capricious character of the collective past symbolized by the taxes levied on individual families by the nobility or the church with the thoughtful and purposive quality of the decisions taken by the cohorts of fathers of his own era. In his eyes, these fathers were keen either to counterbalance the inequalities that natural disorders caused between children, or to reward the uneven achievements of their sons or their daughters.

From this perspective, the pursuit of liberty required the current bourgeoisie to be given preeminence over the church or the feudal lord of the past. Saint Martin stressed the high incidence, and hence the high popularity, of the *preciput* in the Southern part of France, an institution that consists in giving a particular portion of the incoming producing part of an estate to the first child. In doing so, he reminded his colleagues that democracy spells respect for the wishes of the majority. In his eyes then, liberty should be given priority over equality.

In contrast, the champions of equality in the same assembly argued that the moral, emotional, economic, and political consequences of injustice do not stop at the family doorstep. The effects of injustice, they said, are the same *within* as *across* familial groups. In their eyes, the pursuit of equality required the full abolition of wills as a privileged form of transfers *mortis causa* and of the corresponding form of liberty.

This, however, did not resolve the dilemmas encountered by French representatives. Having decried the vices of inheritance, many felt obliged to identify the remedies most appropriate for alleviating the evil. At one end of the political continuum, some representatives proposed to impose equality among children. Mirabeau, whose speech on the topic was read after his death by Talleyrand, asserted that since all heirs would enjoy the same windfall, all would be encouraged to marry and have children. For him, subsequent higher marriage and birth rates would increase the number and the value of income-producing assets. In short, his argument was that forced equality *within* familial groups would both stimulate economic development and force equality *among* these familial groups.

At the other end of the political continuum, however, some Jacobins proposed that the best remedy to the socially negative effects of testacy would be to limit the duration of property rights. Since property is an individual attribute, it should be coterminous with the individual's life span. Further, the preeminence of society over the individual being both logical and chronological, the wealth accumulated by individuals should be returned to the state upon their death.

This stance has three implications beneficial to the pursuit of equality. Today as yesterday, it limits the long-term consequences of interindividual differences in life chances. Each generation is expected to start the race for money and power without any handicap. Today as yesterday, such a stance symbolizes the liberation of current or future generations from the tyranny of the past (for example, from the "authoritarianism legated to Western Europe by the Romans"—to use an expression of Robespierre). Last, even though the holders of this viewpoint were not necessarily aware of its implications, their choice was still the first step toward enhancing the dependence of individuals on a state acting on behalf of the common interest. It was the first step toward policing the family, that is, toward a policy that seeks to liberate the individual from the evil influences imputed to the familial group (Donzelot 1979).

French representatives sought to find compromises between these libertarian and egalitarian aspirations. They decided that the state would specify the amount of the benefits that spouses, children, siblings, and ascendants might obtain independently of the decedents' intentions. They also imposed a ceiling on the sums that decedents could bequeath freely in relation to the size of the estate. Such was the compromise put in systematic form by Napoleon in the civil code. Such is the historical origin of the preeminent status accorded to intestacy in France.

The American Historical Experience of Inheritance

Both processes of diffusion and structural similarities in the tensions that juxtapose liberty and equality account for the comparable dynamics that govern both American and French legal history. As in France, these tensions take on a regional flavor. Early on, the New England colonies became committed to sharing property equally among sons or, at least, to limiting the privileges of the firstborn of them. In contrast, southern colonies abandoned the corresponding privilege of primogeniture later, toward the end of the eighteenth century (Keim 1968; Greven 1970; Alston and Shapiro 1984). The opposite practices of the two regions resulted from both the specific social origins of their respective populations and the distinctiveness of their environments. Primogeniture and the concentration of land in the hands of one single child favored a plantation economy directed toward maximal profits rather than toward subsistence. Even where primogeniture was officially banned, the decline of the practice was neither immediate nor irreversible (Morris 1927).

As in France, tensions over the optimal freedom of testacy were also the results of diverging evaluations of historical precedents. Right after the revolution, American lawmakers were often tempted to condemn explicitly the principle of primogeniture as a symbol of the abhorred British feudal system the colonists had left behind. In 1784, for example, the Tennessee legislature rejected the British common law as being grounded in feudal systems, which "can never apply in this State" (as quoted by Farber 1973). Further, for some American lawyers of the early period, the "American experiment" required the identification and implementation of scientific principles in all legal fields, including intergenerational transfers. Altogether, these lawyers rejected English common law—the trademark of the Dark Ages—in favor of standardized codes. At the same time, others felt sufficiently inspired by pragmatism and by the comfort of retaining a familiar legal style to celebrate the same English common law as the most meaningful trace of the cumulative progress of civilization (Miller 1965; Horwitz 1977).

The multifaceted tensions between faith in progress and respect for tradition on the one hand, and the centrifugal forces of liberty and the centripetal counterweights of equality on the other, are still around.[13] Current debates concerning the transformation of the Napoleonic code to Louisiana offer a case in point (Marcus 1989). Some legislators would like to adopt successoral dispositions closer to those of the other states of the federation, but others prefer to maintain the status quo ante for two quite opposite reasons. To celebrate Louisiana's originality flatters the localism that goes with decentralization. Alternatively, the current sharp increase in divorce rates makes the forced heirship of the Napoleonic code more modern than ever. This is because its dispositions favor inter- over intragenerational transfers and protect children more effectively from the financial turmoils caused by their parents' divorce.

This historical background illuminates the three themes that run throughout the book. First, the preeminence of wills (and hence of testacy) over intestacy and over the uniform application of common norms to all decedents symbolizes the preeminence of liberty over equality. Regardless of the initial doubts about primogeniture harbored by American legal minds, laws concerning intergenerational transfers all postulate the preeminence of the intentions of individual decedents over the morality of the larger society embodied by state laws. This postulate undermines the official and public claim to favor equality.

Second, even though the American Constitution posits the separation of church and state, the preeminence given to testacy is conducive to the metaphysical view that testators' intentions survive their deaths. In this perspective, estates are viewed as the material traces of the individual's immortal soul. As a consequence, the execution of trusts often marks the triumph of the will of their authors over the passage of time and the succession of generations. Insofar as the dispositions of wills are assumed to bind survivors and beneficiaries, the courts limit the number and the type of challenges to which wills might be subjected (Thurow 1975).

Third, the preeminence accorded to testacy accounts, at least in part, for the competence of individual state rather than federal laws for dealing with whatever issues stem from intergenerational transfers. To be sure, the preeminence of state over federal authorities results from a pragmatic concern. Judges, lawyers, and legislators are believed to be more efficient and fairer when they are close to the source of human conflict. The legal resolution of conflicts concerning realty (which was the dominant form of wealth at the time the Constitution was adopted) is deemed more effective when the adjudication process takes place close to the "bone of contention." But American legal decentralization is also an archaism. The virtue imputed to local solutions for solving conflicts concerning territorial boundaries or land titles has been extended, often arbitrarily, to other forms of disputes.[14]

Against this backdrop, the very existence of a federal estate tax, however limited it might be, symbolizes the concern to check and control the extent of inequities passed from one generation to the next. When a legislator at the turn of the century asserted that "the nation must protect itself from abnormal fortunes," he evoked the parallel collective hostility that both monopolistic large-scale organizations and intergenerational transfers have always fueled in the American mind (as quoted by Pessen 1971). Whether these transfers are *inter vivos* or *mortis causa*, they are viewed as threats to interindividual competition and hence to the American dream of a fair and well-deserved upward mobility (Horwitz 1977).

To sum up, the ambiguities of public ideologies toward inheritance both mirror and produce contradictions between liberty and equality as these two ideals are embedded in a romantic and a utilitarian grammar of motives, or in individual and collective interests, such as these develop in the world of corporate capitalism.

Romantic Motives versus Rational Efficiency

The debate concerning the virtues and vices of intergenerational transfers is not only focused on identifying an appropriate balance between liberty and equality. It also concerns the tensions that arise over the relative importance to be given to romantic subjective bonds and to the impersonal efficiency of rationality. Should the logic of the wallet be subordinate to the logic of the heart? Under what circumstances?

To be sure, the focus of the ensuing debate varies across historical eras as well as across societies and social groups. Changes in the sources of wealth, in the distribution of education and hence of skills, as well as of prejudices are paralleled by changes in the profile of the conflicts surrounding familial relations or relations between families and other components of the society at large. For example, when industrialization reduced the role of family groups as units of economic production, these groups ceased to have a significant impact on the resources and the welfare of the society at large. As a result, many scholars keep dismissing the possibility of using assets transferred through the family as a mechanism of social engineering. Some view such transfers as trivial because they involve few testators. Others view these transfers as altogether irrelevant to the common good. Like dowries, bequests are viewed as undeserved windfalls likely to exacerbate the centrifugal effects of freedom and to undermine the stability of the existing social order.

However, keen as they are to avoid giving the appearance of restricting the sacred liberty of both testators and heirs, Americans have always asserted that civilization silences individual passions. In their eyes, the same catalog of "dos and don'ts" prevails anywhere. The stress that the American ethos places simultaneously on rationality, consensus, and conformity reconciles private interests with the common good. In rhetorical terms, this emphasis minimizes the destructive power of liberty by underlining the contribution of rationality to similarities and convergences in the stances that individuals adopt vis-à-vis the distinction to be made between legitimate and illegitimate children, between men and women, and between relatives and business associates.

The Issue of Legitimate and Illegitimate Children

Even though French kings and princes did not necessarily discriminate against their bastards or, to use today's more compassionate vocabulary, their illegitimate offspring, their behavior in this regard was still exceptional. Although these children did not become kings, they were not ostracized either and they often ended up playing significant political roles. In contrast, for the common man in the street, the term "bastard" was (and remains) an insult and a curse. For a long period of time, such an origin caused total exclusion from the familial estate. Further, until the recent past, varying degrees of social condemnation of social illegitimacy as sinful were paralleled by disparities in the claims that children born before marriage, from adultery, or from incest could make on their parents' estates in relation to the claims of legitimate children. Only relatively recently, the demise of the French family as a significant agency of production and socialization, the ensuing progress of individualism, and the parallel triumph of the rhetoric of love over that of cold calculation, have enabled the distinct types of illegitimate children to leave the various closets in which they were locked. They have ceased to be victimized by the "criminal" act imputed to their parents. They have ceased to be restricted in the claims they can make on the latter's estate.

To the extent that ideological views of the family have been less romantic but more utilitarian in the United States than in France, the legal differentiation of legitimate and various kinds of illegitimate children has been and remains less pronounced here. Further, except in Louisiana, where these children are exposed to the same restrictions as in France, the progress of individualism has induced many states to allow them to claim their own shares of their mother's estate. Thus, the number of states that do not introduce any distinction between the claims that legitimate and illegitimate children can make against maternal estates climbed from thirty-four during the period 1860–1879, to forty-nine in 1969. Similarly, only twelve states authorized the claims of illegitimate children to their fathers' estates during the period 1860–1879 as opposed to twenty-eight in 1969 (Farber 1973). The trend is even more marked among the states west of the Mississippi, prodded inter alia by the 1956 changes in the Arizona statutes that have ceased to hold the concepts of "natural," and of "legitimate," as being legally distinct and possibly mutually exclusive.

Since the demise of the family as a unit of production minimizes the consequences of the functioning of this group on the economy as a whole, it allows the progress of individualism and the triumph of romantic views in the western part of the country. As such, it also allows the blurring of distinctions between children as a function of their origin.

The Case of Married Women

The legal status of married women is another illustration of the evolving difficulties encountered by testators as a result of the tensions between a romantic and a utilitarian grammar of motives. To the extent that originally inheritance concerned the transfer of income-producing assets that women were not allowed to manage, parents reconciled romantic and rational motives by providing their daughters with a dowry that was preempted from the estate, but from which land was often excluded (Ditz 1986; Grossberg 1985; Wyatt Brown 1982). This practice, however, took into account love, but not efficiency. The legal incapacity of their daughters obliged fathers to assume that their sons-in-law were sufficiently trustworthy to manage the various assets that formed the dowry.

In the United States as in France, this condition was believed to be met as long as communities remained stable and hence as long as the field of eligible partners was restricted. Matchmakers would identify spouses deemed compatible with one another as well as with their respective families. Limited individual geographic mobility contributed to further enhancing the cohesiveness of communities and this made it easier to punish deviations from expected behaviors. Retaliations could be made against a family unable or unwilling to prevent its son from going astray and gambling away the dowry of his bride.

For two conflicting reasons, American economic development and industrialization disrupted the fragile balance that people had established between romantic and utilitarian views. With the growing geographic and social mobility of the American population, solidarity between in-laws was reduced proportionately. Fathers could no longer keep control of their daughters' husbands. With the rising social costs of ascribing the status of legal minor to married women, they risked both losing part or the totality of the assets they had transferred to their daughters and being obliged to assist their grandchildren. They responded to such threats by empowering their married daughters to manage the resources transferred to them in the dowry. The stress placed on capitalism and thereby on liberty was not divisible and was paralleled by a corresponding stress placed on the equality of the two genders: this made the requirements of rationality and of love mutually reinforcing.

At the same time, since the ideology required by industrialization extolled private property and celebrated its universality, the emerging domestic morality underlined the arbitrary nature of inconsistencies in the status of women. Although allowed to manage the income they might derive from their dowry or their inheritance, women were still incongruously forbidden to manage the income they earned from other sources, especially from their work.

The ensuing contradictions in the requirements of rationality loomed large. The legal power grudgingly yielded to married women in order to neutralize the centrifugal forces created by such contradictions ended up changing their loves or their hatreds, but also their bargaining positions in their families of origin and of destination, as well as in the entire economy. Further, since rationality should be independent of the participants' social position, it was no longer held socially acceptable to restrict the creation of dowries to certain forms of capital; the underlying distinction would be inimical to the universalistic formal efficiency of a modern economic system.

Thus, the logic of capitalism marked the end of the romantic vision of feeble women requiring legal protection from their fathers or their husbands. By the same logic, the freedom of these women could not be divided as a function of the origin of their incomes or of their assets. In the perspective of the new ideology, the capacity to receive gifts was to parallel the capacity to bequeath, to earn wages or salaries, or to manage bank accounts. Even though the new ideology was slowly put into practice, it still sought to reconcile the most glaring contradictions of the properties imputed to liberty and to equality.

Familial Loyalty and Small-Scale Business in the Modern World

Today, some entrepreneurs claim they would prefer to bequeath their factories, their shops, or their tools to their associates and collaborators rather than to their wives or their children, who have never taken part in the daily challenge of their work. In the dichotomy between their work seen as a calling and their family seen as a hornet's nest of greedy dependents, they choose as having redeeming value the solidarity built in the trenches of their economic activities. Thus, many American capitalists argue that transfers based on familial ties ruin the ethic of achievement that permeates American economic life (Kirkland 1986).

This stance rekindles the issue of whether inheritance is primarily about transfers of wealth *within* the family or whether there should be no boundaries in *how much* or *what* individuals are allowed to transfer and to *whom*. Even though people may talk about their business as being their mistress or their love, even though the marriage of love and work looks like a moralistic alliance, the transfer of one's business to one's work associates remains rare. Passionate quarrels between the executors or the assistants and the children of successful artists (De Kooning and Nevelson, for example) or businessmen reveal major ambiguities in the links binding the grammars of romantic and rational motives.[15] Should the solidarity developed by sharing the same esthetic or occupational ideals and pains prevail over familial bonds?

To render the debate even more complex, the importance attached to efficiency justifies the need to distinguish transfers of wealth and transfers of authority. The former is subject to contradictions between romantic and rationalistic views of transfers. The frequent preeminence of the economics of love often implies a parallel commitment to equity. Alternatively, rationalistic views of monetary or economic transfers underscore the power of the views of Adam Smith, for whom limiting the number of beneficiaries was the most efficient way to stimulate the concentration of wealth.[16]

The transfer of authority does not raise such dilemmas. The larger the number of heirs required to share authority, the more unstable the exercise of power and the greater the risks experienced by the entire group. The fights that took place between the Gallo or the Mondavi brothers over the control of their respective familial wineries illustrate the process. More often than not, executives prefer the continuity of power to the continuity of capital.[17] More often than not, heirs of family businesses complain about the slow transition from their father's stewardship to their own (Rosenblatt et al. 1985).[18] In this sense, the transfer of authority requires maximal liberty.

To conclude, the ambivalences stirred by intergenerational transfers reflect tensions between the distinct modes of social interaction inspired by the logics of romantic commitment and of rational efficiency. The first is based on feelings, the second on calculation. Both rely on classificatory systems of objects, but the first invokes tastes and pleasures, while the second invokes the utility or the market value of such objects. Finally, the two logics require the intervention of authority systems that are inconsistent. Love is validated and legitimized by priests; rationality by accountants or by economists.

To be sure, the search for legitimacy is an attempt to reconcile these two logics by emphasizing the merits of precedents. As precedents stress the collective wisdom of past generations, they appeal to both romantic and rational motivations. Yet, the precedents invoked do not remain constant because the moral codes adopted by distinct social groups do not change at the same pace. Some people remain attached to older catalogs of prescriptions, others becoming committed to newer ones. This accentuates the diversity of controversies about the social utility of inheritance. For example, gay couples adopt opposite attitudes toward transfers. Some of them view their current life-styles as liberating them from obsolete practices. But others use inheritance as a mechanism that enables them to legitimize their feelings, however deviant such feelings might be considered by mainstream social segments. All these controversies raise two major questions about the nature of heirship: To the extent that the definitions of property rights are culturally relative, are there parallel variations in the definitions of transfers? Further, are these transfers independent of the relations that citizens should maintain with the state?

Property and Inheritance

Inheritance exacerbates the potential contradictions inherent in the capitalist system. As the perpetuation of the system requires both the number of participants and their commitment to the pursuit of happiness to be maximal, it presupposes a single set of universal rules.[19] Alternatively and for the same reason, economic development makes it necessary to keep bending the rules and adapting them to the features specific to each form of capital.

As a result, the notion of transfer itself has evolved in contradictory ways. Depending on whether transfers are gratuitous or profit oriented, precarious or irrevocable, their respective rules have become more restrictive or more liberal. For instance, current laws give more leeway to sellers and buyers than to lessors and lessees. As another example, gifts *inter vivos* and transfers *mortis causa* are not taxed at the same rate and do not require the same instruments. To the extent that diverging evolutions jeopardize the unity of the concept of ownership, they enhance its relativity, thereby undermining the thrust of capitalist ideology.

Indeed, this ideology posits that to the extent that ownership is synonymous with the notion of dominion, the right to transfer (*jus abutendi*) should be independent of the gratuitous or mercantile quality of the transfer. People should have the right to do whatever they want with what they own, regardless of the nature of the transfer that enabled them to become owners. Similarly, the right to dispose should be independent of *what is* transferred.

This did not raise any problem as long as realty was the primary and quasi-unique form of private capital. With the growing diversification of socially acceptable sources of wealth, the tensions exerted on the notion of property and, indirectly, of transfers should increase proportionately. For instance, the legal sanction accorded to the concept of intangible intellectual property rights (royalties, residuals, etc.), the creation of rights to pension funds, and more recently the formation of banks of human organs or cells (sperm, ovule, blood, kidney, etc.) have all undermined the seemingly immortal nature of ownership, as have the current definitions of "natural" or "social" limits imposed on the beneficiaries of transfers. To allude to a recent example of the contradictions that gnaw away at the unity of the notion of ownership, the issue of whether James Baldwin's heirs should return the advance paid by a publisher for a manuscript that the late author did not deliver raises the problem of the asymmetry between the rights of heirs over the creator's intellectual property and their liabilities for his/her unfinished works under contract.

As another illustration, not only does nature "reject" transplants and hence "prevent" their beneficiaries from enjoying the relevant bequests, but there may also be social challenges to the right of transferring the monetary income earned from exploitation of the human body. The transplant of an ovule may fail. In addition, the proceeds resulting from "renting" one's womb may also remain frozen, as having resulted from an immoral contract (Zelizer 1988). In short, "natural" and "social" taboos may be independent, but they may also reinforce one another.

Inheritance may disturb even further the concept of property whenever it concerns the right to use a scarce commodity without the accompanying right to transfer it. This is exemplified by the transmission *mortis causa*—frequent in certain Eastern European countries or in rent-controlled housing complexes in New York City—of the right to rent an apartment. Such a right may be passed down to heirs, as those are defined by public authorities, but cannot be sold to strangers.

Finally, whenever public authorities specify the beneficiaries of virtual rather than already existing forms of wealth, they reactivate dormant conflicts not only over definitions of the public and private realms, but also over the distinctions between the claims that can be made by successive classes of heirs (past and current spouses, for example) against *existing* as opposed to *future* assets. As noted earlier, in adjudicating the claims that can be exerted on the pension funds accumulated by the divorced spouses of personnel of the military or diplomatic services, the U.S. federal government gives priority to the former wife over the current widow (Weitzman 1985). In this sense, the American community reminds civil servants that they are bound by their private pasts.

To summarize, even though legal minds prefer legal concepts to be both universal and invariant, the distinctions that judges and legislators introduce in the definitions of either the *instruments* or the *nature* of transfers contribute to highlighting the irreducibility of the conflict between liberty and equality. Insofar as property implies the power of transferring *any*thing to *any*body for *any* price, it requires an absolute liberty. Conversely, any restriction in the rights to transfer, whether in relation to the object of the transfer, to its beneficiaries, or to the kind of *quid pro quo* operating, is inspired by the pursuit of equality.

This pursuit, however, involves two distinct objectives. On the one hand, the state may intervene to regulate interactions between individuals acting respectively as sources and beneficiaries of transfers. The distinction that the legislators of some states introduce between the bequests that can be made in favor of legitimate and illegitimate children or of first- and second-marriage spouses illustrates this first objective and the underlying need to keep specifying the socially acceptable boundaries of evolving familial groups. On the other hand, the state may also intervene in order to protect public or private creditors who have not been privy to the agreements passed between testators and heirs. Public authorities rank order the claims that employees, mortgage holders, or the Internal Revenue Service can make against estates in order to ensure the predictability of labor, commercial, or political transactions. Public order requires the protection of strangers from the schemes cooked up by relatives.

To the extent that all forms of public interventions seek to eliminate the contingencies attached to personal agreements, they remind private contractors that they are all *equally* subjected to the good will of the prince. This explains the frequent fiscal undertones of the tension between testacy and intestacy. Inheritance taxes symbolize the actual or even the virtual services rendered by public authorities in regularizing the performance of private rights and obligations. They also reflect the preeminence of the common public good over the divisiveness of private interests, and thus the need to impose discreet forms of intestacy.

Functions of Estate Taxes

Estate taxes stir emotions as strong as inheritance itself. This is evident in the objectives that Americans assign to estate planning and in the emphasis they place on the need to restrict the taxes owed at the time of their death. Both in their discourses and in their practices, they wish to participate in a community with a limited liability. In this perspective, they view transfers *mortis causa* as being the last act of the *private* rather than of the *public* self. For the American public, state interventions should be minimal. As an illustration, it has been suggested that there is a high negative correlation between the taxes imposed by the federal government and the amount of charitable private bequests. Despite the lack of evidence, the underlying political argument is that both multiple and high taxation cuts down the amount of resources that otherwise could be left to philanthropy (Woods 1928; Barber 1983; Chester 1982).

But while estate taxes may be compared to the overhead charges of a broker for the services rendered to holders of wealth, notably by guaranteeing titles that can be invoked against the claims of third parties, they can also be construed as a reminder that individual property rights are favors or privileges conceded out of the eminent domain by public authorities. There are taxes because, ultimately, property rights are only precarious privileges (Halbach 1977).

Although controversies concerning estate taxes share the same implicit agenda about the network of rights and obligations between private actors and the public embodiment of the community at large, they take three distinct forms. First, they are focused on the amount of the taxes levied. For example, the growing deficit of the federal budget has rekindled debates about the merits of income and estate taxes. Not only are the taxes levied on an estate smaller than those levied on an income with the same value, but whereas the proportion that estates represent in the American gross national product keeps increasing, the percentage of estates subject to federal taxes has declined since 1976 (Prosterman and Hanstad 1990). Opponents of estate taxes argue that the proportion of the estate spent in taxes is a valid indicator of the hostility of the state to the very notion of inheritance. The question of whether intergenerational transfers block economic growth and prevent the necessary redistribution of national wealth looms large behind the narrow terms of the debate. Alternatively, the champions of the welfare state emphasize the quality of the social services rendered to individuals by the community to denounce the capricious nature of the help that relatives provide to one another.[20]

Second, controversies are focused on the differential taxes levied on transfers *mortis causa* and on gifts *inter vivos*. The second type of transaction is subject to lower rates because public authorities seem to believe that the duration of physical lives and of estates should be treated as being coterminous. But does the corresponding fiscal distinction also aim at constraining the power of familial groups? Does it seek to stimulate the circulation of wealth across individuals as well as social groups? Are these distinctions based on the belief that it is more difficult to trace gifts *inter vivos* and by the subsequent belief that the losses incurred by the Treasury because of lower tax rates are more than compensated by increases in the frequency of the behaviors taxed and hence, ultimately, by a larger revenue? In short, the questions raised by the use of differential tax rates between estate taxes and gifts *inter vivos* not only concern the bonds woven between testators and their heirs; rather, they are also generated by more practical considerations and by the impact of such differentials on the economy.

The third type of controversy concerning estate taxes is focused on both the feasibility and fairness of variations in their rates by classes of beneficiaries as well as on the equity of the relevant policies. These debates lead to conflicts over the social usefulness of distinguishing between the population of the decedent's relatives as a whole and the private or public cultural, social, or economic agencies that benefit from the decedent's riches. In short, should the taxes levied on estates be independent of their destination? When one argues that destination makes a difference, should in-laws benefit from less favorable fiscal conditions than the decedents' relatives, and should the answer depend on the type of relative considered?

To make the debate even more complex, the deduction of gifts to educational, cultural, or social private institutions may be seen as symbolic of the triumph of the private over the public sector and thus as another symbol of the preeminence given to liberty over equality. To empower decedents to choose the sectors that may benefit their generosity is to symbolize the triumph of private interests over the common good (Teltsch 1990). The decedents' apparent generosity may be viewed as a ploy that enables them not only to reduce the taxes owed by their estates, but also to create dynasties that weaken even further the authority of the state.[21]

This array of observations throws additional light on Durkheim's (1957) belief that the *number* of beneficiaries of familial transfers *mortis causa* as well as the *amounts* of money involved are likely to decline with industrialization. With the declining role of the family as a significant economic agency, Durkheim argued, individuals should be tempted to make bequests in favor of voluntary professional organizations (museums, hospitals, schools, welfare agencies, research institutes geared toward the formation of human capital).

If one believes in the scientific merits of Durkheim's analysis, one might wish to accelerate the declining flow of economic transactions between generations, either by accompanying bequests made to professional organizations with appropriate fiscal incentives, or by imposing additional fiscal burdens to those bequests made to relatives. Like other taxes, estate taxes constitute a powerful instrument for inhibiting certain types of transfers or stimulating others.

Yet, regardless of the conditions under which such taxes act as *negative* or *positive* reinforcements, the fact is that Americans seem to have a limited knowledge and understanding of the role played by the state in transfers *mortis causa*. Analysts are often themselves victims of collective ambivalences toward inheritance and toward the state. Many of them underestimate the attachment of the American populace to the symbols of familial continuity and liberty. The polls of the then presidential candidate Senator McGovern took a dive when his advisers suggested a stiff rise in estate taxes (Chester 1982).

The Outline of the Book

The major purpose of this book is to identify the most significant sources of variations in the amount and the direction of transfers *mortis causa* in the contemporary United States. As such, it is based on a variety of secondary sources. But it involves also more directly a systematic comparison of a sample of 232 estate tax returns collected from decedents who passed away in 1920 and 1944.

The analysis of estate tax returns and of the data collected on preceding as well as subsequent periods will enable me to suggest that the study of inheritance highlights the two major difficulties of any sociological work. The first one, inherent to all social analyses, concerns the dialectics of the bonds between subjects and objects, in our case, between testators and heirs. It is easy enough both to affirm the rights of the former and to denounce the arbitrary privileges of the latter. But to inherit is also a particular form of achievement, since there is a network of reciprocal patterns of identification between decedents and their beneficiaries. In the same way that Maine (1954) noted that the horse of the fallen knight was transferred to the best surviving rider, one should identify the symbolic equivalents of this type of transfer in the modern world in order to ascertain what exactly stimulates the imagination of potential heirs and "makes them run." What does it mean to be a "favorite son" or a "beloved daughter" in the modern world? Are there changes in the role played by birth order, gender, or matrimonial status in determining what is expected of children and siblings? How do changes in the expectations attached to familial role shape individual behaviors? In short, it is not valid to treat individuals or groups as loose atoms, since their practices are unavoidably embedded in larger structures with which they keep interacting.

The second difficulty concerns the multiplicity of time dimensions that should be incorporated in the study of social phenomena. I have suggested that inheritance reproduces both relations within familial groups and the rank order of these groups in the larger society. In order to explore this notion of social, cultural, and economic reproduction, the analysis must distinguish between the variety of time dimensions within which social phenomena occur and differentiate the effects of (a) the life cycle of the decedents and their beneficiaries on their respective needs and their accumulation of wealth, and (b) short- and long-term economic or political changes on the structure of symbolic and material exchanges between relatives. In this sense, the book represents a focused exploration of the interaction between life cycle and period effects (Ryder 1965). The two samples of 1920 and 1944 decedents mimic two adjacent generations. They also tell us something about the impact of wars, depressions, and other historical disjunctures on intergenerational solidarity.

These considerations illuminate the major theoretical dilemma underlying analyses of inheritance. Transfers *mortis causa* may respond to the *immediate* constraints and opportunities experienced by both decedents and their potential heirs in their environments. Conversely, as inheritance symbolizes the long-term stability of familial assets and commitments, it is also conservative. However, documents do not specify what it is that inheritance perpetuates: Is it the power structure of the family and its hierarchy? the network of domestic loves and hatreds, and thus the range of relations between ascendants and descendants as well as between siblings? the abstract familial structures that the larger society imposes willy-nilly on familial groups by defining the bequests that can be claimed by varying classes of relatives? or the actual social hierarchy with its inter- and intrafamily inequalities?

To raise such questions links the notion of social, cultural, or economic reproduction to the importance of doing things the right way and hence to the notion of legitimacy. This makes it necessary to sketch the general profile of the subcultures most likely to intervene in transfers *mortis causa*, and more pointedly to identify the role played in this regard by national origin and to a certain extent social class, before speculating as to whether gender is a by-product or a determinant of heirship practices.

Are women discriminated qua women or as passive objects of the class, the religious group, or the nationality to which they belong? More generally, then, Chapter 2 is devoted to a systematic exploration of the notion of reproduction, its agencies, and its limits.

Chapter 3 summarizes the difficulties of doing work on contemporary American heirship. These difficulties are threefold: First, there is the challenge of creating an appropriate sample and focusing on a representative component of the relevant populations. Is the sample supposed to mimic the entire universe of decedents or only those with appropriate resources? Second, the study of heirship highlights the weaknesses of the methodological individualism typical of the American social sciences and hence of questionnaires. Whereas sociologists often base their conclusions on the verbal accounts of subjects, they are cagier about the use of official documents. The second thrust of the chapter is not only to assess in what sense estate tax returns are less obtrusive than typical sociological instruments, but also to see what difference this makes in the results obtained. Third and last, to the extent that national origin is deemed to be a major determinant of cultural reproduction and thus of the perpetuation of domestic morality, the chapter is also devoted to the difficulties underlying the identification of the national origin of individual decedents, in this case as Germans or as Irish.

Chapter 4 focuses on the determinants of both the *amount* and the *form* of the assets accumulated, since the wealth accumulated commands the wealth bequeathed. Indeed, the logic governing the division of estates should be largely dependent upon the nature of the assets accumulated by individual decedents as well as by the economic profile of the larger society to which they belong. Hence, I examine the role played in this regard by macrosocial factors such as the level and rate of development of the national and local economy as well as the history of the various social classes, nationalities, and religious denominations.

Chapter 5 is devoted to the analysis of the instruments of transfers. Their purpose is to overcome the constraints that death creates in imposing unpredictable temporal limits on human activities and in separating human beings from one another. Thus, the chapter has two major objectives: The first is to evaluate how these instruments reveal distinct orientations toward time. Some human beings want their gifts to be inspired by the spirit of the moment. Others prefer them to symbolize the durability of their power and influence. The second objective is to show how instruments of transfers symbolize the complementarities binding the rank ordering of objects with the hierarchy of persons significant to the decedent.

Chapter 6 focuses on an examination of the distinctions that testators establish among their children and their surviving spouses. Thus, the chapter is devoted to the evaluation of the differentiation of heirs and an analysis of its determinants. Centered on the notion of inequality and on the variety of forms it takes, the chapter assesses the changing significance of gender and matrimonial status and examines the differential impact of structural and cultural forces on the choices made by testators as a function of the gender and the matrimonial status of their possible heirs.

The conclusion of the book deals with the possibility of generalizing to the contemporary scene the results obtained on the samples of IRS returns. As such, it involves both substantive and methodological concerns. From a substantive viewpoint, the analysis underlines the need to rethink the sociology of generational bonds, as it is informed by age and gender. In this sense, the analysis underlines the need to show how the impact of the tensions between liberty and equality on inter- and intragenerational bonds evolves with changing times.

From a methodological perspective, social analyses suffer too often from the selectivity governing the choice of the phases of the life cycle deemed worth investigating. There has been a sociology of child-rearing practices (which is, incidentally, becoming obsolete); there has been more recently a sociology of aging unduly focused on aging as a cause of poverty (unduly because it leads sociologists to overemphasize a particular segment of the socioeconomic continuum at the expense of others and to forget that aging is a universal phenomenon); there has been an even more recent discovery that there are "passages" between adolescence and retirement (Sheehy 1978; Schlossberg 1983). Despite these successive revolutions, analysts act as if children, elderly, and adults were differing and independent "tribes," rather than interdependent components of the same social systems. In effect, this trend is reinforced by the conscious or unconscious preeminence accorded to the free market ideology in the social sciences. Even though such a preeminence assumes a selfish and egocentric vision of the world, it is still highly successful in intellectual circles.

Thus, the book is also a meditation about the strengths and weaknesses of current sociological tools.[22] As such, it is an invitation to pay more attention to the multifaceted dimensions of time in the analyses of current American familial practices. It is at this price that sociology may help Americans to learn how to transcribe the legacies of the past into contemporary challenges related to changes in both the assets accumulated by individuals and their relations with the other gender or the other age groups.

2
Inheritance and Reproduction

The social face of death is Janus-like. On the one hand, it marks the most dramatic disruption in the relations between specific human beings. On the other hand, it evokes also inertia and the restoration of the most basic natural or social equilibrium. As such, it evokes the continuity of social relations beyond the accidents of individual lives. Aside from its reference to monarchs, the meaning of the well-known expression "The king is dead, long live the king" echoes the following remarks of Proust, "We, the living, are merely dead people who have not as yet begun to exert their functions."[1] The English language mirrors the two opposite faces of death with two complementary verbs. The verb "pass away" evokes the extinction of life, the verb "pass on" or "pass down" refers to the bonds interwoven between generations.

Insofar as inheritance concerns the second aspect of death, it represents a key process of physical, social, cultural, and economic reproduction. After a brief historical review of the use of the term in the sociological literature, I will underline the three major theoretical challenges raised by the concept of reproduction and, more specifically, by the continuity of social institutions and social bonds. The first one is to ascertain *what* material and symbolic assets endure and hence, to distinguish biological, cultural, and economic forms of capital from one another. Always selective, reproduction involves only some of the institutions and solidarities that form a particular culture.

The second challenge is to ascertain *who* makes things endure and *how*. Far from being automatic, reproduction requires appropriate agencies that tap distinct sources of legitimation to render socially acceptable the individual transfer of the various forms of capital owned by individuals or groups.

The last challenge consists in ascertaining the duration of reproductive processes. The notion of reproduction highlights perhaps the intrusion of the past into current social life. Yet, such an intrusion is temporary. Since reproduction involves human actors who have their own foibles or vanities, these actors miscalculate at times, indulge at times in pipe dreams, and at times, too, harbor unduly modest aspirations. As a result, some practices or some beliefs persist longer than expected but others disappear faster than anticipated. In short, the more one stresses the weight of reproduction, the more one risks denying the dramatic disjunctures that history introduces in social relations.

Reproduction: The Historical Background of the Term

Keen to introduce a diachronic dimension into the analysis of capitalist systems, Engels distinguished reproduction from production. While specific modes of production foster corresponding patterns of social exploitation and dominance, the perpetuation of these patterns requires appropriate child-bearing and child-rearing activities. Children of slaves must learn how to be slaves; children of masters, how to become masters.

Thus, reproduction represents the physical as well as sociocultural processes by which both oppressing and oppressed domestic groups perpetuate themselves. As long as the family is a major unit of production, the private spheres of production and reproduction are supposed to be managed by women under the ultimate authority of male elders (Cornell 1988). Women produce what is necessary for the subsistence of their families. They are the almost exclusive agents of socialization of their offspring.

With industrialization both malehood and seniority cease to act as universal or unique sources of wealth and power. An increasing number of women leave the private sphere of reproductive activities to participate independently in the public world of production. Their very appearance on male turf causes problematic shifts in the allocation of productive and reproductive tasks, on the one hand, and in the systems of social control used to maintain patterns of dominance, on the other. As industrialization accentuates cleavages between private and public spheres of interaction, more specifically, between the household and the factory or the store, it fragments the authority that men claim over women and that elders aspire to impose on children. In short, capitalism and patriarchy cease to foster convergent attitudes or practices.

This evolution accentuates both the macro- and microsocial tensions opposing liberty to equality. As such, it heightens the problematic nature of the linkage between inter- and intrafamilial inequalities. The dominance of men over women in the public sphere ceases to imply their dominance in the domestic realm. The same holds true of relations between generations. The power derived from seniority in the workplace does not say anything about familial relations. ("A lion in the office, a lamb at home," as the saying has it.) Correspondingly, the impact of bequests on social stratification as well as on domestic relations becomes more uncertain because of greater variations in the amount and the destination of the sums involved. In this instance as in others, economic development accentuates the complexity of the links between society at large and the family.

As long as the distinction between productive and reproductive spheres remained blurred and the relationship between genders was one of dominance, heirship served primarily to link generations to one another. At best, a widow got a life bequest that was to be returned at the time of her death to the estate of her late husband. The purpose of inheritance was to transfer assets from parents to children rather than between spouses. It was to keep the identity of descent groups separate rather than to facilitate their combination. Conversely, as soon as families ceased to monopolize economic functions and as soon as the entry of women as autonomous agents of production empowered them to become both testators and heiresses, there developed distinct variations in *who* transfers *what, when, how,* and *to whom*. Reproduction ceased to be simultaneously a macro- and microsocial process. Correspondingly, the roles played by inheritance for the familial group and for the larger society ceased to be automatically complementary. For example, beneficiaries of a rich bequest no longer automatically enjoyed a higher social status.

Bourdieu (1964, 1970) elaborates on Engels's work to identify the mechanisms that individuals and groups use to maintain their dominance over others in the modern world. His analysis emphasizes much more the perpetuation and the endurance of existing modes of social control than their atemporal intensity. In his perspective, today as yesterday, the perpetuation of patterns of dominance depends on the rules of appropriation imposed by elites and the resources they mobilize to get things done their way. But as the use of raw power is costly, this reproduction is also contingent on distributive rules and, more specifically, on the legitimacy that all segments of society assign to the allocation of resources. Herein originates the importance, for those who hold public or private forms of power as well as for their subordinates, of believing that the perpetuation of existing arrangements is in the order of things. Indeed, this perpetuation is legitimated to the extent that it is deemed to be "natural" (Newby, Bell, Rose, and Saunders 1979).

Since the link Pierre Bourdieu established between reproduction and inequality is what made him so popular in this country, notably among sociologists of education who have used the concept to assert that the function of formal schooling is to ensure the persistence of the privileges accumulated by elites, the disregard for inheritance and its relationship to the notion of reproduction is startling.[2] The more liberal a society, the more subtle the forms of control used to ensure conformity and the greater the number of positive as well as negative reinforcements used to keep people in line. The more diversified are the functions served by inheritance in this regard.

Of course, many underlying forms of control originate with the state. For example, public authorities vary the conditions and rates of estate taxation to accentuate or to blunt the existing economic rank ordering of distinct families. Also, when these same authorities spell out the size of the share that cannot be taken away from spouses or from children, they seek to perpetuate the domestic arrangements they deem best suited to the political or economic needs of the larger society.

Familial groups enjoy the same opportunity to control the behavior of their individual members—by disinheritance of a prodigal son or promiscuous daughter at one extreme, or by an exclusive bequest to a favorite son or beloved daughter, at the opposite.

The point is that it is bad sociology to assume that abstract social structures perform reproductive functions. For it is to indulge in the same vice for which the French philosopher Peguy criticized Kant, that is, for having elaborated disembodied and, as such, armless as well as harmless ethics. In effect, while reproduction represents above all a seemingly conscious individual or collective strategy aiming at dominating others, dominant actors use distinct mechanisms or ploys. Their strategies toward potential heirs and toward bureaucrats cannot be the same. These strategies vary also with the behaviors to be controlled. For example, as long as the behaviors expected from male and female heirs differ from one another, parents—mothers as well as fathers—are most unlikely to make the same use of "the carrot and the stick in dealing with their sons and their daughters.

Inheritance and Reproduction: The Challenge

Transfers *mortis causa* constitute material symbols of the perpetuation of moral rights and obligations as well as feelings between relatives. As such, they ensure the survival of the identity of familial groups in the eyes of decedents' relatives as in those of outsiders. This view is shared by a number of legal scholars. Thus, when Friedman suggests that "laws of succession allow social groups or societies to reproduce their economic and social institutions each new generation" (1966:25), he echoes the remarks of Tocqueville, who wrote that "the laws of inheritance lay hand on each generation before it is born" (1961:44). In this sense, inheritance and the underlying beliefs and behaviors are molded by "the lost world of the past" (Shammas, Salmon, and Dahlin 1987:4).

In the United States as elsewhere, transfers *mortis causa* epitomize therefore the multifaceted perpetuation of individual as well as collective, and material as well as symbolic, assets. Such a perpetuation requires the motivations of decedents and their beneficiaries to be, at least partially, congruent. These motivations are usually twofold. On the one hand, material transfers symbolize the continuity of the group, and the beneficiaries may experience the obligation to pass down to the succeeding generation a capital equal or even superior to what they received (Gotman 1988). This is the origin of the verb "to pass on."

On the other hand, the concerns of both testators and heirs may be selective and centered on the fate of specific individuals or specific objects. Children may forgo their own claims to a particular asset and yield their rights to only one of their coheirs in a way deemed highly valuable by the decedent. For example, the transfer of a summer home may go to the one son or daughter who either lives close by and promises to keep the property in good standing, or who agrees to act as the new host of his or her surviving parent and siblings (Gotman 1988).

The Conscious or Unconscious Nature of Reproduction

As a source of reward and a mechanism of social control, inheritance involves two conflicting principles. To differentiate among heirs by relying on their strengths or their foibles maximizes the liberty of testators. In contrast, to distribute one's estate equally to all heirs highlights the obligation for testators to treat all their beneficiaries fairly.

The incompatibility of these two ideas renders reproduction problematic. Inequalities within or among familial groups jeopardize existing social arrangements to the same extent as collective indifference to individual needs and achievements. In both cases, but for opposite reasons, individual commitment to kinship or to the community at large keeps declining. Extreme inequalities in the form or the amount of bequests alienate victims. Alternatively, the lack of incentives inhibits many potential achievers from proving themselves.

Different cultures keep inventing their own solutions for preventing the converging negative effects of these two opposite forces and for keeping the corresponding tensions within optimal limits. In traditional societies, heirship practices are overtly dictated by customs over which individuals have little control. Heirs are designated by the community's elders speaking in the name of tradition. To depart from such customs is to take a blasphemous stance toward the sacred properties imputed to ancestors. Even today, these customs continue to represent long-term patterns of selective retention and mutation caused by environmental changes. As such, they correspond to unconscious (because collective) processes of reproduction.

With the triumph of individualism that the American Revolution symbolizes, individuals have become overtly empowered to allow their loves and hatreds to dictate what assets go to whom, when, and how. Correspondingly, the voluntaristic and deliberate properties of wills and of testacy in the American modern world contrast with the transcendental and uniform quality of the rules that governed succession in medieval European societies. When one wants to evoke contemporary American forms of transfers, this evolution makes the concept of replication more appropriate than reproduction. For the word *replication* symbolizes the growing role assigned to free will in social interaction. Yet, to use the word *replication* in order to highlight the individualistic aspirations of Americans does not mean that they are fully aware of the influences that make them repeat the same decisions as their parents. Free will may be an illusion. Indeed, the evolution of American heirship practices highlights how Maine's metaphor (1954) for describing successions becomes ambiguous in the modern context.

Today, the legal clothing to which Maine alludes is mass manufactured in some instances, tailor-made in others. To die intestate, that is, without a will, may be a symptom of indifference or acquiescence to the dispositions taken by the state in the name of the community at large. Alternatively, while some decedents rely on testacy to confirm such dispositions, others use wills to deviate from them, although their "conscious" choices may unwittingly mirror the values of their respective reference groups.

These contrary outlooks account for the changing nature of the contrast between testacy and intestacy. In Illinois, as already seen, successive generations of German-American farmers have not only relied more often than their Yankee counterparts on testacy, but in addition, most farmers who did write wills during the period of reference did so to assert a commitment to equality that simply confirmed the dispositions of the law. Yet, where the German-Americans were primarily anxious to maintain the traditional values of the province from which they originated in Germany, their Yankee counterparts were probably deviating from the exceptionalist ideology that should have been theirs. Alternatively, the rising number of German-Americans who have used testacy to introduce differences among their children suggests a growing erosion of the initial heirship model of this population and its underlying commitment to egalitarianism (Carroll and Salamon 1988). In this sense, the meaning of the contrast between testacy and intestacy has changed over the years.

All this is said to emphasize that when one views wills as a by-product of free will, "free" may mean that the distribution of the relevant decisions in the population at large follows a random pattern; alternatively, the notion of "free" may be illusory, the distribution of the dispositions of wills being systematically structured by the age, the gender, and the social circumstances of their authors. Thus, today, the notion of reproduction remains appropriate only insofar as the distributions of feelings, ideas, and values mirror the existing social structure and its major forms of differentiation. Since the logic governing American inheritance laws, the successoral ideologies specific to the religious or national groups present in the United States, and the actual heirship practices of individual decedents are all based on postulates that are at least partially independent of one another, reproduction is limited (Berkner 1976:71–74).

The Three Components of Reproduction: What Endures?

Interaction among family members is governed by three kinds of constraints and opportunities: (1) their respective genetic makeup, as this makeup helps define the range of values within which physical appearance, emotions, and cognitive skills are deemed to be socially acceptable; (2) the economic resources available to them for taking full advantage of their physical or social endowments or to compensate for their weaknesses; and (3) the body of values and rules that specify the functions and objectives of social interactions and govern the underlying language.

The Biological Aspect of Inheritance

The notion of reproduction has primarily a biological meaning. It is dictated by the notion of "inclusive fitness" and more specifically by the propensity of individuals to maximize the number of copies of their own genes within the population" (Smith, Kish, and Crawford 1987:172). In other words, reproduction refers first to the physical continuity of individuals. In this sense, the impact of biology on inheritance is twofold. On the one hand, there cannot be inheritance or reproduction if there is no heir. Correspondingly, the continuity of families requires the existence of blood bonds and, in their absence, the legitimation of adoptees as appropriate substitutes. The Chinese practice of adopting sons-in-law when families could only beget daughters is not unique. The same practice prevailed in many other patrilineal societies and is documented, for instance, in some parts of the Pyrenees.[3]

On the other hand, the biological reproduction at work in inheritance also involves the perpetuation of specific physical qualities across generations. Not only is the "favorite son" often the look-alike of the testator, but there is also a more unconscious form of genetic selection of heirs. The genetic transmission of certain impairments such as hemophilia induces the differential morbidity of children who consequently do not enjoy similar chances to accumulate riches and to benefit from their parents' bequests.

The same genetic transmission operates also with regard to specific cognitive functions. Thus, correlations between the intelligence tests of siblings reared apart are higher than comparable correlations between strangers (Dobhzanski 1968; Jensen 1969). To the extent that siblings are more alike than strangers, the social or economic trajectories of the relevant pairs of individuals are likely to show a definite stability in differences in life chances *among* families. But to the extent that there are also stable differences in the abilities and motivations of siblings, these differences are often used to justify inequalities in their respective bequests (Lindert 1977). In a nutshell, heredity influences inheritance under two conditions: Interindividual differences in life chances must have a genetic origin. Further, these differences must be socially acknowledged and valued (positively or negatively).

The Economic Aspects of Inheritance

Inheritance evokes also the reproduction or perpetuation of existing economic activities and arrangements. Thus, transfers *mortis causa* sometimes enable children to take over the very occupations of their parents, becoming farmers, shopkeepers, artisans, and even professionals (medical doctors, lawyers, or architects). In other words, transfers of land, stores, equipment, or networks of clients contribute in part to the intergenerational continuity of the American occupational structure and of the ensuing inequalities.[4]

As already noted, the political agenda of debates concerning the reproductive functions of inheritance is about whether money can be anything but old and about why or how poverty breeds poverty. But this is not all. The perpetuation of occupational structures and of the parallel distributions of income or wealth may be imputed to contrasts in the genetic capital of discrete familial groups or in the differential methods and values of socialization they use. In other words, this perpetuation depends, in part, on how effective familial groups are in socializing their offspring to the mannerisms that are supposed to go with success.

Thus, whether the link between inheritance and reproduction concerns the perpetuation of inter- or of intrafamily inequalities, the basic question remains to ascertain the extent to which such disparities are the by-products of a stable series of differential sets of interactions between decedents and heirs. Understanding these differences makes it necessary to ascertain at what point of their life cycles heirs are chosen and groomed for the roles they will assume later on. By the same token, it is also necessary to ascertain whether the selection of heirs is based on the empirical observations that testators make about the distribution of vices and virtues among their potential survivors; or whether this selection reflects the collective wisdom accumulated by successive generations, regardless of the perceptions and preferences of individual testators.[5]

The Cultural Aspects of Inheritance

The preceding observations make it clear that inheritance reproduces primarily the existing cultural capital of familial groups. Legitimate intergenerational transfers reveal the normative structure of familial groups, that is, the rank ordering of feelings that relatives are expected to experience toward one another in function of the symbolic distance that stands between them (Craig 1979; Schneider 1980). To come back to examples already mentioned, contrasts in the amount, the form, and the timing of bequests made in favor of legitimate as opposed to illegitimate children, of legitimate spouses as opposed to lovers, or, increasingly so, of first as opposed to second or third spouses, say a great deal about overlaps and cleavages between the actual passions of decedents and their sense of what their families should look like.[6] Today as yesterday, to use here the words of Jack Goody, "the manner of splitting property is a manner of splitting people" (1976:8). Today as yesterday, the trajectories of specific objects such as jewelry, silverware, family Bibles, paintings, and clocks within as well as across generations reveal the need for successive individuals to assert the enduring quality of their feelings or of their commitments. In other words, the rank orderings of survivors and of objects are interrelated.

The underlying familial models involve the mix of ascriptive and achievement-based practices. For instance, the transmission of first names across generations or the transformation of last into middle names (as is sometimes the custom in the South) is based on ascription, because they are patterned as a function of the gender and birth order of children (Rossi 1965: Wyatt Brown 1982). At the same time, insofar as the attribution of names requires children to identify with their namesakes and imitate the latter's behaviors, the underlying transfer also involves achievement or, more specifically, the performance of a role the standards of which are set up by people other than the actors themselves (Vernier 1989).[7]

Thus, when familial models rank-order relatives within a same kin group, they use an implicit or explicit hierarchy of skills and knowledge. For example, specific assets of the estate are attributed, say, to male rather than female heirs, both because their use is deemed to require highly valued talents and because the distribution of such talents is supposed to be gender sensitive. These skills and knowledge cover a wide range of arenas from speech patterns to table manners. Stendhal's observation that the Catholic hierarchy in seminaries could detect among seminarists the "pious [and hence] proper way of eating a boiled egg" (as quoted by Bourdieu and Passeron 1970:150) parallels recurrent anecdotes about the importance for New Yorkers living in California to take speech lessons in order to dissimulate their geographic or social origins.[8] Success within the familial group as well as within the larger world requires individuals to mimic the behavior of those with power and influence.

In short, the cultural capital of a family refers to the conduct that its members are allowed or even encouraged to use in order to pass economic or political ordeals and achieve goals that are highly valued by the most significant actors of these familial groups (Cuddihy 1974). In the same way that the Kennedy sons were expected to win the presidency, their less fortunate "Smith" or "Brown" counterparts of today are expected to be the first ones to go to college, to attend Harvard, or to become medical doctors, as the case may be. Material inheritance contributes to the perpetuation of this cultural capital, but only insofar as the objects transferred *inter vivos* or *mortis causa* are associated with the evocation of sharply focused feelings toward particular relatives, toward the behaviors or ideas the latter epitomize, and toward the ideals that such behaviors symbolize. In this sense, inheritance is the repository of collective memories or values (Lichtman 1982; Hyde 1983). Thus, inheritance is about specific heritages.

Interaction among the Genetic, Economic, and Cultural Components of Inheritance

Heredity, inheritance, and heritage, as forms of transfer, respectively, of genetic, economic, and cultural capital, interact constantly with one another. Thus, long-term cycles of upward or downward economic mobility have a double effect on the developmental opportunities and constraints of successive generations. Since these cycles affect patterns of exogamous marriages and more specifically the economic, social, and cultural distance separating the respective familial groups of conjugal partners, the same cycles broaden or restrict the genetic pool of the populations under consideration. As such, they modify the limits of the human capital that individuals can acquire.[9] Yet these long-term economic forces also influence life-styles, notably with respect to nutrition and health, and thus the actual mobilization of this human capital. In a nutshell, economic growth facilitates the systematic development of human capital but, in turn, interindividual variations in the accumulation of this particular type of asset account for differences in the creation and upkeep of material wealth.

The preeminence of cultural over other forms of capital comes from the very fact that culture represents both "the rules and the stakes" of the game (Bowles and Gintis 1986:119).[10] Indeed, the very notion of genetic capital, any understanding of its components, and their evaluation are all the by-products of a stock of knowledge, beliefs, and practices that are differentially distributed across various subgroups and do not remain constant. Correspondingly, the definition and the manipulation of this particular form of capital are both a determinant and a result of power.

Similarly, the two types of economic exploitation (of nature and of other human beings) as well as the accumulation of the relevant forms of capital are contingent on knowledge, on its transformation into marketable skills, and on values (notably those concerned with innovation). The introduction of kiwifruit into the American diet offers a case in point. The feasibility of introducing the appropriate tree had to be determined. It was then necessary to find suitable production sites and to identify relevant marketing strategies. In this sense, the monetary profits to be derived from the exploitation of this exotic fruit were contingent on the preceding mobilization of the stock of data pertaining to food production and consumption. Even though economic resources have their own impact on culture, affecting both the dominant features and the variability of all sorts of arrangements, they cannot operate without the a priori cultural evaluation of the goals and processes involved in the corresponding economic activity. Similarly, culture affects both the criteria and the outcome of the selection of key social players (for example, who is supposed to marry whom, who is best suited to enter a specific job, or who is expected to succeed whom). Thus, nobody is indifferent to the characteristics of who sets the relevant rules or who enforces them. The mayor or the judge can make a difference in the lives of all sorts of private citizens. Who controls the rules would like to control the stakes and vice versa.

To conclude, the perpetuation of genetic, economic, and cultural forms of capital and the persistence of corresponding interindividual differences raises two significant challenges. On the one hand, it is never sufficient to document the persistence of inter- or intrafamilial contrasts in the distribution of material or symbolic resources. This documentation must be accompanied by an analysis of the material, cognitive, emotional, and normative strategies that human actors use in order to maintain or accentuate their privileges. In other words, it is not sufficient to observe that some people are, say, richer than others. It remains necessary to ascertain the type of wealth most valued by the rich, the knowledge they have of the risks involved, and the type of risks they are ready to take. Thus, the notion of reproduction is meaningful only insofar as it fosters a dynamic view of social relations, that is, a view that acknowledges the likelihood that humans might commit errors in the games they are playing and abide selectively by some of the relevant rules, but subvert others.

On the other hand, the dialectics between the choices of individual actors within the confines of familial groups, and the modes of cooperation and competition among their families must be identified. To be sure, reproduction involves individual choices and actions. But various social groups hold distinct views of paternal, maternal, or conjugal roles, and they also use distinct systems of rewards and punishments in order to keep parents, children, and spouses in line. As a result, for individuals, choices and actions are informed by the collective stocks of knowledge, skills, emotions, and values that major reference groups (gender, age cohort, social class, national origin, religious affiliation, etc.) develop about major events of human life, from sunrise to sunset, from the first to the last day of the year, and from birth to death.

As a result, the preeminence of cultural capital as a determinant of heirship practices precludes the existence of one and only one form of rationality. In the same way that economists describe segmented labor markets that have their own rules, there are distinct inheritance "markets" that reflect the impact of the variety of assets accumulated by individuals and by groups on patterns of bequeathing. The term *market* refers here to the systematic bodies of specific prescriptions and proscriptions concerning what to bequeath to surviving spouses as opposed to children, to sons as opposed to daughters, to first- as opposed to late-born children, or to married as opposed to unmarried children. In this sense, all families have their own cultural capital, which is the object of envy as well as scorn by others.

What is most problematic then is to identify the conscious as well as unconscious mechanisms that shape the sphere of influence of distinct cultural capitals and enable the actors of the relevant groups to impose their own models of behavior on other human beings. More specifically, what is most problematic is the time lag separating economic or demographic events from the changes they trigger in heirship practices (Ogburn 1955). As these events modify the opportunities to acquire wealth, and hence, the "rules" governing their acquisition, they also modify its distribution, and hence, the relevant "stakes" (Collins 1975:414).

The identification of the conscious and unconscious mechanisms that govern reproduction reveals yet two independent pitfalls. Whether in the domestic or in the public sphere, whether within or among families, reproduction cannot be the exclusive result of oppression through violence. To stress the exclusive use of violence by oppressors would be to underestimate the possibility of overt as well as covert rebellion by the oppressed. Alternatively, to view reproduction as being the exclusive result of oppression through corruption would be to underestimate both the greed as well as the dignity of the underdogs. In either case, one exaggerates the intelligence and the power of the elites. In either case, one undervalues the mobilizing abilities of the oppressed.

The Specificity of Reproduction in American Society: The Evidence

Before seeking to avoid these two pitfalls in exploring the determinants of reproduction, it is necessary to take stock of the evidence available as to how exceptionalism and the faith in intergenerational mobility it generates affect American heirship practices.

Even though exceptionalist views emphasize the independence of generations vis-à-vis one another, a particular member of the American elite noted during the Jacksonian era that success was contingent upon the "privileges of birth, formal education, and a cosmopolitan outlook on the world acquired through extensive travels" (quoted by Pessen 1973:154). The first step of the analysis consists then in ascertaining the relative stability in the distribution of these three types of valuable assets in the American population at large.

Reproduction in the Inequality of the Distribution of Wealth

As far as the privileges of birth are concerned, and hence as far as inheritance money is concerned, the pre–Civil War period was characterized by the strengthening of existing patterns of social stratification. Between 1833 and 1848, the percentage of wealth owned by the 1 percent wealthiest Bostonians climbed from 33 to 37 percent. Between 1826 and 1845, the corresponding figures went from 29 to 40 percent for New York and from 22 to 42 percent for Brooklyn. Moreover, these figures seem to have been the same for the entire American urban landscape of the period (Pessen 1971, 1973; Jaher 1982). Later on, the wealth hierarchy became even tighter. In 1925, over one-half of the rich had been born in rich families, against only one-third of their deceased predecessors (Sorokin 1925). Today, *Forbes* magazine suggests that no less than 59 percent of the richest Americans owe their wealth to their ascendants and there is evidence to suggest that the distribution of income is increasingly polarized, the proportion of families with the highest incomes increasing at the same rate as the percentage of familial groups falling below the safety net keeps climbing.

This current polarization of the American social structure makes it even more important to evaluate the form and the amount of transfers *mortis causa* among middle classes. The poor have nothing to transfer.[11] The very rich use uniform strategies not only because they rely on the advice of the same type of specialized lawyers and because they are subject to similar tax pressures, but also because their life-styles induce convergence in their stance toward survivors. Of all the groups, it is thus the middle classes who are the most likely to play a significant role in the redistribution of the remaining wealth. But this role is also problematic since the same middle-class families have been instrumental in the diffusion of the Horatio Alger myth, many of them believing in the discontinuous progress of successive generations.

Reproduction in the Inequality of the Distribution of Human Capital

The fortunes of one generation are shaped not only by direct transfers of nonhuman wealth, but also by human capital investments, as these are dictated by perceived inherited traits (Rosen 1988). Indeed, parents must decide how much money they intend to spend to booster the "natural" cognitive and emotional skills of their various children. Correspondingly, changes in the educational requirements of economic organizations and in the role of human capital as a source of wealth make it necessary to assess the evolving distribution of formal education within and across families (Langbein 1989). With economic development, there has been a simultaneous growth in college enrollment. The percentage of the total age group entering college has gone up from 6 percent in 1920 to 46 percent in 1980. To be sure, increases in college enrollment have been associated with a parallel decline in the differential participation of the various American social classes in higher education. There were practically no lower- or working-class college students until 1940. In 1980, no less than 90 percent of the children of upper and upper middle classes were enrolled in institutions of higher learning, as opposed to no less than one fourth of their male and one fifth of their female counterparts at the bottom of the social hierarchy (Levine, Mitchell, and Havighurst 1984).

However, these emerging convergences should not mask the transformation of educational disparities among the various segments of the American population. With the tightening of the links between educational and occupational markets, the rising national demand for higher education and the ensuing increase in college enrollment have been associated with a corresponding rise in tuition fees and overall college costs. There has been a subsequent accentuation of the differential college trajectories of individuals according to gender, socioeconomic level, or ethnic origin (Adams and Meidam 1968; Steelman and Powel 1989). In the past, what differentiated the rich and the poor educationally was whether they went to college. Today, what differentiates them the most is what kind of institution they attend. These institutions vary in terms of their locations, the private or public nature of their status, the number and depth of the programs they offer, and the socioeconomic or intellectual composition of their student bodies.[12] In effect, with rising postsecondary enrollment, the devices used by upper classes to maintain their advantages have become more subtle. This is akin to what Diana Crane (1972) called the "invisible colleges" in another context, the informal networks of information or rumors about what schools are "in" and what schools are "out." Differences in the pace with which families adapt to the subtle changes in the hierarchy of colleges are revealing of the place they occupy in the social as well as the cultural hierarchy.

What is less known, however, is how American parents choose to allocate increasingly scarce resources to the educational plans of their various children. Torn between the differentiation of tuition fees among colleges and the increased variability of the returns attached to distinct types and sources of degrees, parents must choose between the ideals of equality and identity as determinants of the educational strategies they adopt toward their children. Their decisions may reflect the differential distribution of abilities and achievements in function of birth order and gender, but they may also be dictated by the traditions governing the transmission of valuables. In the same way that the fathers of yesterday gave the farm to their oldest son, the urbanized middle-class parents of today may send their first-born sons to Harvard, and restrict, implicitly or explicitly, the range of educational opportunities available to their younger children.

Reproduction and the Inequality of the Distribution of Travel

The influence of travel on success is less obvious and less documented. Despite protests to the contrary, many Americans are concerned over the legitimacy of their achievements. In the United States as elsewhere, it is important to avoid appearing provincial and to adopt speech patterns and mannerisms that are typical of communities where money has always been supposed to be old. Henry James has described the travail undergone by the rich Americans of the last century in order to "pass" among established European elites. In many arenas and notably in the cultural sphere, success required Americans to be legitimated by significant European kingmakers. Painters and musicians were heralded as being successful only after they had gone to Europe and had "made it" in the right circles.

However, the days are long gone when cruises to Europe were only for the mighty and the affluent and when American-European marriages brought together the daughters of American empire builders and economically impoverished European noblemen. But in the same way that mass education transforms patterns of educational stratification, mass travel modifies the mechanisms used by the upper class to perpetuate its ranks through travel. What counts more and more is the place visited in relation to the season of the visit. April in Paris gives one quite a bit more prestige than August.

To conclude on the role of assets, of formal schooling, and of travel as sources of success, what is most remarkable about the contemporary American scene is the gap between the stability of the *actual* distributions of wealth and symbolic valuables and their *ideological* elaborations, which keep emphasizing success stories and keep underlining opportunities for mobility by indicating the various recipes that should make wealth and happiness universally accessible.

Determinants of Reproduction

To document the inertia of social life and its tendency to perpetuate itself does not explain it. To the extent that the writers who stress the importance of reproduction underline the stability of relations of dominance, their major task is to identify the factors that prevent or facilitate the perpetuation of existing arrangements.

Originally, inheritance was a key component of patriarchy. Modes of division of labor and of wealth within and among families reinforced one another. Patterns of marriage and of intergenerational transfers enabled families to retain both their internal structures and their dominance over the outside world. Whatever forms of transfers *mortis causa* most people adopted were alike. There were few deviations from the model set by the larger society.

Later, the predominance of corporate capitalism required the free circulation of money, of persons, and of ideas. As such, it required the diffusion of a liberal ideology that emphasized the universality of personal property rights but condemned inheritance as irrelevant or even as inimical to further development. With most families losing their grip on major means of production, who gave what to whom ceased to make a difference on the wealth and the income of either the average man or the larger society. Reproductions of social stratification and of familial structures became independent processes. While inequalities between bequests continued to modify interindividual differences in the form or the amount of wealth accumulated, their relative impact on the economic identity of familial groups has kept declining. Dynasties are limited in number.

To conclude, even though the choices of testators cease to have a uniformly significant impact on the national economy, these choices continue to serve essential private functions. As such, they are more than ever determined by the quest for legitimacy, that is, by the sense that people have of "the right thing to do." Historians and moralists refer to it as "noblesse oblige." In equivalent forms, this applies to a variety of social groups during a variety of historical periods. The desire to do the right thing, usually defined by precedents, and hence by the exemplary choices of forebears, is universal.

This is what Weber (1968) referred to when he observed that even though the Poles and the Germans cultivate the same land, with the same constraints and opportunities, they do not follow the same inheritance practices. To emphasize in this regard the role of the "irrational" and hence of the quest for a legitimacy rooted in the past is, of course, to underline the importance of crucial particularist sets of interaction between successive generations. Poles and Germans have distinct heirship systems because of differences in their histories and in their interpretations of the environment they are currently sharing.

The same irrationality is a fortiori evident in the United States because patterns of social differentiation and the ensuing diversity in the background of the population maximize the diversity of the sources of legitimation invoked. Because of this very diversity, the first step of the analysis consists in identifying the universal sociopsychological factors that operate as forces of reproduction.

The Role of Identification

Insofar as reproduction requires the conscious imitation of the beliefs and practices typical of preceding generations, it is a by-product of the identification of children with the more functional of their parents, that is, with the one who controls the material or symbolic resources they value most (Winch 1963). This assumption fosters two distinct propositions. First, testators select as beneficiaries the children who they perceive identify most closely with their own practices and beliefs. Alternatively, this very selection is itself influenced by the identification of the testators with their own ascendants. In this sense, distinct modes of identification are not necessarily mutually exclusive. Rather, they represent successive moments of the life-cycle of individuals who seek to elicit the generosity of potential testators and act "dependent" on them, before imitating the latter's practices or beliefs in dealing with their own heirs.

These two patterns of identification at work between testators and their beneficiaries can be positive or negative (in the latter case, deviations from prevailing parental strategies of inheritance represent covert or overt condemnations of the financial abilities of the parents, of their commitment to justice, or to equity, etc.). Identification patterns may also cover a narrow or a broad range of practices and interactions. The "heir" may imitate only the occupational activities of the testator, or he or she may also seek to imitate all the behaviors, speech patterns, or gestures of the character.

While the corresponding variations depend on the functionality of testators, that is, on the economic or socioemotional resources that they monopolize and that make the most dramatic difference in the lives of their heirs, they are also contingent on the organization of society at large and more specifically on the functions assigned to familial groups.

The Role of Regression

While the proximity of death should tighten the extent to which individuals imitate their own ascendants in their behavior toward their own survivors, their motivation should also be inspired by the regression that goes with fear. Thus, one can generalize here the argument of Whiting and Child (1953) about the effects that the positive and negative fixations experienced by the majority of children during their formative years exert on the collective interpretations of the causes and cures of illness in their cultures. For these authors, in the same way that the original indulgence displayed toward oral, anal, genital, dependent, and aggressive behaviors during childhood commands the cultural explanations of remedies, the subsequent repression of these five systems of behavior may help account for cultural explanations of illnesses.

Mutatis mutandis, cultural representations of death and survival may trigger analogous regressions. Thus, the negative fixations experienced by individuals during their childhood may help explain the cultural construction of the threats that death represents, the positive fixations experienced by the same individuals accounting for the elaboration of the strategies deemed most appropriate for countering these threats.

In short, the question is whether it is possible to transcribe the framework of Whiting and Child to identify the personal, albeit universal, components of reproductive processes. The desire to deserve the approval of the "significant dead" by imitating their practices serves as the psychological basis of the search for legitimacy and hence, for precedents.[13]

The Role of the Material Environment

Even though patterns of reproduction reveal the continuing influence that the significant others of preceding generations exert as role models, the actualization of such an influence still depends on the material bases of social life (Gregory 1989). Heirship strategies vary as a function of the impact that economic innovations have on the main sources of legitimation.

As long as there are *no* dramatic technological revolutions that create new opportunities and *no* ensuing transformation of relations of dominance in specific sectors, social arrangements perpetuate themselves, simply because alternative solutions are too costly to come about. Thus, the reproductive processes present in heirship strategies should be more marked during certain historical eras. In the United States, there should be few variations and few changes in heirship practices in the case of communities with limited rates of innovation. Such practices should persist longer among agricultural rather than among nonfarming families. Among the latter, these practices should also prevail in the case of familial groups engaged in occupational activities whose profits grow steadily rather than in the case of occupations subjected to dramatic up- and downswings.

In short, reproduction should be greater in the case of communities with lower rather than higher levels of complexity. It should also be more marked for those with lower rather than higher rates of technological change, or for those with linear rather than nonlinear patterns of change. Further, to the extent that technological and economic revolutions foster parallel innovations in heirship practices, these innovations may or may not be irreversible. Indeed, they may change individual means, but not their ends.

The Role of Cultural Isolation

The relative isolation of the populations under study contributes also to determine the extent to which their familial arrangements perpetuate themselves. Cultural isolation involves three distinct forces that affect the variety of contacts that individuals retain with their alikes. The effects of *residential* isolation are enhanced by continuing *endogamy* since their combination facilitates linguistic and religious stability and thus, faithfulness to distinctive norms and practices (Alba 1988, 1990).[14] The effects of *occupational* segregation along ethnic lines are analogous, since they homogenize the networks of constraints and opportunities enjoyed by initial settlers and facilitate the retention of common cultural and notably legal components.

Take the case of the Germans. The heirship practices adopted by initial waves of German immigrants in America during the later part of the eighteenth century were inspired by their continuing interest in inheriting from their own parents in Germany and by the ensuing difficulty of dealing simultaneously with the strategies best suited to the American economy and ideology and those strategies they learned in the old country (Roeber 1987). Since these settlers were scattered in homogeneous pockets throughout the country, they had little knowledge of American law and often relied on their own German priests to translate the dispositions of their wills in terms compatible with the local common law.

Yet, those Germans who best managed to preserve some of their inherited legal culture were the ones who were sufficiently educated to use most effectively, if selectively, the relevant mechanisms of English inheritance law. Their behavior in this regard confirms the validity of Maine's views on the innovative functions of wills. Insofar as testators write wills in order to depart from prevailing rules and models, they must know such rules and models, and hence be sufficiently educated to adapt easily to the legal culture of the host country.

There are reasons to believe that what was typical of the first waves of German immigrants can be generalized to the first waves of migrants who subsequently arrived in the New World, from the Italians or the Greeks of the nineteenth century to the Cubans or the Vietnamese of the more recent past. In the world of today, the high concentration of Vietnamese in certain occupations exposes them to a variety of similar technical and economic risks, especially in view of their continuing residential segregation. As a result, they retain a common symbolic vocabulary, especially since the linguistic effects of these two forms of isolation are reinforced by their endogamy.

The combined effects of residential and occupational segregation and the various forms of endogamy on individual communications underscore the contributions of religion, ethnicity or national origin, social class, and gender to the patterns of reproduction at work in transfers *mortis causa*. Indeed, these five factors constitute the major sources of legitimation operating in American society today. The range of behaviors involved in this identification is larger whenever familial groups play a significant economic or social role, but it gets narrower and less institutionalized in response to any decline in the economic or political functionality of these familial groups.

The Effects of Religion

Historically, the church influenced heirship as it sought to convince European decedents to limit the amount of transfers made in favor of relatives and alternatively to increase bequests made to its charities, monasteries, and schools. In return, the church was willing to guarantee the validity and enforcement of individuals wills, notably by giving them the appropriate written form (Aries 1981; Goldthorpe 1987). The meaning of the word *testament* is twofold in this regard. Today as yesterday, it has economic referents. But as the document is also a testimony to the faith of the decedent, its sacred character requires witnesses. This was precisely the role played by the clergy from the Middle Ages to the end of the eighteenth century. In other words, today as yesterday, the word stands to remind us that the legitimation of the emotional bonds highlighted by heirship requires the visible or invisible presence of a third party.

Even today, religion remains a major source of reproduction because it continues to alleviate the anxieties stirred by illness as well as by death. In France, for example, the notions of estate and of legacy help to differentiate Catholics from other religious subgroups. More than Protestants or atheists, Catholics emphasize their commitment to preserving the symbolic capital handed down to them (Michelat and Simon 1977, 1985). Evidence is more spotty in the case of the United States. Yet, variations in the religious orientation of Americans continue to be associated with parallel contrasts in transfers *mortis causa* and in the perpetuation of the major activities of familial groups. For example, since Apostolic Christian residents in Illinois practice church endogamy and follow patrilocal arrangements, they place wives and daughters in a subordinate position vis-à-vis both their husbands and their mothers-in-law. In contrast, their Mennonite neighbors follow much looser rules of mate selection and allow all women to enjoy more economic and social autonomy. The first group views transfers *mortis causa* as a means of both maintaining economic security and perpetuating a religious way of life, in contrast to their Mennonite counterparts, who are more committed to fairness among their children regardless of gender. The first type of community is further apart from the American mainstream than the second one, but in its attempt to perpetuate cultural ideals that are more marginal, it also ensures more successfully the perpetuation of existing economic arrangements (Salamon and Davis Brown 1988).

In urban environments, religion should continue to play the same role as a reproductive agency, whenever or wherever the relevant parishes are organized around ethnic lines and are served by clerics with the same national origin as their flock. In other words, the persistence of the legitimating power of religion depends on the organizational profile of individual churches.

The Effects of National Origin

National origin represents another source of legitimation of the heirship practices of Americans for two distinct reasons. On the one hand, national origin perpetuates the image that American society at large and its influential opinion makers harbor of a particular population. As this image commands the range of permissible behaviors and beliefs, ethnicity or national origin tends to be coterminous with social class (Lieberson 1980). Individual shares of the pie vary with the amount of prejudice displayed by the majority of immigrants already in the market. On the whole, these shares tend to increase with the relative Americanization of the populations under study.

On the other hand, national origin represents also a crucial component of self-identity, especially when it entails the retention of a language other than English. In this sense, national origin or ethnicity reproduces distinct ideologies that are independent of the immediate material conditions of social life. In this sense, national origin and religion are closely intertwined, even in the case of Catholicism, the forms of which differ between Italians, Irish, Germans, and Mexicans. In the central part of Illinois, where the land has a relatively uniform value and offers the same opportunities, Irish-American, German-American, and Yankee farmers tend to practice distinct heirship strategies that are influenced by the specificity of their respective cultural backgrounds (Salamon 1980; Carroll and Salamon 1988). The first group retains the same rule of impartibility that prevails in Ireland; the second group retains the same rule of partibility that is typical of the northern part of Germany from which the group originated[15]; finally, the third group has been more indifferent to the problems associated with intergenerational continuity.

To be sure, these cleavages may be restricted to farming. In contrast to other occupations, farming facilitates the perpetuation of specific familial ideals because it is often associated with occupational inheritance and with the continuous socialization of children by their parents to a specific life-style. But the same forces should account for the persistence of ethnic discontinuities among all occupations where the entire family remains involved in the production of income, and thus also in fishing, shopkeeping, craft, and a variety of small businesses.

The differential perpetuation of these ideals seems, however, to be contingent on other factors. In the state of Rhode Island, for example, not only do Irish-Americans tend to be concentrated in specific occupations, but they tend also to marry at a later age and to display marriage patterns that differentiate them strikingly from the other nationalities (Italian, Portuguese, and French Canadians) present in the state (Kobrin and Goldscheider 1978). These contrasts may parallel the differential opportunities and constraints faced by Irish-Americans and other ethnic groups in the region, but they may also stem from the specific material bequests and symbolic legacies passed down to individual Irish children of successive generations as a result of their birth order, their gender, or other personal traits.

In short, the point is that in elaborating distinct representations of familial roles, national groups construct distinct models of inheritance. Further, these groups differ from one another in terms of how long they retain the practices corresponding to such models after departing from their native land. They also differ from one another in terms of the processes that govern the selective retention of these practices.[16]

The Role of Social Class

The relative reproduction of social classes depends on the same mix of forces as national origin. Insofar as social class evokes the perpetuation of differences in income, expenditure patterns, or wealth accumulation, it is a by-product of the network of constraints imposed by other social classes (Parkin 1979). But the reproduction of social class also reflects contrasts in both the demands that parents impose on their children and the techniques of rewards and punishments they use to achieve their goals (Miller and Swanson 1958, 1960). As noted by Goblot (1980) quoted by Le Wita (1988:133), "one belongs to a family before belonging to a social class. A middle class born person becomes middle class through and with his/her family". In this sense, the concept of social class also evokes the concept of culture, because it refers to intergenerational continuity in how much individuals learn to acquire, what they acquire, from whom they are expected to inherit, in whose favor they are taught they should bequeath, and in what form.[17]

To the extent that the *form* of wealth owned is as important a determinant of beliefs and practices as its *amount*, the reproductive power of social class should decline over time with the contradictions of interests that the differentiation of the economy creates within the same class. For instance, while the profits derived from land investments and commercial ventures by their ascendants enabled many second generations of rich Americans during the Jacksonian era to participate in new industrial activities, the ensuing segmentation of the sources of wealth has also contributed to create autonomous subcultures and to weaken the initial solidarity of the mighty and the affluent.[18] The heirship strategies of the "landed aristocracy" cannot be the same as the logic of the "industrialist entrepreneurs" or of the contemporary managerial elites of large corporations: their respective patterns of consumption and hence of savings differ. So do the attitudes of these three groups as to the optimal links between specific assets and specific eligible heirs.

Similarly, insofar as the entrepreneurial and bureaucratic families of some thirty years ago adopted distinct child-rearing practices, they created distinct personality types, each with its own psychological traits. To the extent that these entrepreneurs and bureaucrats were successful in legitimizing their respective life-styles, the ensuing differences have probably persisted until today (Miller and Swanson 1958). The first type of familial group should continue to emphasize material transfers, the second one being more inclined to stress the financing of higher education. The former should see education as a narrowly defined investment, the latter as a source of status and access to fruitful social networks.

The Role of Gender

The sociocultural reproduction of gender depends on both the particular modes of identification between daughters and their mothers and the patterns of exclusion used by men to maintain their sisters, wives, or daughters in relations of subservience.

Thus, as in any other castelike hierarchy, the perpetuation of gender stratification requires the simultaneous intervention of conflicting criteria. These criteria are universalistic whenever they work in favor of the dominant group. Alternatively, they become centered on ascription when the elite doubts being able of perpetuating its dominant status.[19] Likewise, the reproduction of any gender hierarchy requires a mix of achievement- and ascription-based ideologies, depending on whether men feel certain of their superiority.

Further, this reproduction requires a significant asymmetry in the bequeathing behaviors of male and female testators toward their sons and their daughters. Patriarchy requires the "betrayal" of female testators, who should not hesitate to discriminate against their female eligible heirs. The fact is that American mothers do not entertain the same expectations about the behaviors of their male and female children. During the early phases of the life cycle, their expectations concerning the formal education of sons are more elaborate than those concerning the schooling of daughters (Gasson et al. 1988). Further, their desire to see their daughters "reproduce" their own behaviors depends on the latter's birth order (Kammeyer 1966). Later in the life cycle, they also expect more in emotional or instrumental terms from their daughters than from their sons (Wolf 1984).

In short, the reproduction of gender reflects both the complicity of adult men and women, and the lack of female solidarity within the confines of familial groups and in the larger society. Thus, American mothers are more often sensitive to variations in the behaviors of their daughters than of their sons. More egalitarian vis-à-vis the latter, they exclude or reward their female children for particularistic reasons (Rosenfeld 1974).

The Limits of the Notion of Reproduction

Up to now, I have examined the various reproductive processes embedded in inheritance. Yet, the perpetuation of any cultural or social arrangement is always limited. As already noted by Wilbert Moore, "the wheel of time turns not only on itself, but also on a changing terrain" (1964:338) or to quote Bowles and Gintis, "society is both a reproductive and contradictory totality' (1986:18).

Strangely enough, few sociologists pay enough attention to these two remarks, which emanate clearly from the two opposite ends of the political continuum. Such neglect entails a reification of the concept of reproduction for two opposite reasons. The implicit ahistoricity of functionalist writers and the stress they place on self-reliance or achievement force them arbitrarily to view inheritance as being obsolete or even socially dysfunctional. Alternatively, the obsession of conflict sociologists with the power and the wealth of current elites leaves them no room for taking account of errors or subversions. Yet, these errors and subversions exist. The consequences of loves and hatreds weigh evenly on all social groups. But while no one can escape history, the influence of history is not automatic either (DiTomaso 1982). The tyranny imputed to a chameleon-like socialization parallels the tyranny imputed to history.

To acknowledge these two opposite sociological perspectives underlines the need to appreciate the dual nature of transfers *mortis causa* as reproductive processes. On the one hand, the structuring of successive generations aims at counteracting the centrifugal forces of history in order to maximize the continuity of social relations. In this sense, transfers *mortis causa* are located in a sociological time, that is, in a time made of equivalent units that can be easily manipulated. For example, trusts seek to keep intact the rank ordering of successive generations and of children, independently of their respective intentions, resources, and life spans. Again, bequests made in favor of sons facilitate the perpetuation of the existing gender hierarchy, both within and between familial groups.

On the other hand, these transfers occur also in an historical time, that is, in a time where things can never be the same and where change is unpredictable. This is the origin of the two notions of a changing terrain or of a contradictory whole, as well as the source of the paradox that Americans often impute to the French, "Plus cela change, plus c'est la même chose." The more powerful the winds of change, the more the family acts as a buffer against the turmoil of the outside world. But this role of the family as a buffer is effective only insofar as the forms and the timing of intergenerational transfers become more differentiated.

Mechanical versus Interpretive Forms of Reproduction

This constant tug of war between the desire to keep things the way they are and the need to adapt to a constantly changing environment creates two distinct (mechanical and interpretive) forms of reproduction (Bourdieu and Passeron 1970). Mechanical reproduction involves strict homologies between each component of the original and of the new figure. In the case of transfers *mortis causa*, heirs enter the totality of the roles performed by the decedents. In Africa, the son (or sons) takes over the father's farm or business and marries the latter's widow.[20]

On the other hand, interpretive reproduction involves symbolic equivalents between the original and the new figure. For example, in the rituals associated with mourning, the Nisei follow the Japanese rule of etiquette, which imposes on the extended kin the obligation to feed the close relatives of the deceased. Since the Nisei mourn in the United States, however, money is substituted for rice (Yaganisako 1978). The rule remains the same, even though its overt manifestations change. Similarly, transfers *mortis causa* continue to foster the perpetuation of the existing rank ordering of relatives and, hence, the dominance of spouses over children, or of sons over daughters, or of first- over later-born children, but the perpetuation of the hierarchy is contingent on the choice of appropriate material symbols. Since the environment evolves, so do the material symbols of success. As already noted, in the same way that the oldest son of yesteryear got the farm, his counterpart of today may get his tuition to Harvard paid.

Mechanical forms of reproduction are likely to prevail in stable communities where rates of demographic or economic changes are moderate. Even in communities where these rates are higher, they should persist in the case of occupations or social groups with a minimal sensitivity to the forces of a market economy. Thus, they should persist longer among farmers and among small businesses geared toward their own survival rather than to profit. In the United States, as already suggested, mechanical forms of reproduction are at work in the successoral practices of specific groups of Illinois farmers and their Mennonite neighbors, or in the case of German as opposed to Yankee farmers.

But there are also recurrent manifestations of interpretive reproduction, as unwittingly observed by Tocqueville when he noted that with the sons of the great landowners of New York now becom[ing] merchants, lawyers, or doctors, the last traces of hereditary rank and distinction have been destroyed (1969). Unwittingly, because he assumed that there is only one form of reproduction and that heirs inherit land, wealth, and power all at once. In effect, the rich landowners of New York to which he referred understood that the emergence of new forms of wealth would be acquired through what would be called much later "human capital." Correspondingly, many of their sons owed their legal training to the resources that their ancestors had acquired by exploiting the land. Whaling, commerce, and insurance formed the other and more recent bases from which subsequent familial fortunes originated (Pessen 1973). With the systematic development of human capital and the simultaneous increase of large-scale economic organizations, the number of strategies used for maintaining the wealth and/or the power of familial groups has kept increasing. Patterns of reproduction have become even more interpretive.

But insofar as interpretive reproduction prevails in communities characterized by high rates of change, it involves a variety of risks. Indeed, both errors and subversions keep generating discontinuities in the dynamics of social stratification. Even though the relevant evidence is available exclusively outside the United States, it still highlights the processes by which both demographic and economic constraints modify the current forms of intergenerational solidarity (Cole and Wolf 1974; Stys 1957). For example, among rural societies that have adopted the practice of bequeathing equal shares to male children, patterns of marriage and fertility rates tend to be high until a sufficient number of families begin experiencing the effects of land scarcity. As a result of these pressures, not only do these families delay the marriage of their children, who themselves have fewer children, but in addition they tend also to violate increasingly overtly the prescription of equality among children.

Alternatively, the increased availability of land and the presence of additional opportunities for profit introduce significant counterweights to the restrictions associated with impartibility. Families become more committed to equity and underplay the role of gender, birth order, or matrimonial status because they have enough to endow all their children with the resources necessary for surviving in distinct environments. In short, whenever the material bases of social life keep changing, the ensuing up- and downswings of the economy introduce discrepancies into heirship ideologies and practices. This is what Tocqueville observed in the case of the farmers of New York State.

The challenge remains to ascertain the conditions under which these discrepancies are reversible or follow a cumulative pattern. Regardless of whether the findings are relevant to the American scene, comparisons between two small islands, one in Western Europe, the other in the Caribbean region, show that whenever local economic conditions generate both emigrations and exogamy, the original rules of inheritance followed by local populations lose their grip and become irrelevant (Brennan, James, and Morrill 1981). *Mutatis mutandis*, the perpetuation of the heirship practices and beliefs of immigrants in the United States should disappear with their integration into the socioeconomic or cultural mainstream. For instance, the Connecticut communities first integrated in the market economy and having first adopted a commercial mode of agricultural exploitation were also those that first adopted the individualized and egalitarian heirship strategies typical of the modern exceptionalist ideology (Ditz 1986).

Yet the irreversible effects of the market in this regard may be slowed and blurred by the peculiarities specific to intergenerational feelings and bonds. From one *odd* to the next *odd* generation (grandparents and grandchildren), there is often a partial restoration of the commitment to the catalog of original prescriptions and proscriptions. Because these generations feel close to one another in their ambivalences toward their *even* counterparts (the sons of the former and the parents of the latter), they can understand better the norms and values of the old country.

To sum up, the limits governing the reproductive processes inherent in transfers *mortis causa* involve patterns of convergences and divergences in the practices of decedents and of heirs. There are convergences because American economic development facilitates the expansion of middle classes. There are also convergences because the growing complexity of the law induces an increasing number of testators to prepare wills through lawyers. In other words, the legal subculture tends to supersede the variety of distinct occupational, religious, or national ideologies. Finally, there are also convergences because the behaviors of originally distinct subgroups are inspired by uniform definitions of legitimacy. For instance, as homosexuality becomes more acceptable as an alternative life-style, "informal cohabitation partners" (to use the appropriate expression) are increasingly keen to draw wills in favor of one another. In drawing wills rather than making gifts *inter vivos*, they choose, however, to legitimize their bonds and to place themselves in the mainstream. In this sense, they reproduce the very "patriarchal" arrangements they have rejected.

Alternatively, the accentuation that economic growth introduces has mixed effects on existing patterns of differentiation. For example, the differentiation of assets and occupational roles keeps modifying patterns of wealth accumulation. As another example, the increasing frequency of divorces is probably paralleled by the creation of one or several subcultures that attempt to introduce variations that differ from the model of the typical nuclear family. For instance, the partial restoration of loyalties between grandparents and their grandchildren seems to be more pronounced for divorced than for stable families. And the restoration is more marked on the maternal than paternal side.

Summary and Conclusions

The link between transfers *mortis causa* and reproduction highlights the three basic ambiguities underlying relations between generations. First, while these relations may be governed by patterns of socialization and hence by the differential stress placed on specific values and the differential use of rewards and punishments, they may also reflect the basic components of the existing social structure and hence the current distribution of the opportunities and constraints confronted by decedents at the time of their deaths.[21] While the combination of these cultural and structural forces tends to create constant tensions between the reproductive and innovative facets of transfers *mortis causa*, these tensions are most acutely experienced toward the middle of the social hierarchy. It is there that heirs make most of their parent's bequests. It is there that they also squander most frequently the trust and the resources of their parents. Thus, it is the analysis of middle-class heirship practices that is most important for understanding the relative rigidity of patterns of social stratification.

Second, while intergenerational relations evoke the continuity of familial loves and hatreds and, through such feelings, of the values embraced by specific familial groups, they also evoke the hierarchy of ideas, feelings, and values defined by society at large. Hence, what counts in the analysis of transfers *mortis causa* is to identify the links between what goes on within the family and what goes on between individuals of such a family and the outside world. Hence, the analysis must focus on the interaction between testators and their surroundings. Interrelations between these two facets of the family underline the need to identify the boundaries of the family as a "reproductive unit" and to ascertain what happens when these boundaries cease to be coterminous with those of the family as a "production unit" and those of the family as a "consumption unit" (Dupont and Dureau 1988).

Finally, reproduction is always imperfect. Seeing inheritance as exclusively determined by the past ends up arbitrarily glorifying an arbitrarily defined tradition. Alternatively, however, emphasizing the responsiveness of inheritance to current opportunities and networks ends up benignly neglecting the major sources of legitimacy. Thus, the need emerges to assess both the temporal and functional limits of reproduction. In this sense, it is important to ascertain specifically what endures and for how long. Is it the wealth itself that stays somehow in the hands of the same families? Or is it the rules that make the difference between the most and the least fortunate familial groups or relatives? The ensuing explanation requires the analysis to encompass at least two adjacent generations.

3
The Burden of Proof in the Study of Heirship

The validity of any study concerning variations in patterns of wealth accumulation and transfer is contingent on two conditions: the representativeness of the samples used as sources of evidence, and the instruments used for obtaining the information one seeks.

The high cost of data collection obliges social scientists to rely on miniatures of the real world. But what do these miniatures represent? One easily forgets the distinct aspects of the notion of representativeness. The sample must represent the whole range of beliefs or behaviors deemed problematic. In other words, the "internal" validity of the study depends on the extent to which the sample mirrors the full link deemed to exist between the suspected causes and their effects. This mirroring is not always perfect. The range of behaviors recorded in the sample may lead one to over- or underestimate the power of the force suspected of acting.

In addition, the sample must also represent the incidence of the range of beliefs and behaviors considered worth studying in the population at large. In other words, representativeness concerns also the "external" validity of the study, that is, the extent to which the results obtained can be generalized to other populations and other seasons.

Many social scientists are trained to believe that randomization contributes to enhancing the representativeness of samples. Yet they often forget that the effectiveness of this strategy requires specific assumptions about the normal distributions of physical, psychological, or social traits in the population at large. Sometimes there is no a priori evidence to support these assumptions.[1] Much too often, the search for representative samples is an empty ritual, because it is not informed by a theoretical concern for the project. In such a case, the quest for methodological purity becomes simply formal.

The second major condition concerns the validity of the instruments used. As such, it depends on the biases that the *form* of the data introduces in their *content*. Much too often, social scientists forget that the opposition encountered by Galileo and Einstein concerned as much the procedure used for collecting the evidence as the theories defended by these two scientists. The former was challenged for his use of the telescope; the latter for his use of the camera. If one fears the consequences of the artifactual nature of the evidence used in astronomy or in physics, that fear should be even more pronounced in the social sciences. Human subjects react more swiftly and/or more intensely than other creatures to the instruments purported to measure their behaviors. Further, in the social sciences, it is difficult to distinguish predictions from self-fulfilling prophecies or from rationalizations. Individuals may respond to an objective stimulus; they may respond to what they think is the stimulus, confirming thereby its reality; and they may also construct a reality that satisfies their needs or reduces their frustrations. To the extent that the conclusions of many social scientists are based on the written or verbal accounts that the subjects themselves offer of their beliefs or their actions, how can researchers decide whether such accounts mirror faithfully the behavioral or attitudinal reality they stand for? What do these traces tell us about the actual world? How do we distinguish in what sense they offer justifications rather than explanations?

Self-generated accounts like wills may be more reliable than externally induced reports, precisely because they represent public statements of their author's intentions that cannot be modified after his or her death and become therefore accountable.[2] The adversarial procedures used for the execution of wills constantly test the "truth" concerning the value of the assets accumulated by the decedent, his or her choice of heirs, and the form or the amount of his or her bequests. In contrast, one can never be sure about the origin, the direction, or the extent of the biases introduced in responses to interviews or to questionnaires. The anonymity of respondents does not always guarantee the quality of their responses.

The Representativeness of Samples

As suggested, the notion of representativeness raises questions about the link between the sample and the universe from which it is derived. In order to better understand transfers *mortis causa*, the sample need not mirror the entire population of individuals who passed away during a particular year. The information sought pertains only to the behaviors and practices of those persons who have actually accumulated wealth and were empowered to make bequests. Since the study concerns the cultural and economic determinants of the choices facing individuals at the twilight of their lives, the sample should be representative of adults rather than of children. Few children have an estate. No minor has a say as to what to do with it. By the same token, it should be representative of the universe of estates rather than of decedents. By definition, the poor do not leave anything behind them.

To make these distinctions is not to indulge in a mere academic exercise. The universes involved have distinct sizes. Decedents who leave an estate represent only a segment of all decedents. Decedents who leave an estate and can choose the destination of this estate are even fewer.

The procedures used to draw samples that represent various aspects of intergenerational transfers also differ from one another. So far, research on inheritance has involved four distinct sampling strategies. In their comparative analyses of testacy in Los Angeles and Bucks counties during the eighteenth, nineteenth, and twentieth centuries, Carol Shammas, Marilyn Salmon, and Michael Dahlin (1987) have drawn a sample of probate documents (hence of estates sufficiently large to be taxable) before assessing how this could tell them something significant about the population of decedents at large. Only subsequently did these researchers ask themselves whether their sample fit the universe of all the adult individuals who died during the three periods of reference.

Alternatively, in their study of heirship practices in Cleveland, Marvin Sussman, Judith Cates, and Daniel Smith (1970) started their enquiry from a sample of death certificates before identifying in a second step which of these certificates were associated with the registration of a will. In other words, they followed a strategy opposite to that adopted by Shammas and her coauthors, by moving from a partially relevant but large population to the specific target of their queries.

Other analyses rely on differing sets of preliminary assumptions. In her analyses of heirship practices of German-American, Irish-American, and Yankee farmers, which I use extensively, Sonya Salamon relies on the names of individuals registered as holding titles to distinct pieces of land to define the population she wants to study. In doing so, she satisfies the requirements of internal validity only insofar as her use of family names as indicators of national origin is validated by some other source (such as the type of church attended or the language abilities of her subjects). She does not, however, make any claim concerning external validity. Thus, she does not say anything about the possibility of generalizing her findings to German- and Irish-Americans engaged in other economic pursuits elsewhere in the United States, or to other national groups. Similarly, in his study of heirship attitudes and behaviors among the inhabitants of retirement homes in New Jersey, Jeffrey Rosenfeld (1979a and b) focuses his analysis on a circumscribed locale in order to see the influence of the environment on the differential bonds that elderly patients establish with their survivors and with their care providers. He does not claim, however, that his conclusions can be generalized to other populations.

A last strategy consists in reconstructing both bequests and estates from the accounts of heirs. This strategy has been adopted by Jencks (1979), but most significantly by Tomes (1988), who challenges the conclusions of Menchik (1988) regarding the practices of American testators.

Contrasts in the construction of these samples entail variations in the nature and the quality of the data. Clearly, the first study cannot yield immediately reliable information on the effects of education or religion on patterns of accumulation or distribution of wealth, since the raw data do not include any relevant information in this regard. Researchers are obliged to rummage through other sources in the hope of extracting the missing pieces of the puzzle they have already elaborated. Alternatively, the other studies to which I have referred may help in evaluating the impact of schooling or occupation, but the information they offer on variables such as estate size or composition may be suspect whenever the relevant data are generated through direct interviews with respondents.

To conclude, the representativeness of the analyses derived from any sample is always relative. For example, Salamon's conclusions concerning heirship practices in rural Illinois are indicative rather than demonstrative of the perpetuation of national models of inheritance in the contemporary United States. Is the persistence of contrasts between the heirship practices of German- and Irish-American farmers due to the particular mode of agricultural production prevailing in this specific part of the Midwest? Can the differences observed be generalized to other populations of self-employed decedents, to other regions, or to other national groups?

The questions raised highlight the opposite concepts of control in social analyses. At one end of the continuum, the notion of control is based on the use of chance. In allowing as much irrelevant "noise" or as many random variations as possible in the equation, the researcher seeks to capture the significance of central tendencies. With this type of control, one seeks primarily to ascertain the *average* response of the subjects to the stimulus presumed to act on their behaviors. One is interested to test how much the link deemed to exist between independent and dependent variables departs from random variations.

At the other end of the same continuum, control consists in reducing as much as possible the variability of the dependent and independent variables. In so doing, the researcher seeks to assess whether the relationship deemed to exist between the two sets of factors stands up in spite of systematic restrictions on the variance of the distributions of the phenomena studied.

In contrast to the first strategy, which offers an overview of the relationships pertinent to the phenomenon one seeks to explain, the second is exploratory. It is often used at the very onset of a research project. But it also helps to rely on deviant cases in order to achieve a better understanding of the dynamics at work, once the major links between dependent and independent variables have been identified.

As we shall suggest, the challenge of this second strategy is to ascertain whether the results obtained are alike for all the parts of the distribution. For example, when one observes that the frequency of one particular heirship practice, say, partibility and the ensuing equality among heirs, increases with estate size, even though one has deliberately skewed the sample toward the lower end of the wealth continuum, the question is to ascertain whether the relationship holds true for higher parts of that continuum or even for the continuum as a whole.

The Choice of a Sample of Estate Tax Returns

An evaluation of the variety of sampling strategies reviewed here helps in delineating two solutions worth considering. The first consists of drawing a sample of wills from the registrar of wills, from surrogate courts, or from the organization that plays the same role in other parts of the country. This solution is advantageous insofar as the relevant documents fall in the public domain. This facilitates the use of a large *current* sample. Yet, the solution also presents shortcomings. The drawing of the sample would involve quite cumbersome procedures since there is no listing available from which one might draw names that would be relevant for the purpose of the study. Thus, there is no way to know the size of the universe from which one wants to draw a sample. In addition, the sample would be necessarily local since the registrar of wills or any similar public entity is only competent over a restricted geographic space.

The second solution consists in drawing a sample of federal estate tax returns. The sample is easier to draw as long as IRS authorities are willing to produce a list of the returns potentially available for various years. Further, these returns facilitate a large-scale study since they cover the entire United States. At the same time, it is necessary to take into account limitations on the documents collected by IRS. Estate tax returns always serve administrative rather than scholarly purposes. Their first function was and is the collection of revenues. Hence, scholarly analyses of these documents are a secondary by-product. While the data collected must be precise in order to collect as much tax as possible from the estates under scrutiny, the file does not include variables that would be useful to the researcher but to which public authorities would be indifferent.

The IRS intergenerational wealth transfer file has two origins. First, it includes all wealth holders with an estate over $1.5 million and a sample of decedents who died during a year ending with the digit 8, 9, or 0, the likelihood for such decedents to be included being a reverse function of their estate size. But the file also contains a sample of decedents for the years 1944 and 1945 that was initially collected for another survey of American wealth, but with the same guiding principles.

The file begins in 1920 (there was no federal estate tax before 1916), a date that constitutes therefore the lower time boundary of the history of American testacy that can be explored. At the current end of the historical continuum, both the rules against disclosure and the costs of transforming recent individual returns into a fully computerized database make it impossible to study populations who passed away after 1950, a date that represents therefore the upper time boundary of the history of American testacy that can be examined. Thus, the use of the file is subject to time limitations. It provides potential information on the relevant practices of decedents who belong to a relatively recent, but not immediate past. The findings remain nevertheless useful as guidelines for exploring current inheritance practices.

The absence of any systematic information on the inheritance practices of successive generations of the American population leads me to base the identification of the small sample used for the study on the three following principles, which all reflect recurrent tensions between the rationality and the legitimacy of the decisions that decedents take with regard to the accumulation of their wealth and its transmission to their heirs.

The Importance of Estate Size

The specific profile of the distribution of wealth in the United States renders the concept of average wealth meaningless. As elsewhere, the very top of the distribution of national wealth is concentrated in relatively few hands. The composition of this group remains stable over historical time. The list of the richest Americans established by *Fortune* still includes a large number of individuals whose forefathers were already at the top of the distribution (Kessler and Masson 1988a,b). Conversely at the bottom of the socioeconomic ladder, poverty seems to reproduce itself. The higher mortality rates of the poor do not prevent them from begetting poor children. It is the middle of the socioeconomic distribution that is both the most elusive and unstable. It is this very middle that acts both as the source and as the target of the Horatio Alger myth. In this sense, it is the very population for which it is most crucial to test the extent, the form, and the limits of the reproductive processes at work in inheritance.

To concentrate on the middle part of the wealth continuum (relatively speaking) corresponds therefore to two distinct objectives. This study seeks to illuminate the relevant practices of a *larger* number of Americans. It seeks also to explore the *maximal* tensions faced by decedents. In short, the choice of the sample is informed by Jack Goody's remarks (1976) about the greater importance that decedents with limited resources attach both to the amount of the bequests they make and to the profile of their beneficiaries. Indeed, one can generalize Goody's remarks to the choices that decedents make in the composition of their estates. Does the relatively precarious nature of their wealth induce them to concentrate or, alternatively, to diversify their portfolios?

To be sure, the middle part of the wealth distribution is difficult to define. In 1920, a study of the Federal Trade Commission conducted on twenty-four counties of thirteen states concluded that almost three-quarters of adult decedents left no estate (Woods 1928).[3] Insofar as this finding is reliable, the lower limit of middle-class wealth is higher than is usually believed. Middle classes represent a more exclusive "club" than the ideology praising upward mobility would induce us to believe. At the upper end of the continuum, the same study showed that the estates of over $500,000 represented less than 1 percent of the total number of estates but 26 percent of their value. In this sense, the upper boundary of middle-class wealth is probably lower than is usually accepted. The claims of many rich Americans to be middle class are ill-founded. If one takes these figures seriously, middle-class populations are clearly less numerous and wealthier than is usually argued; the Estate Tax Law passed in 1916, which fixed the floor below which estates could not be taxed at $40,000, was directed at the upper rather than the middle classes.

In 1920, the number of estates with a value between $25,000 and $100,000 represented less than 2 percent of the entire population of estates and 24 percent of the transmitted wealth. They represented 4 percent of those probated and 25 percent of the wealth probated. By comparison, in 1983, the lowest class of taxable estates represented 55 percent of all estates, but 26 percent of the entire wealth transferred *mortis causa*.[4] As the same proportion of wealth is therefore in the hands of a larger number of decedents from the first to the second date, there seems to have been a slight democratization of wealth. This makes it even more important to achieve a better understanding of the variety of modes of intergenerational transfers.

The Effects of Time

Inheritance constitutes an instrument of social or economic reproduction only insofar as it causes the relevant attitudes and behaviors of adjacent generations to be alike. This continuity cannot be assumed. It does not make sense to aggregate cohorts of decedents as if they were parts of a homogeneous population.

Attitudes and behaviors concerning inheritance have two conceptually distinct origins. In the short term, these attitudes and behaviors are dictated by rationality, and more specifically by the network of immediate constraints and opportunities experienced by individuals. One acquires what is immediately available and produces immediate profit. One divides the estate according to the nature of the assets accumulated in order to minimize the taxes owed by the estate and to optimize the returns that each asset is likely to yield. In short, as the search for rationality underscores the short term, it also underscores the importance of historical time, that is, of a time made of discontinuities.

In contrast, the quest for legitimacy, which emphasizes the value of precedents, underlines the importance of sociological time, because it reflects the enduring ideological body of prescriptions and proscriptions that inspire the choices made by individuals as a function of their religion, their national origin, their social class, or their gender. The effects of rationality and of legitimacy coincide only insofar as the economic constraints and opportunities of society at large remain stable. Alternatively, the effects of these two factors differ when there is a critical amount of change. Opportunities for accumulating wealth and the representations concerning the creation or the upkeep of capital do not evolve at the same speed. The ensuing time lag and the underlying test of the stability of reproductive processes require comparisons of cohorts of decedents that are sufficiently apart from one another in time.

The Influence of Sociological Time. In sociological terms, the very concept of reproduction and its relevance to the continuity of familial practices justify comparing populations whose dates of deaths are sufficiently apart to evoke intergenerational differences. In the present case, the 1944 decedents are proxies for the children of those who died in 1920.[5] In view of the constraints attached to the use of the IRS files, there is no alternative to 1920 and 1944. The underlying twenty-four-year time interval cannot be duplicated for subsequent or earlier periods.

This pairing facilitates a first approximation of the extent to which patterns of wealth accumulation and of bequeathing perpetuate themselves. If there is any economic and cultural reproduction, the practices of the two subsamples should be alike. The assumptions underlying this test are even more compelling since the introduction of national origin in constructing the sample reduces the variability of norms and values among those individuals who died the same year.

The Influence of Historical Time. While 1920 and 1944 represent two generations, they also symbolize two sets of events. First, passing years symbolize economic growth and complexity. Individuals enjoy additional choices in their investments and their risks are subject to more diverse forms of rationalization. In this perspective, differences between the two cohorts of decedents are cumulative. For example, cars were more numerous and cheaper in 1944 than in 1920.

However, this cumulative view of history as a unilinear and evolutionary development contrasts with the image of economic life as a succession of cycles or revolutions. The population that passed away in 1920, just after World War I, experienced the thrust of the initial phases of industrialization. Active during the three preceding decades, individuals included in the subsample were likely to have a direct knowledge of the booms experienced by the American economy during that era. In contrast, not only did people who passed away in 1944 live in a more complex and differentiated economic context, but they also experienced World War II and, before that, the depression. During the period, they witnessed revolutions in the definitions of the forms of capital most in demand. Life insurance policies offer a case in point. This type of investment, which was frowned upon in 1920 as a form of gambling, became very popular in 1944.[6]

In short, the choice of 1920 and 1944 facilitates two tests. The behaviors of the two subsamples may simulate those of two adjacent generations. The patterning of differences between their behaviors concerning the accumulation as well as the distribution of wealth may also symbolize the discontinuities of modern American history.

The Effects of the Sources of Legitimacy

Far from being exclusively determined by a homogeneous rationality, behaviors governing the accumulation and the distribution of wealth are segmented as a function of the cultural norms of decedents and of the competing definitions of legitimacy by which they abide. Norms that shape the definitions of the best ways of making money and of sharing the ensuing benefits are articulated around the wisdom acquired through religious, national, social, and sexual affiliations. Since IRS files or, for that matter, death certificates do not offer information on the religious background of decedents, the exploration of this variable would require a different strategy than the one used here.[7]

The Role of National Origin. The fact that IRS files contain the names of estate holders facilitates the elaboration of inferences concerning their national origin. My selection of nationalities has been based on two considerations. The first is theoretical. One of the rationales of the study is to ascertain the extent to which differing European heirship traditions survive in the United States. In parts of Germany, people adhere to the rule of partibility and divide estates equally among their male children. Conversely, in Ireland, as in other parts of North West Europe, the rules of impartibility prevail, providing the oldest or youngest son with a preeminent heirship status. Does the distinction persist in the New World?

Far from being gratuitous, the question reflects what is already known about the current populations of German- and Irish-American farmers of the central part of Illinois or the partial survival of some Irish social traits in New England. The Irish-Americans follow the old model of impartibility, whereas, as already suggested, German-Americans tend to be divided in this regard (Salamon 1980; Kobrin and Goldscheider 1978). Some German-American subpopulations follow the rule of partibility, but the decedents of other areas divide their estates into unequal shares among their male children.[8] As a minimal hypothesis, one can therefore expect fewer variations in Irish- than in German-American inheritance practices.

The relevant contrasts, however, may be contaminated by disparities in the migratory patterns of the two national groups. Even though both the initial waves of German and Irish migrants arrived in the United States at the same time, toward the end of the eighteenth century, the decedents included in the 1920 and 1944 sample do not necessarily belong to the same generation of immigrants. The differential Americanization of their familial groups should be associated with differences in their respective occupational or residential opportunities. Unfortunately, IRS files do not offer any clue as to the date of immigration of the decedents' families.

The second consideration has been practical. German- and Irish-Americans were also chosen because of the relative ease with which their names can be identified.[9] A systematic inspection of the listing of estates for the years chosen showed that there were too few Italian or Polish names to justify their inclusion in independent subsamples. Further, French names (there were very few of them anyway) evoke too diverse a history of preceding French migrations (not only toward Canada, but also toward Protestant countries in Europe or toward colonies during the sway of Richelieu or as a result of the revolution) to represent a homogeneous subculture.

Two criteria have been used to identify the national origin of the German- and Irish-American decedents registered by the IRS. German-American decedents have been chosen because their last names appeared on the list of passengers of a ship that transported immigrants from Europe during the eighteenth century.[10] In addition, their first names also had to be German (e.g., Wolfgang, Ludwig, Otto). Similarly, Irish-Americans were chosen as such not only on the basis of the appearance of their names in the dictionary of Irish names, but also of their first names (e.g., Patrick, Rose) (MacLysaght 1985).

To the objection that the construction of the sample unduly eliminates decedents who have changed family names, one can retort that the very fact *not* to retain one's family name constitutes a *prima facie* indication that one has not kept intact one's culture of origin. The loss of one's family name should entail the loss of familial traditions as well. In this sense, analyses of the sample used here are based on a conservative assumption. Should there be no significant difference between the practices of the Irish- and German-American decedents sampled here, one might suspect that the lack of contrasts would be even more glaring for Irish- and German-American subjects who have masked their national origin.

To conclude, the lack of sharp cleavages between Irish- and German-American decedents may be due to two distinct factors: a faulty methodology and the surreptitious introduction in the sample of respondents of the wrong national origin. But it may also result from substantive forces. Thus, it may correspond to the heterogeneity of successoral models in the country of origin, to changes affecting inheritance practices in a new environment, or to the erosive influence of mixed marriages. In other words, the rejection of hypotheses concerning the importance of national origin remains fraught with equivocations. The data do not enable us to decide what might have caused the partial or total decline of differences in the inheritance patterns of migrants to the United States.

Alternatively, should the study reveal sharp differences between the populations assumed to be German-American and those assumed to be Irish-American, the contrasts cannot be necessarily generalized to other segments of the American population. The only claim I could make in the context of the present study is that German- and Irish-American behaviors concerning the accumulation and the transmission of wealth are different. These differences may be related to the differential position that the two national groups occupy in the American social structure. To the extent that the two subsamples retained belong to the same segment of the wealth distribution, it is more tempting to assume that the culture of origin of American families persists longer than is usually claimed by social scientists.

The Role of Social Class. There is no systematic information on the social class of the decedents included in the sample nor, therefore, on their level of education or on the income and occupation of their parents. The only relevant information, which is unfortunately not systematically available, concerns their occupation as farmers, self-employed businessmen, or executives.[11]

To the extent that within these broad occupational categories, individual investments or bequests differ from one another, I will be able to suggest that, in the United States as elsewhere, social class is not only about discrete positions in the socioeconomic hierarchy, but also about the specific cultures that specific occupational groups are able to create. To share the same occupation means to share the same environment, the same timetables, feelings and hopes, and thus the same discrete modes of perceiving opportunities and constraints. Correspondingly, the existence of occupational variations in the composition of the estate or in the number and destination of bequests *within* the same wealth categories should be seen as an indicator of the diverging forces that affected the patterns of social stratification prevailing in American society during the two periods.

The Role of Gender. Whether the analysis concerns 1920 or 1944, American wives enjoyed limited occupational opportunities. They did not have the same experience of the matrimonial market. Nor did they face the same legal constraints. Dissymmetries in the status of married men and women make it even more important to compare the patterns of wealth accumulation and of bequeathing typical of men and women. Yet, the interaction between gender and national origin may be difficult to ascertain in view of the particular use of patronymy in the United States. Despite the precautions taken with regard to first names, there is no guarantee that married women listed as Irish- or as German-Americans belong to these two groups. Nor is there any guarantee as to whether their decisions concerning wealth formation and bequests are informed by the traditions of their husbands.[12]

To summarize, the sample reflects four deliberate choices: (1) It is biased in favor of small estates. (2) It is focused on two cohorts of decedents that may be regarded as two adjacent generations, but that may also be seen as having experienced differing phases of economic growth or distinct short-term up- and downswings in the economic cycle. (3) While the sample probes differences between German- and

Irish-Americans, the study does not make any claim as to its external validity. Its findings cannot be generalized to other national groups or over time. The conclusions of the study stand on their own, *only* to highlight the importance of introducing specific historical or cultural factors in the analysis of intergenerational bonds. (4) Finally, as the sample includes approximately the same number of men and women, it says little about the differential wealth of the two genders. But by the same token, it provides a rich source of information concerning the differential strategies that men and women adopt in accumulating and bequeathing wealth.

The Overall Demographic and Socioeconomic Profile of the Sample

Despite the Great Depression, estate tax returns increased markedly between 1920 and 1944, from 12,492 to 17,723. In order to highlight the importance of the stakes faced by decedents, the subsample used here has been drawn from a listing that eliminated both the largest estates (above $4 million), and the youngest decedents (less than 50 years of age). The listing reduced the number of decedents eligible to 5,002 in the case of 1920 and 2,334 in the case of 1944.

From the 1920 listing, 217 names of German-American male and 72 German-American female decedents were extracted as well as 158 names of Irish-American male and 49 Irish-American female decedents.[13] In the case of the 1944 listing, 76 names of German-American male and 30 German-American female decedents were extracted as well as 65 names of Irish-American male and 23 Irish-American female estate holders.[14]

The constitution of the final sample has been the result of two strategies already noted. On the one hand, it was deemed important to reduce the range of estate size, thereby eliminating those individuals who were too rich. On the other hand, instead of mimicking the relative importance of German- and Irish-American populations in American society, it seemed more important to collect the same number of German- and Irish-American estates for the two years of reference and to engage in a corresponding fourfold comparison. For the same reason, it seemed important to minimize the differential visibility of male and female decedents.

The sample is comprised of 118 cases for 1920 and 114 for 1944. In 1920, the sample includes 69 men and 49 women, 64 German-Americans and 54 Irish-Americans. In 1944, the sample includes 74 men and 40 women, 55 German-Americans and 59 Irish-Americans. Translated into constant dollars, the average estate is $99,104 for the subsample of 1920 and $99,181 for the subsample of 1944. The variance is approximately the same in both cases ($50,030 for the first year and $55,135 for the second one).

However, the sampling strategy introduces biases in the data. Large estates are much less numerous for the two subsamples than for the populations at large from which they are derived. For 1920, returns for estates over $100,000 represent 62 percent of all returns included in the IRS file against only 42 percent of all returns included in the subsample for that year. Similarly for 1944, the same category of returns represents 72 percent of all estates processed, but only 32 percent of the subsample.[15] Even though this contrast does not affect the results of this study, it is noteworthy that in relative terms, differences between subsamples and the corresponding universes are greater for 1944 than for 1920.

Sampling strategies used also explain differences in age distributions between the sample and the universe. The decedents included in the sample are significantly older than the total populations recorded by IRS for the two years of reference. For 1920, decedents over 70 years of age constituted 57 percent of all the individuals included in the sample but only 47 percent of all the returns recorded for that year. For 1944, the corresponding figures were 62 and 54 percent, respectively. This should not come as a surprise in view of the conflicting effects of age on wealth. To be sure, wealthy individuals tend to be healthier and live longer than the general population (McCubbin and Rosenfeld 1989a,b). At the same time, however, the oldest estate holders of the two years of reference reached the phase of their life cycle when a declining health obliged them to disinvest. Hence, their estates were smaller than when they were younger. Their estates were also probably smaller than those of younger persons who died the same year.

As already indicated, since my purpose is to compare the patterns of wealth accumulation and distribution of the two genders, the sampling principles used here have deliberately minimized differences in male and female wealth levels. Thus, the gender ratio of the sample has been artificially lowered. There are only 140 males per 100 females in the 1920 subsample and the corresponding figure is 185 for 1944. By contrast, in the 1920 full population of tax returns, there were 321 males for every 100 female decedents, but the corresponding figure declined to 220 for 1944. In this sense, the female component of the 1920 population should be considered as being even more deviant from the mainstream than it appears. The relative increase in female wealth between the two dates corresponds to changes in the organization of American familial groups. It reflects the strengthening of conjugal or "horizontal" bonds at the expense of intergenerational or "vertical" loyalties. It also reflects the increased gainful employment of American women.

The residential profile of the sample mirrors the changes that took place in American society between 1920 and 1944. Thus, 38 percent of the decedents sampled in 1920 lived in villages and small communities, as opposed to 24 percent of their counterparts sampled in 1944. In other words, shifts in the geographic distribution of the American population have been associated with shifts in private wealth.

In the same way, there has been a marked decline in the relative number of returns originating from farmers between the two years of reference, from 16 percent to under 9 percent, while there was a concomitant increase in the proportion of managers and executives, from less than 3 percent to over 9 percent. The corresponding shifts mirror actual changes in the occupational structure of the American population, but they also represent changes in the control that federal authorities have been able to exert on the movements of distinct types of capital.

The search for German- and Irish-Americans has not introduced marked biases in the geographic distribution of IRS returns (Table 3.1). For 1920, the universe and the sample are alike. For 1944, decedents originating from the East North Central part of the country (Michigan, Illinois, Indiana, Ohio, and Wisconsin) represent 31 percent of the full sample, but only 19 percent of the universe. However, in both the sample and the universe, the South Atlantic states have experienced a significant rise in the number of estates between 1920 and 1944, with a concomitant decline in the wealth accumulated in Iowa and the Dakotas.

Table 3.1. Distribution (%) of Estates by Region

	1920		1944	
	Subsample	Total Pop.	Subsample	Total Pop.
New England	7.7	9.9	10.5	9.9
Middle Atlantic	27.2	25.4	23.7	26.7
East North Central	23.1	22.5	30.7	18.7
West North Central	25.6	18.6	7.9	9.0
South Atlantic	4.2	7.9	7.9	10.1
East South Central	0.0	3.6	4.4	6.8
West South Central	3.4	3.6	4.4	6.8
Mountains	3.4	0.0	2.1	2.3
Pacific	5.3	11.4	6.7	13.1
N	114	12,492	118	17,723

The regional distribution of decedents is also sufficiently diversified to facilitate a first evaluation of the influence that the distinction between community property states and those states where the assets of the spouses remain individual property should exert on patterns of wealth accumulation and heirship strategies. In the case of the universe, the relative impact of this distinction on the size of the population of testators does not change between 1920 and 1944. In contrast, as far as the sample is concerned during the same period, the incidence of decedents coming from states where the properties of husbands and wives are kept separate jumps from 35 to 47 percent. This jump has differing implications on the size of male and female holdings. Thus, the average estate of post–World War II female decedents is slightly higher in community property states than in common-law property states. In contrast, male estates are more sizable in the case of common-law property regions.

Since the legal characteristics of the environment affect investment choices, they should also influence individual decisions regarding testacy or those regarding bequests made in favor of surviving spouses. For example, decedents may make some investments to protect themselves from the claims of their partners or alternatively, to ensure the latter's long-term well-being.

Both in the sample and in the universe, both in 1920 and in 1944, a little over 40 percent of the decedents resided in states where, regardless of their gender, surviving spouses could claim one-half or one-third of the decedent's estate. The question is to ascertain whether individuals committed to conjugal equality originate from such states and use testacy to confirm the collective choices made by the community; or whether they originate from states that imposed an inferior status on women and use testacy in order to overcome what they consider to be unfair inheritance policies.

To conclude, the profile of the sample should facilitate a first assessment of the impact of the socioeconomic and cultural characteristics of decedents and of their environments on inheritance strategies. The small size of the sample presents, however, two drawbacks. It limits the number of independent variables that can be introduced in the equations and this restriction obliges us to compare the relative explanatory power of distinct sets of variables rather than to examine the conditions under which these sets can be mixed in order to obtain a more refined picture. In addition, it prevents the use of certain tests. For example, in order to explore the relative discrimination faced by daughters, it is necessary to limit the analysis to families with at least one male and one female child. This reduces even further the number of cases available and limits in turn the possibility of using multiple-regression analyses.[16]

The Validity of the Data

No alternative sampling strategy could be used because of the absence of data on the gender of children in the IRS file.

The Validity of the Data

Most social scientists have no qualms about relying on verbal accounts of *any* of the behaviors they are interested in studying. Even though many methodologists have underscored the variability of such accounts as a function of the relationship between the gender, the age, or the social status of interviewers and that of interviewees, many researchers act as if anonymous surveys were necessarily unquestionable sources of valid information. And these scientists retain the same optimism as to the reliability of the information collected, regardless of the issue under consideration.

Yet, refusal rates vary both with the socioeconomic status of respondents and the nature of the questions asked. Surveys dealing with accounts of sexual activities, with specific esthetic tastes, or with money matters are characterized by high rates of refusal, especially among wealthy persons (Tickamyer 1981). But this is not all: Their accounts are not necessarily trustworthy.

Specificity of the Problems Raised by Inheritance Surveys

To the extent that transfers *mortis causa* involve both a donor and a beneficiary, an understanding of both the practices involved and the supporting motivations requires the analysis to be concentrated on families rather than on individuals (Collins 1975; Curtis 1986). However, studies concerned with the accumulation and the transfer of wealth always take one and only one perspective. When the individuals interviewed by Jencks (1979:214) reported having inherited nothing or less than $10,000, nobody dared to ask for confirmation from potential or actual donors. Yet, this confirmation would have been critical in a culture that praises benefactors and frowns upon beneficiaries. Similarly, when Henretta and Campbell (1978:1209) assert that, for the majority of the population, net worth is an *attained* (italics mine) status, it is unclear whether this is an observation of a verifiable fact, an article of faith on the part of the American populace in general, or, as suggested by Gouldner, an article of faith of the sociological profession itself. In short, the celebrated American generosity should be only treated as a myth as long as the accumulation of wealth remains too difficult to capture, as long as beneficiaries remain so elusive, and as long as so many of them seem inclined to underestimate the amount of the bequests transferred to them.

The neglect of disparities between definitions of what is given and what is received illustrates the methodological individualism typical of American social sciences. In effect, its effects are amplified whenever positivist orientations underestimate inter- and intrapersonal variations in the definition of the situation in order to make some sort of measurement (McNamee and Miller 1989). For instance, American parents, American children, American fiscal authorities, and American social scientists are not similarly inclined to consider the financing of higher education as an intergenerational transfer.[17] The immediate beneficiaries—the college applicants themselves—may consider such financial aid a part of nonnegotiable parental obligations. Should they take such a stance, they are unlikely to enter the sums at stake in their estimates of the bequests they have ever received. For other reasons, fiscal authorities take an analogous view since they treat the sums payed to colleges merely as expenses rather than as gifts or preempted bequests.

In their desire to create unequivocal measurements, many scientists not only ignore the variability of the definitions of the situation offered by distinct categories of actors, but they also frequently underestimate the variability of the assets accumulated and its consequences. In their interviews, social scientists ask questions about homeownership, banking practices, or the possession of cars and other expensive equipment, but they do not explore the possession of more rewarding and more easily negotiable investments, such as stocks and bonds. In other words, their fear of facing refusal on the part of interviewees induces them to limit the range of financial behaviors to be probed.

Further, the same scientists tend to disregard differences between virtual and actual situations or dilemmas. Thus, economists ask respondents how they would invest their savings (if they had any), rather than seeking to determine how people actually did invest (Solmon 1974). In the same way, sociologists ask respondents how they consider boundaries between social classes without probing first the actual nature of the interviewees' immediate environment and contacts (Kluegel and Smith 1986). Finally, sociologists also ask respondents how they would prefer to divide their estates should they have a surviving spouse and surviving children, or a surviving spouse and a surviving sibling or ascendant.[18] In all these cases, no attempt has been made to distinguish ideological views prompted by a hypothetical situation from actual practices.

Yet the diverging results obtained by Cheung Moon Cho (1989), a researcher analyzing the heirship practices of Korean immigrants to the

United States, depending on whether he used hypothetical situations or the concrete experiences of his respondents highlight the fallacies of relying on hypothetical choices. He did not get the same responses when he asked his informants how they would divide their estate among their sons and daughters *before* and *after* probing whether they had male and female children (Cheung Moon Cho 1989). Professed commitment to equality among children regardless of their gender or their birth order varies when Korean respondents living in the United States are confronted with an abstract dilemma, and when they evaluate this dilemma in relation to their concrete experiences as parents. There is no reason to assume that the disparities observed among Koreans cannot be generalized to other national groups.

To summarize, studies concerned with the accumulation as well as the transmission of wealth suffer from two complementary weaknesses: (1) They do not differentiate actual from imaginary situations, and (2) they unduly treat individuals as loose atoms instead of treating them as integrated into institutional networks. In short, they do not take account for the fact that, like many other strategies, heirship choices constitute responses to the immediate environment. Estate holders do everything they can to avoid taxes; they also do everything they can to prevent favored creditors (their former spouses when they are divorced, for instance) from gaining access to their capital.

The Use of Official Documents

In view of these pitfalls, it is preferable to base the study of American heirship practices on the documents that the executors of the estate must file to close the accounts of decedents. The use of probate documents or estate tax returns poses, however, three problems: First, it is necessary to use other sources to document the causes of any radical shift in the patterns of accumulation or transmission of wealth. Interviews may enable the researcher to probe why respondents cease operating in a particular way; in contrast, federal estate tax returns or probate documents provide only cold facts. This makes it necessary to identify the laws that were passed around 1920 and 1944 that may have induced decedents to change the form of the wealth accumulated or the form of their bequests. Laws on joint tenancy offer a case in point.

Second, the elaboration of files has changed over time. For example, as the returns filed in 1944 include death certificates, the information provided is richer than that derived from the returns filed earlier (notably with regard to the decedents' birthplace and occupation). Thus while estate tax returns facilitate the construction of time series, such a construction is often still hampered by changes in the definitions of the information expected from executors. Similarly, the highly decentralized nature of the entire American administrative structure implies relatively large regional variations in the handling of estate tax returns. For example, wills are not always present in the files of decedents reported to have died testate. Also, there are marked regional variations in the number and quality of the inventories of personal property, or in the quality of the data concerning the matrimonial status of decedents. Yet biases are probably more randomly distributed in the case of administrative documents as opposed to more classical survey instruments, because they involve a larger number of potential sources of errors.

Finally, there are—anyhow—unavoidable biases in such data sources. As we shall see, certain types of assets are likely to be overrepresented in any sample of returns, while others are underrepresented. For instance, cars and real estate probably offer more precise evaluations of American wealth at a particular moment both because they are registered and their markets are structured. Not only is it easy to know whether an individual owns a car, but the existence of a *Blue Book* makes it easy to ascertain the range of values within which any transaction concerning the car has taken place. Today, the same holds true of stocks and bonds since all transactions are recorded and since their prices do not vary from one place to the next. But all financial transactions were much looser then than now.

Alternatively, it is difficult to pinpoint the causes of the underrepresentation of most personal property items. This underrepresentation may be an artifact, the decedent or his/her executor having disposed of jewels, furniture, and clothing before the inspection of the estate by fiscal agents. But the absence of such personal items may also be imputed to the spartan American life-style of the period. In a society devoted to mobility, individuals kept few items likely to be impediments. As people prepared for their deaths, they jettisoned whatever was not immediately useful to the satisfaction of their immediate needs.

To render things even more complex, interindividual variations in the type and value of items of personal property entered in the return may reflect variations in the quality of the lawyers who were called upon to draw up the will. Since overt bequests involving personal property enhance the likelihood of a more systematic evaluation of the whole estate, many decedents may be tempted to make gifts *inter vivos*.

Against these drawbacks, fiscal documents also represent the equivalent of unobtrusive measures, since their use for administrative and for scholarly purposes involves two different logics that do not contaminate one another: The documents are unobtrusive, because the information created is totally independent of the purpose of the research. For instance, stocks or bonds in individual estates are enumerated to verify the taxes owed by executors rather than to assess the extent to which decedents spread their economic risks across various ventures.

The research is also unobtrusive since the documents do not yield any information on decedents' characteristics that are deemed irrelevant to their ability to pay. Indeed, insofar as the interests of IRS are more fiscal or economic than demographic, the file assembled tends to be focused on top wealth holders. As such, the data gathered concern the composition of their estate rather than the history of the decedent's familial life.

Finally, the adversarial nature of the probate process and the conflicting nature of the interests defended by the lawyers representing the parties involved constitutes at least as good a guarantee of scientific rigor as the classical precautions taken by the authors of most surveys.

Conclusions

The purpose of this chapter is to remind readers that scientific studies are as much about the quality of the tools used as about the world they intend to explain. In the same way that Galileo was expected to prove both the validity of the world theory he was proposing and the accuracy of the measures provided by the telescope, social scientists have to indicate what precautions they have to take to lower the biases inherent in their measurements.

The very nature of administrative documents such as estate tax returns enhances the quality of the data that generate public revenues. As such, their use protects researchers from both under- and overestimating the contrasts they are looking for. At the same time, these documents are not void of human presence. Insofar as taxation rates depend on whether transfers are made *mortis causa* or *inter vivos,* and on whether benefactors anticipated their deaths whenever they gave away a particular item of the estate, some returns include passionate accounts of decedents' choices and behaviors. For instance, an IRS agent confirms the presence of an epidemy of influenza in the community of a decedent whose estate he is probing by evoking the "endless rattle of hearses on the thoroughfares of the city." In another case, a widow reminds an IRS agent that her late husband had the custom of offering her a number of roses on her birthday equal to her age. More to the point, he had also adopted the custom "since roses get wilted, to offer her the same number of stock certificates."

In the present case, I have attached to the record of individual decedents data concerning my interpretation of the wills they made. Since we know little about the structure of wills, I have elaborated a large battery of dichotomous codes for exploring their functions and the forms of inequality created among children. For the time being, identifying whether a particular feature is present or absent remains the safest way to determine the form of inequality (ties) sought by will writers. In other words, it is necessary to rely on qualitative methods and on the presence of characteristics deemed crucial before assessing the relative inequality of bequests in quantitative or monetary terms.[19]

Further, I also have assumed that individual strategies are inspired by the characteristics of the environment. Thus, to each record, I have attached data concerning the level of economic development achieved by the state of residence of the decedents for the two years chosen as points of reference.[20] Similarly, I have also attached data concerning the level of urbanization observed for these same two years.[21] Finally, I have attached data pertaining to how various states divide the individual assets acquired by husbands and wives prior and subsequent to their marriage between their respective estates and how the same states define the intestate distribution of such estates.[22] In short, for each state, I have generated *one* geographic code, which reflects the general political, economic, and demographic profile of the population; *two* measures of urbanization; *two* measures of economic development; and *two* legal measures.

To conclude, administrative documents offer a basic framework around which researchers may add data coming from other sources as well as data derived from reanalyzing the information present in these documents. I am sure all these remarks may sound pedestrian to those scholars familiar with this type of research strategy, but I ask them to ponder why, then, the field of sociology of the family seems to be so resistant to the use of such documents and why practitioners increasingly prefer the faceless contact of telephone interviews.

4

On the Variety of American Wealth

The main objective of this chapter is to lay the groundwork for evaluating how assets affect the instruments of transfer Americans choose, and the form as well as the amount of bequests they offer to specific heirs. For testators with few resources or for those who own only few types of assets, the most significant challenge is to decide what to transfer to whom. Scarcity renders people more sensitive to the consequences of whatever power they hold on the lives of others. But are the effects of the size and the composition of the estate in this regard independent of one another? Or, rather, are they complementary?

Since the first step of the analysis consists in assessing how much money decedents leave at the time of their death, it is important to summarize initially what is known and not known in this regard. The thrust of the argument is that the value of estates depends not only on the sociodemographic characteristics of their owners, but also on the network of opportunities and constraints of the immediate environment. Contingent on individual savings, this value is also a function of the level and the form of economic development of the community. A state where mining represents the most significant economic activity does not offer the same risks and the same rewards as a state of the corn belt.

Thus, analyses that transform wealth and estates into mere monetary terms fall prey to the fallacies of reductionism.[1] To the extent that people are what they have, to use the expression of the French philosopher Georges Gusdorf, our understanding of distinct social classes depends on our knowledge of what they possess. For example, even though stocks and bonds might have the same nominal value, they are not negotiated in the same markets. They involve distinct sets of risks and rewards.

The Relevance of the Theory of Segmented Labor Markets

To stress the variety of capital markets serves as a rationale for the attempt to generalize to a new realm the line of reasoning used by the theorists of segmented labor markets. In the same way that these theorists challenge the existence of a single homogeneous labor market, I suggest here that there are discrete forms of capital. In both cases, the argument originates in the suspicion of Marx that "upon the different forms of property, upon the social conditions of existence, rises an entire superstructure of distinct and peculiarly formed sentiments, illusions, modes of thought, and views of life" (cited in Newby, Bell, Rose, and Saunders 1979:24). This suspicion usually serves to justify contrasts between the worldviews of workers and of capitalists. It may serve as well to justify the empirical examination of variations in the worldviews of distinct types of capitalists.

Segmented labor market theorists seek to demonstrate not only that differing types of jobs and employment produce differing wages, but also that these differences result from distinct logics or strategies. One is not rewarded for the same reasons in the various markets. No theorist, however, seems able to decide whether contrasts across labor markets result from (1) the distinct requirements of discrete occupational roles or (2) the specific social and psychological outlook of the populations attracted toward or forced into these roles. The assumptions underlying the first alternative are materialistic and allow for *faster* changes in the direction and the intensity of the determinants of success. What is most problematic is the level and form of individual adaptation to this environment. What counts are the evolving properties of the tasks attached to a particular job, and the effects of the underlying changes in the power relations between workers and capitalists.

In contrast, the assumptions underlying the second alternative tend to be more cultural and highlight the preeminence of legitimacy as the key determinant of the decisions about the placement of individuals in the occupational hierarchy, or of the decisions concerning the financial rewards they can claim. As the second set of assumptions underscores the role of precedents and the importance of continuity in shaping the individual choices made by entrepreneurs and by workers, it minimizes the pace of change.

In generalizing the reasoning developed with regard to labor markets and applying its logic to distinct markets of commodities, the purpose of subsequent analyses is to determine whether differences in the material and symbolic returns to various forms of capital result from the distinct logics governing their production and circulation; or alternatively, whether such differences emerge because of the specific rhetorics developed by the populations they attract. In the first case, the specificity of the risks inherent to the possession of, say, land as opposed to paintings produces specific bodies of beliefs and practices. In the second, objects have no intrinsic qualities and their respective owners create differing ideologies in order to justify their choices and to distinguish themselves from the common man (Thompson 1979).[2] This second argument is not necessarily new or heavily theoretical. Common sense, for example, distinguishes between old and new money. During the past century, the landed gentry criticized the boorish life-style of industrial innovators, who in turn made fun of the conservative orientation of their peasant rivals. Like the mythical phoenix, the practices and beliefs that Moliere derided in *Le Bourgeois Gentilhomme* are constantly reborn in other eras and other places.

In short, the second purpose of this chapter is to assess the evolution of contrasts in the value and type of the assets accumulated by individuals. Real estate, stocks, bonds, promissory notes, copyrights and patents, royalties, pension funds, paintings, precious metals, jewelry, and furniture do not offer comparable yields. Nor are their owners faced with the same constraints: They do not require the same care, their transfers are not subject to the same restrictions; and they are not similarly taxed.

The first part of the chapter concerns the *amount* of wealth accumulated by individuals; the second, the *forms* taken by this wealth. In both cases, I examine first the variety of micro and macro factors that have been identified as influencing what people do, before analyzing the actual behaviors of the two cohorts of decedents included in the sample and assessing whether such analyses confirm what is already known.

On Patterns of Capital Formation

Both what should enter in the evaluation of the wealth accumulated by families and the determinants of the relevant behaviors are subject to uncertainties. Definitions of capital are relative, from both an institutionalized and informal viewpoint. As already seen, it is not clear whether economists are entitled to count as a particular component of an individual estate the monies put aside for the schooling, more specifically, for the higher education, of children. The resources corresponding to the payment of college tuition have not always been purposefully set apart for that purpose. Nor is the date of the underlying decision clearly ascertained. Further, the various parties interested in evaluating wealth do not all agree that the payment of tuition stands for a bequest that the college applicant might expect to receive later on. Most important in this regard, phenomenological accounts of the decisions taken by individuals are closely linked to the institutional framework within which they operate, that is, to the definitions that tax authorities impose on the situation. For instance, the reluctance with which parents view the payment of tuition as a form of bequest or gift *inter vivos* may be a mere rationalization triggered by the hostility of the IRS toward such a stance.

As another illustration, the acquisition of jewelry or of paintings may be viewed by some as indicating strong emotional attachments, while others may see it as just another variety of economic investment. Currently, some cultural elites feel upset about the skyrocketing values of impressionist paintings, for example, because they feel that this perverts the art world, which should be exempt from monetary considerations.

The determinants of wealth accumulation are sources of uncertainty as well. The relationship between income and wealth remains difficult to interpret because the concentration of capital and the production of income do not evolve within analogous time dimensions and do not mobilize the same economic or cultural factors. Income evolves more or less on a yearly basis, whereas changes in capital require more time and are not as cyclical. As a result, not only are the rankings of wealth holders and income earners different, but in addition the two distributions have differing profiles.

Models of Wealth Accumulation

The equivocations underlying relations between income and wealth explain the variety of models that have been successively proposed in order to explain how individuals accumulate wealth (Kessler and Masson 1989b). The first model defines the current economic climate as preventing capital formation, because it makes it impossible to contract extensive long-term debts. For the most part, individuals save little and borrow only limited sums for acquiring relatively modest non-income-producing forms of capital. In the United States, for instance, they borrow and pay annuities over long periods of time before acquiring full ownership rights on their homes or their cars. Put another way, they take possession of these items but make final payments at different moments in their life cycles. As the corresponding distinction limits what people may acquire, the model minimizes the role of transfers *mortis causa* in the creation of wealth because there is little to be transferred. Further, even though assets such as cars are treated as important components of individual wealth, they depreciate rapidly in the short term before becoming antiques and being reevaluated accordingly.

A second model emphasizes the control that individuals exert on their budgets in their efforts to rationalize their patterns of consumption over time. Basically, this model sees people as preparing themselves for the last years of their lives. In contrast to the behaviors identified in the first model, the subjects of the second one see savings as depending on the extent to which individuals anticipate both declining resources and additional expenses, rather than on the decisions of the banks or credit companies that granted them loans in the first place. Like the first model, the second one views intergenerational transfers as playing a modest role in the welfare of a specific generation since parents and children are supposed to be independent and prepare their respective retirements from scratch. Whatever individuals transfer to their children are the leftovers of financial planning that turns out to have been unduly stringent. Indeed, the second model sees transfers as linked to the accidental creation of a surplus in the war chest accumulated by individuals. It denies intergenerational solidarity and sees the survival of parents and of children as independent challenges.

The third and last model highlights the transfers that individuals seek to make in favor of their ascendants, their descendants, or their adult siblings. In this context, all familial decisions are supposed to evolve within time dimensions that are significantly larger than individual life cycles. Some of the relevant behaviors are said to be inspired by the desire to create dynasties, others by the simpler commitment to perpetuate what already exists (Gotman 1988). Decisions to invest are based on long-term considerations of profits that may be reaped much later by the descendants of the original investor. For example, during the nineteenth century, some New York heirs held on to the land passed down to them, while others preferred to take immediate advantage of the industrial or urban development that occurred at the time and reinvest the proceeds of the sale of their realty in stocks or bonds. Meanwhile, those heirs who inherited parcels of land in Manhattan during the nineteenth century and sold them right away could hardly have expected that the profits they derived from their sale would be minimal compared to the prices that their descendants could demand a century later.

The relative validity of the three models differs both across eras and regions, because of variations in the place that bequests occupy in the wealth accumulated by differing generations at various moments of their lives. When one uses a diachronic mode of analysis, the third model illustrates most accurately the agrarian societies of the past, while the first one fits best the postindustrial United States of today. When one chooses a cross-sectional approach, each model represents accurately the behaviors typical of a particular social class or ethnic group. The various cultures corresponding to these groups do not entertain the same notion of intergenerational solidarity and hence of parental or filial obligations.

For the time being, the lack of evidence allows economists to make mutually exclusive—because unverifiable—assumptions about the validity of these models and on the role played by intergenerational transfers in the accumulation of wealth. Modigliani asserts that 80 percent of the wealth accumulated today results from the savings of the current generation, but Kolikoff and Summers take the opposite position and claim that 80 percent of the current wealth has been inherited (Kessler and Masson 1988a).

The Determinants of Wealth Accumulation

The variety of models used to predict the accumulation of wealth makes it even more important to identify the concrete factors that shape the distribution of wealth. This distribution depends, of course, on factors over which individuals have little control. Thus, the distribution of life chances across the various segments of society at large has little to do with individual aspirations or deeds. This is because conscious improvements in, say, nutrition cannot be expected immediately to lower the likelihood of falling prey to a particular epidemic. As another illustration, getting a degree will not necessarily erase the negative stereotypes that others attach to one's identity. As a last example, interindividual or intergroup differences in wealth accumulated also depend on the timing of the additional resources earned by individuals as a result of technological revolutions or of the bequests made in their favor by the preceding generation. The earlier in a lifetime one receives bequests, and the greater the value of the corresponding windfalls, the more significant the investments one can make later on. From this vantage, the current forms of economic development minimize the economic impact of bequests since they are transferred too late in the life cycle of heirs.

Even though wealth and income represent distinct economic phenomena (the first is like the power of the water held behind a dam, the second is akin to a flow), the way people accumulate assets depends on their cumulative savings, and on the influence that their life cycle exerts on their earning and consumption patterns.

During the initial phases of an individual's active life, the effects of rising earnings are partly erased by the additional expenses caused by raising children. In contrast, during the later phases of the life cycle, the combined effects of occupational seniority and declining needs are amplified by the enhanced likelihood that individuals may inherit from their parents, or other ascendants. In this country, less than 8 percent of individuals under 25 years of age are said to have ever inherited, as against 41 percent of their counterparts 75 years and older. Further, the bequests received by the former are significantly smaller than those received by the latter (Lansing and Sonquist 1969). Conversely, savings are supposed to dwindle as soon as one reaches retirement, because of the additional expenses resulting from old age, the need to enjoy new pleasures, the desire to make gifts *inter vivos* to those of the children who need additional resources, and finally the partial or total loss of salaries or wages.

Patterns of wealth accumulation also vary with gender and hence with the differential education, occupational, and even matrimonial history of American males and females. Thus, patterns of hypergamy (marrying up in the social ladder) enable women to be less underrepresented at the very top of the distribution of net worth (the top 0.01 percent) than at the next rung (1 percent), even though their position in relation to those of men at the apex declined between 1962 and 1972. Indeed, the wealth owned by the top 0.01 percent richest men almost doubled from $4,690,000 to $7,340,000 during those ten years, whereas the corresponding figures for the richest women in the top 0.01 percent grew moderately, from $3,220,000 to $4,530,000 (Brittain 1978:40–42). Further, recent changes in divorce laws have accentuated divergencies in the accumulation of wealth by American men and women. These shifts have made it harder for women to acquire some share of the not yet completely paid for assets acquired by the couple under the rules of joint tenancy.

Patterns of wealth accumulation also depend on education (Solmon 1974). Regardless of the historical period considered in the United States, individual average net worth is greater for populations with a college education than for those who did not go beyond grammar school. The contrasts indicate the differential evolution of earnings over the life cycle. But they also result from the impact of formal schooling on risk-taking behaviors. As formal schooling modifies time orientations, it modifies both the propensity to save and the choices of investments.

Far from being stable, however, relationships between age or educational attainment and wealth vary across historical periods. For example, the annual growth rate of the wealth generated by human activities increased systematically up to 2.2 percent during the first part of the nineteenth century, remained stable at 2.5 percent between 1850 and 1900, declining to 1.3 percent between 1900 and 1950 and falling even further since (Soltow 1975a; Chiswick 1978). In analyses of wealth, it is hence improper to treat time series as if years were all alike and as if the wealth acquired each year did not vary with specific events.

The Economic, Demographic, and Political Determinants of Changes in the Growth and the Nature of Wealth

Both the growth rate of wealth and the differentiation of assets vary with technological innovations as well as with the efficiency with which the economy runs. Discontinuities in these rates reflect the emerging impact of new forms of energy and means of communication on the structure of economic exchanges of various regions and segments of the population. Scientific or technological revolutions change what individuals desire and what they can amass or conserve. The transplanting of organs offers a recent example of the emergence of new forms of assets (Zelizer 1988).

Growth rates of reproducible wealth are also related to changes in the demographic profile of the American population. For example, the erosion of the differential employment opportunities enjoyed by American-born citizens and their immigrant counterparts has been accompanied by the parallel blurring of the contrasts in the relationships between age and wealth holding for the two populations. As long as the flow of immigrants remained abundant, until the end of the nineteenth century, the curvilinear relationship between age and wealth was significantly more marked for foreign-born than for locally born populations (Soltow 1971:37). Immigrants expected less from kin networks or social programs than their counterparts born and raised in the country. With a slowdown in immigration rates and the concomitant growth of the economy, the melting pot became generally more of a reality than of a myth.

Similarly, variations in the size of successive cohorts are also associated with differences not only in the actual opportunities enjoyed by their respective members, but also in the attitudes they hold toward the future.[3] The larger the group of individuals who are born in the same year, begin their education at the same time, and look simultaneously for jobs, the more severe the competition that pits them against one another, and the more nuanced their attitudes toward the future. Thus, when economists banked on the relationship observed between savings and schooling to predict that the growth of the educational system would entail a continuous increase in the savings accumulated by Americans, they forgot that the consequences of education are time relative. Educational benefits depend as much on the scarcity of school graduates as on the content of their educational experiences. The educational explosion of the last decade has been conducive not only to a steep rise in the costs of a college education, and hence in the amount of money borrowed to cover them, but also to a sharp decline in the saving abilities of educated Americans. Returns to educational investments are lower than they used to be, since schooling has become a collective good claimed by all. Further, increases in the stimulating effect of education on consumption have proportionately reduced its contribution to net individual worth.

Finally, changes in the growth rate of wealth reflect changes in the public policies concerning the allocation of risks and the distribution of profits in the general population. Prior to the passage of the Social Security Act and to the diffusion of pension programs across an increasing number of economic sectors, the savings that the elderly made in anticipation of their retirement did not prevent them from being consistently at the bottom of the American income or wealth distributions. Years went by before successive cohorts of elderly began to enjoy the fruits of the diffusion of the relevant public and private programs. As late as 1970, grandparents of a family still had fewer savings than their children and their adult grandchildren. The forms of their savings were also less differentiated (Hill 1970). They were more likely to have savings accounts or money market instruments than stocks.

Variations in mortgage rates and down payment requirements represent another illustration of the impact of public policies on the growth of wealth. These two factors modify the age at which individuals can enter the home ownership market and hence the age at which they become able to shift in other budgetary directions the relative resources initially assigned to housing. Furthermore, the consequences of individual educational attainment vary with the educational level of the populations examined and with changes in the differential expenditures attached to successive years of schooling. Thus, within the 1929-born cohort of college-educated individuals, 67 percent became homeowners when they were under 35 years of age as opposed to only 58 percent of their least educated counterparts. In contrast, within the 1900-born cohort of college-educated people, 67 percent reached the same residential status when they were 65 years old, whereas 58 percent of those with a grammar school background acquired a home before they were 56 years of age (Lansing and Sonquist 1969).

In short, a late entry in the labor market has not always had positive effects on the processes of capital formation. More recently, during the 1970s and the early 1980s, sharp increases in mortgage rates and in the down payments required in local real estate markets, or in the tuition fees charged in the world of higher education, have contributed to narrowing patterns of wealth accumulation and to altering the enduring effect of education on saving behaviors.

As a last example of the consequences of public policies on patterns of wealth formation, one might speculate as to the implications of the 1987 changes in the deductions allowed on credit cards. Before the reform, deferred payments allowed lower taxes. The reform may have stimulated savings by dampening consumption, but it may also have lowered the overall level of economic activity, reducing overall individual incomes, and minimizing thereby the likelihood of individual capital formation.

To conclude this overview of public policies on the formation of individual wealth, the conjuncture of laws and regulations concerning housing and educational markets commands the overall productivity of the national economy and the amount as well as the timing of the most significant familial expenses. At the same time, these effects also depend on tax policies, which determine not only what enters public and private pockets, but also the division of the fiscal burden between the rich and the less rich.

Determinants of the Wealth Held by 1920 and 1944 Decedents

Since the major assumption of the study is that scarcity makes choices more difficult, I have chosen two cohorts of decedents with similarly limited estates. As already seen, the two corresponding distributions have the same limited means and variances.[4]

However, it is not because variances are small that they are necessarily undetermined. In the present case, socioeconomic factors (occupation, age, income level of the state) account for 7 percent of the variance of the 1920 distribution of wealth, with farmers making less and businessmen more than the population at large. For 1944, the corresponding percentage of the variance explained declines to less than 1 percent, which suggests that the contribution of occupations to this particular part of the American wealth distribution has declined even further over the years. For both cohorts, estate size is independent of the urban or rural character of the decedents' residence. In 1944, however, estates are larger in the case of decedents residing in states of common-law property where conjugal assets are kept separate and where individualism stimulates the taking of risks.

Insofar as the absence of overall significant differences between the two cohorts suggests that the two subsamples represent a single homogeneous wealth class, the choices of investments and of bequests should respond similarly to the environment. To make this inference raises, however, the question of whether the notion of wealth class is determined by how *much* people have, rather than by what they have.

On the Distinct Forms of American Wealth

The development of the American economy and its increasing technological complexity have been accompanied by a parallel differentiation of the assets accumulated by individuals or groups. Thus, there has been a parallel differentiation of risks, markets, and property rights. This differentiation has involved three successive phases.

The Dominance of the Land

Originally, the most important source of wealth resided in the land. With its plantations, the South participated in the world economy to a larger extent than the North and enjoyed therefore a larger financial surplus. Insofar as the plantation economy generated trading activities with Europe and with the Caribbean and other regions of the New World, shipping and its ancillary activities, like maritime insurance, already represented significant alternative source of income. At the time, personal property referred to a much smaller number of items than today and they were all essentially functional. These items included the tools that enabled men and women to exert their functions and to live as comfortably as possible, even though the richest segments of the population transformed their savings into precious metals and jewelry.

The Effects of Industrialization

Industrialization has been paralleled by a differentiation of the forms of wealth. The creation of industrial plants and warehouses has fostered a parallel transformation of the patterns of land use. With divergences in the requirements attached to the acquisition of the lands used for residential, commercial, industrial, and agricultural purposes, as well as in their respective returns, the distributions of landowners and of their real estate investments have evolved differentially. Landownership ceased to be an exclusive privilege of farmers. On the one hand, it became the concern of individuals keen to reduce their housing expenses. On the other hand, it became an investment enabling people to take advantage of urban development, and to think in terms of both the profits expected from future sales and of the income that the land might generate.

With the continuous growth of American cities, dwelling units purchased originally for residential uses have become significant financial investments. Yet the distributions of homeowners in the general population and of their respective investments have evolved differentially. Almost two-thirds of homeowners close to retirement own their houses debt-free, and from 1970 to 1990, the median price of a single-family home jumped from $23,000 to $92,500 (Blumberg 1980; Kolko 1962; Tuckman 1973; Farnham 1990:73).

Industrialization has also been conducive to the differentiation of both the risks that individuals are willing to take and the returns they expect or are able to obtain. Timetables of risks and profits are less contingent on the seasons in industrial than in agricultural ventures. In addition, initially at least, captains of industry thought that their profits would vary as a reverse function of the wages of their workers. They rejected the view that low labor costs would limit demand in a variety of sectors and that the combination of unfavorable economic and demographic circumstances could weigh heavily on small-scale enterprises that were too weak to ride out economic storms. Because of their strategies, the growth in the value of certain assets proved to be cumulative, but other fortunes and riches remained highly vulnerable to the vagaries of the market.

Since industrial ventures require the mobilization of a large amount of capital, individual entrepreneurs have sought associates or loans. Despite the growing role played by banks in this regard, the demise of the family as a unit of production did not immediately cause its end as a source of financial aid. A system of mortgages and promissory notes originating from individuals has persisted in spite of the growth of stocks and bonds. In other words, the expansion of a capitalist economy has not necessarily occurred by leaps and bounds. Rather, as we shall see, it has been articulated around the mobilization of capital by regularly growing networks of relatives or residents of specific neighborhoods.[5] One of the challenges of the analysis is to identify the pace at which the number of individuals willing to lend capital with or without security has declined. The challenge is also to ascertain when the sums committed to that type of investment dropped sufficiently dramatically to cease to have an economic impact.

This research agenda rests on the assumption that the evolution of American wealth has been slower than is usually acknowledged. Despite the emphasis placed on anonymous capitalist structures, 90 percent of American businesses remain family-owned today. Family-owned businesses absorb the majority of job applicants on the labor market and produce 40 percent of the GNP. Even at the top of the wealth distribution, 175 of the 400 largest corporations remain owned by a single family (Rosenblatt et al. 1985). The persistence of familial enterprises underscores the need to know more about the role of intergenerational transfers in the circulation of productive and nonproductive forms of capital.

The Consequences of the Abstract Society

The notion of "abstract society"—the term coined by Anton Zidjerveld (1970)—epitomizes the sociopsychological effects of the emergence of postindustrial societies and subsequent postmodern ideologies. The lengthening of the production and commercialization processes has enhanced the physical, temporal, and functional distance separating investors from the loci of the enterprises to which they lend their monies.

In the early phases of industrialization, stockholders lived close to the companies they would finance. They could anticipate the short-term results of their investments and they knew the gamut of products or services marketed. Similarly, the relationship between the gross product of the firm, the dividends offered, and the demand for fresh capital took place within a highly structured time dimension. In contrast, today stockholders have little knowledge of the activities of the organizations they support and they cannot anticipate the ups and downs of their fortunes.[6]

Most importantly, the development of the abstract society is associated with the growth of a variety of intangible assets. During the early stages of industrialization, American lawyers were somewhat reluctant to assert the private nature of patents, copyrights, and other forms of intellectual property because they feared that this would inhibit the development of the infrastructure necessary for economic growth. In other words, they believed that such an infrastructure (notably in the intellectual field) should be managed by the state in order to facilitate private ventures (Miller 1965; Horwitz 1977).

At the very same time that the acceleration of technological change has been associated with a parallel increase in the number and value of patents, the concomitant development of the cinema, of recording industries, and of advertising has fostered a parallel growth of royalties and residuals, which represent new forms of wealth that are governed by their own rules. In contrast to stocks, for instance, the value of these rights and of all forms of intellectual capital varies with the frequency of their use; they yield income over a limited period of time (usually, over the lifetime of the artist or writer and the 50 subsequent years) and they are not readily negotiable (Finkelstein 1954).

The systematic growth of the tertiary sector and more specifically of commercial, transport, leisure, and administrative activities has also been conducive to the emergence of human capital. With these particular sectors requiring the services of an increasingly educated labor force, there has been a parallel growth of individual investments in formal schooling. This particular form of capital cannot be sold. Yet in very recent times, institutional links between human and more economic forms of capital have become more complex and more numerous. A number of courts, for example, now oblige divorcing medical doctors or lawyers to reimburse their former wives who entered the labor force in order to finance their husbands' studies. In a symmetric fashion, when courts abolished the notion of lifelong alimony, they also adopted a system of short-term educational subsidies enabling divorced women to acquire the skills necessary for reentering the labor market.

As the development of the economy typical of the abstract society has also been conducive to a redistribution of social risks, it has facilitated the creation of corresponding new forms of assets. These assets may be public, as illustrated by the institutionalization of social security and retirement programs. Wage earners accumulate deferred rights to an income they receive at the end of their occupational lives. As a result of the diffusion of these programs and of the generalization of fringe benefits to an increasing part of the labor force, the elderly have ceased to be the poorest age group of the American population.

Abstract assets may also be private and take the form of life insurance. While the secularization of society has been accompanied by a greater acceptance of gambling, the accentuation of the division of labor along gender lines has allowed the diffusion of beliefs concerning the particular financial vulnerability of widows. The conjunction of these two forces facilitated the accelerated penetration of American families by life insurance companies. From specific forms of protection covering limited types of risks, policies became another variety of financial investments (Zelizer 1979).

Finally, the technological development typical of the abstract society has also implied the emergence of a new property right that concerns the possession and the transfer of parts of the human body. The vocabulary used by Americans acknowledges the underlying evolution. In contrast to blood transfers, that were once described in terms of *donations* (e.g., blood donors), biotechnology has transformed the human body into another source of income. There are sperm *banks* and other human organs can be stocked to be transplanted over longer periods of time to an ever-increasing number of beneficiaries. Alternatively, the introduction of life support technology represents another source of liabilities, and transforms the notions of contract or of solidarity. Indeed, should heirs be held accountable for the enormous expenses associated with the use of such technologies? To raise this issue is to raise the question of whether the logics underlying the transfers of liabilities and of assets are the same.

Consequences of the Distinction between Types of Assets

The continuous emergence of new forms of assets has a variety of economic consequences, because it modifies the nature of both estates and transfers *mortis causa*. First, the markets where these various types of assets are exchanged have different structures. Real estate markets remain local, even though computers have facilitated their rationalization. Further, real estate transactions involve a variety of go-betweens (lawyers on both sides, real estate agents, title companies). In contrast, while stocks and bonds are increasingly negotiated on national and international markets, they require fewer intermediaries, despite significant variations in the size and the activities of stock brokerage firms or institutional funds on behalf of their clients. Conversely, despite the growth of the market, antiques and works of art remain negotiated through particularist channels, which enhances the risks taken by collectors with regard to both thefts and forgeries.

Second, the extent of property rights varies across types of assets. In the case of real estate, the effect of sales on ownership rights is immediate and is independent of the social identity of sellers and buyers. The same holds true of stocks and bonds. Alternatively, royalties and residuals can only be claimed for a definite period of time, before the relevant properties enter the public domain. More important, the corresponding rights can be claimed by the natural dependents of the creator but they cannot necessarily be sold. Rights over human capital are subject to even tighter restrictions, even though the monetary costs assigned to its acquisition can be evaluated and redistributed. Similarly, regardless of variations in the duration and the amount of the pensions accumulated by individuals, there are also restrictions on the transferrability of the underlying rights. Such rights may be enjoyed by the surviving spouse and minor children, but by no other relative. In the case of individuals who have accumulated pension credits their remarrying implies the automatic transfer of parts of that principal or of the revenue to their divorced partner.

Third, there are differences in the taxes levied on the various forms of capital. The acquisition of human capital is financed in part by income taxes and hence by the revenue acquired by preceding generations as a result of their own formal education. But as educational revenues are mostly derived from property taxes or from tuition fees, the acquisition of human capital is financed primarily by students themselves or by their parents.[7] As another illustration, dividends were until recently taxed at a special rate, and today IRAs are still subject to some fiscal exceptions. As a final example, ownership of stocks, bonds, or personal property is not taxed per se, in contrast to realty, which is subjected to annual taxes whose rate depends on the use of the property and the general economic level of the community.

Finally, distinct types of wealth are subject to differing types of public control. Ownership rights are subject to greater restrictions in the case of land than of stock. The state can expropriate landowners and prevent them from constructing the buildings they have in mind. Alternatively, individual stockholders have little recourse against the consequences of mergers and takeovers. As another example, while students have some guarantee as to the quality of the education they receive through the accreditation process of the institution they attend, they are less protected as far as the tuition they have to pay.

In summary, there are objective contrasts in the risks or profits of, and threats to the property rights of the increasingly distinct types of assets available to contemporary Americans. These differences make it questionable to identify wealth classes and the practices of their individual members exclusively in terms of the *values* accumulated. But to assert the significance of the *form* of the wealth accumulated in this regard raises the question of the origin of individual choices.

Cultural Variations in the Type of Wealth Accumulated

There are sociocultural variations in the American responses to the dilemmas raised by the ownership of differing kinds of assets. These assets do not only have intrinsic economic or social qualities, but they also have qualities that vary with the social characteristics of their owners and change with the history of the society to which they belong. For instance, following a significant decline between World War II and 1980, the number of farms in the state of New Jersey rose by 9 percent between 1982 and 1987, with an increase in the number of part-time farmers who cultivate a limited part of their land and lease the remaining part to full-time agriculturalists (DePalma 1989). In brief, at least on the eastern seaboard, the concept of farming has evolved.

Even in a society as devoted to progress as is the American society, individuals continue to hold particularist standards in evaluating the returns they expect from their investments. These differences are informed by experience, but also by ideology. For example, an aversion toward gambling may lead investors to prefer the stability of bonds to the unpredictable nature of dividends and capital gains. Some investors may also prefer to buy the stock of small-scale companies located close to their place of residence, rather than invest in large-scale companies that may be exposed to friendly or hostile takeovers. Others may feel more secure investing in blue chip stocks, even if their limited resources oblige them to buy odd lots. In a nutshell, the rationality governing the preferences of individual investors toward specific forms of capital or toward one particular asset in the same category of investment is not universal.

Instead, this rationality is shaped by both the experience that the most significant American social groups have of time or of risk and by their respective sense of legitimacy. In this sense, this rationality varies with the profile of the "significant others" who influence individual lives—decisions are likely to be influenced by the "wisdom" of relatives. Even when they consult "experts" (e.g., brokers and accountants), access to such experts is still conditioned by particularist forces and by the advice offered by associates, friends, neighbors, or relatives.

Yet one knows very little about the determinants of individuals' differing tastes for specific forms of property. Paradoxically, despite the relatively low economic value of personal property, the social determinants of the various components of this type of possession (clothes, cars, etc.) are often better documented than the acquisition of other types of assets (Csikszentmihalyi and Rochberg Halton 1981).

Gender is highly significant in this regard: Television and stereo equipment, vehicles, tools, and sporting goods are more often mentioned by men, while women refer more frequently to plants, china, glassware, and clothing. In general then, men and women are not attracted by the same symbols. Further, they also differ from one another in terms of the risks they are willing to take.

Attraction toward objects is also determined by the unfolding of the life cycle. Musical instruments, TVs, stereos, vehicles, pets, aquariums, refrigerators, sports equipments, toys, and stuffed animals are more likely to attract the attention of children than of their parents or grandparents. Conversely, visual art, sculpture, and appliances are more often a concern of parents, whereas the value assigned to china and silverware seems to increase as one moves higher up the ladder of generations. Of course, as the information has been collected once and only once, it is difficult to ascertain whether these contrasts reflect life cycle or cohort effects. For instance, the meaning of refrigerators has evolved over the years. Treated originally as a valuable oddity by adults, the appliance has become something raided by children in search of snacks. Further, as with gender, aging means both evolving commitment to distinct symbols and changing definitions of risks.

Similarly, the type of assets accumulated also varies with the national origin of wealth holders. By way of illustration, there have been marked differences in the patterns of home ownership between the early waves of immigrants in the American urban fabric. The Irish of Boston or the Poles of Pittsburgh originated from a rural society and believed that home ownership was the first compulsory step toward their social integration into the new world (Thernstrom 1964; 1973; Bodnar et al. 1982; Laurie 1980). In contrast, Jews had had enough experience of discrimination and violence as well as enough of a sense of the interrelations between geographic and socioeconomic upward mobility to feel that it was safer to invest savings in more easily movable human capital (Thernstrom 1973). As another example, black and white residents of Washington, D.C., do not have the same attraction for real estate and life insurance, after one controls for their wealth. Similarly, different national groups hold distinct views of the same type of asset. Thus, in Illinois, attitudes and practices of farmers vary by national origin. Yankee farmers tend to "camp," leaving their farms behind whenever they find more promising opportunities. By contrast, their German-American neighbors subordinate their farming to the perpetuation of the specific sociocultural order in which they believe (Salamon 1980; Carroll and Salamon 1988). In the first case, economic endeavors represent an end in themselves; in the second one, they represent means to help perpetuate cultural ideals.

Finally, there are contrasts in the attitudes of the various social classes toward valuable objects. Visual art, stereo systems, and fine carpets catch the fancy of the upper middle class, but radios, plants, and clocks mobilize the imagination of the lower middle class. Material possessions embody an ideal, and are thus worth acquiring for the first category of respondents, but their possession results from gifts in the second case. However, the usual notion of social class is insufficient to account for the distribution of tastes. "Better because older" and "better because newer" correspond to time orientations that differ both across and within classes as they are usually defined (Feyerabend 1975). Thus, among individuals with the same resources, some buy fluorescent lighting in order to look modern, while others prefer to give the impression they are traditionalist by purchasing lamps modeled after the candlesticks of past centuries (Thompson 1979). Similarly, university students whose academic success enables them ultimately to enter an elite socioeconomic stratum do not necessarily share that elite's evaluation of modern art. Individuals who are born into that elite tend to judge contemporary forms of expression more favorably than do their counterparts who come from a more modest background. The former use the criterion of modernity to distinguish themselves from the latter (Bourdieu and Passeron 1970).

There should be comparable differences in the value of the assets accumulated by different classes. For example, stocks represent 8 percent of the wealth of individuals who have less than $5,000, but 66 percent of the wealth of those with over $100,000. Alternatively, real estate represents almost two-thirds of the capital *accumulated by* the lowest wealth class, but 12 percent of the wealth accumulated by those with over $100,000 (Smith 1975).

To conclude, even though the selection of investments is less "rational" than neoclassical writers would like us to believe, the documentation of the ensuing variations remains spotty. For example, we know that home ownership does not occupy the same role in the patterns of wealth accumulation of blacks and whites (Henretta 1979; Terrell 1971; Smith 1975). Similarly, we know that the motivations governing the selection of colleges, and hence of specific experiences of human capital, are not the same for the various social classes. To the extent that undergraduate studies are a status marker for students from favorable social circumstances, they are likely to attend institutions where fraternities or sororities are sufficiently active to stimulate a lively social life and the creation of appropriate social networks. Alternatively, to the extent that undergraduate studies represent an investment for adolescents from a more modest background, they are more likely to choose institutions according to the reputation attached to the specific academic programs in which they happen to be interested. Yet one knows little about the specific processes by which students finalize their choice of a specific institution. The same holds true a fortiori of the choices of more significant forms of investment.

As already noted in the introduction, this ignorance results from the methodological difficulties inherent in undertaking the relevant type of research. However, this ignorance also serves a social function. The more "irrational" the origin of wealth is deemed to be, the more acceptable it becomes. One cannot be angry when the goddess of chance winks in the direction of a fortunate neighbor.

The Variability in the Composition of Estates in 1920 and 1944

Decisions concerning the composition of estates involve a succession of choices. The first choice pertains to whether it is appropriate to buy a particular type of valuable and to enter the corresponding market. With the increased complexity of economic life, Americans may decide to buy real estate, stock, state bonds, federal bonds, bonds of private companies, or life insurance. They may also decide to lend money in the form of notes that may or may not be guaranteed by mortgages. While they may deposit their monies in the bank, they may also purchase personal types of property and invest in antiques, rugs, jewelry, or works of art. The purpose of the subsequent analysis is to assess the statistical significance of contrasts between those who do and those who do not hold a particular asset, the relevant decisions being analyzed in terms of logit equations, that is, of statistical analyses that seek to explain dichotomies.

The second choice faced by decedents pertains to how much they should invest in each category of assets. This is a twofold choice: Investors decide the value of each investment in real dollars. In addition, since they are also concerned with the opportunity cost of such an investment, they must decide how much they should assign for the purchase of one type of asset in relation to their estate as a whole. This entire second set of choices is analyzed with the help of multiple regressions in order to examine how much interindividual variation in the amount of resources invested in one type of asset can be explained by the individual characteristics of the decedents and those of their surroundings.

The third choice, to which I alluded earlier, pertains to the diversification of the estate. Wealth holders must decide how thin they should spread their risks. In view of the variety of logics operating in distinct markets, is there an optimal way of concentrating savings in a limited number of types of ventures? Similarly, for each type of investment is it wiser to diversify the number of titles held rather than stick to one secure form of wealth? For example, some stockholders prefer to spread their risks among a variety of companies, but others think it is more reasonable to put all their eggs in the same basket by buying only blue chips titles. The same holds true a fortiori for individuals who lend money to others. The more numerous their borrowers, the greater their risks, but the thinner they are spread. In this case, too, analyses of individual choices involve the use of multiple regressions.

The Socioeconomic Determinants of Choices

The decisions to enter into a specific market and to invest a certain amount of dollars are inspired by structural factors, more specifically, by individual and collective economic variables. At the individual level, age tends both to increase income and reduce patterns of consumption. Overall estate size affects the degrees of freedom enjoyed by decedents and the resources they could mobilize to enter new ventures or selectively reinforce some of their holdings. Similarly, occupation reveals the selectivity of the information and of the funds that they dispose of. Further, these choices also depend on the diversity of the risks that people take and thus on the number of individual titles acquired within a single category of assets. Finally, in collective terms, these decisions depend on the networks of opportunities and constraints offered by the immediate environment, as measured by the level of economic activities of the state where decedents reside, and hence by the income taxes paid by individuals for 1920 and 1944.[8]

The Familial Determinants of Choices

Decisions concerning wealth formation are also shaped by the models of familial relations to which decedents subscribe.[9] Their decisions should vary with their gender since this variable commands both patterns of consumption and experiences of the various markets. Their decisions should also vary with the number of children since this number reduces the capacity to mobilize the resources immediately necessary for entering a successful venture. The more children individuals have, the less leeway they have for postponing certain expenditures. Given the differing expectations attached to the roles of sons and daughters, individuals' decisions should also depend on the composition of their offspring. In the same way, the matrimonial status of daughters is also relevant. Since marriage was and remains a key instrument of social mobility for American females, parents may vary their investments according to the matrimonial status of their daughters.

Yet the relevance of the gender of the decedent and of his or her offspring should also vary as a function of national origin and of the underlying immigration experience. Both factors influence not only the amount and the type of economic opportunities to which each gender has access, but also the image that people hold of gender and generations as determinants of estate formation. The combination of the relevant structural and ideological factors accounts, at least in part, for contrasts in the orientations held by differing types of Americans toward women, notably as these manifest themselves in their heirship practices.[10]

Finally, decisions are also shaped by two major aspects of the law to which the estate is subject. Depending on the state where the decedent lived at the time of death, the share to which the surviving spouse is entitled may be independent of or vary with his or her gender. In the first case, the value of that share may range between one-third and one-half of the estate. The implications of these institutional constraints, however, also depend on whether assets acquired after marriage are automatically parts of the community property or remain the dominion of each spouse. It is one thing to spell out how to divide between spouses, another to spell out what should be divided.

Thus, the study seeks to test the limits of the postulate that American individualism is sufficiently powerful to dictate how people invest their monies in order to triumph over the state. Is is really true that Americans say, "Me on one side, the IRS on the other," to use the words of the president of the Rockefeller Foundation (Farnham 1990:77)? Clearly, such a test requires evaluating the limits within which individual choices are independent of the legal opportunities and constraints set up by state authorities.

Modernizing Experiences as Determinants of Decisions

The third set of equations includes three sets of variables tapping the relative modernization of the populations examined. Granted the ambiguities attached to the term, one can hypothesize that it evokes the complexity of the information made available to individuals. Hence, a first measure of modernization includes the size of the community where individual wealth holders were residing, since this variable determines their exposure to new ideas and strategies. A second measure involves the urbanization level of their states of residence, because this level says something about the maximal density of social networks in which individuals may partake and hence about the channels of information available to them. A third measure includes geographic clusters, notably contrasts between the eastern seaboard (Pennsylvania, New York, and New Jersey)–considered the most urbanized part of the nation during the period under study, the South (from Maryland to Louisiana)—the least urbanized region, and the remaining part of the country. In the case of the 1944 cohort, one can also introduce the decedents' patterns of mobility since this commands exposure to new ideas and new values and the ability of anticipating the twists and turns that individual fortunes might encounter.[11]

The purpose of these three sets of analyses is to compare the respective contributions of economic, cultural, and social factors to the individual decisions governing the accumulation of wealth. The same sets of variables are used in the equations concerning each type of asset, which makes the results more easily comparable.[12]

For each type of asset, it is then possible to determine the extent to which the variance of the distribution of the relevant choices and its determinants remain stable over time, and are alike for the two cohorts of decedents. This makes it possible to assess the extent to which the stability of the patterns of capital formation allow individual decedents to use transfers *mortis causa* to ensure an effective reproduction of existing familial arrangements.

The Composition of the Estate: An Overall Picture

The distribution of wealth involves two measures. While it is necessary to evaluate the relative *popularity* of differing types of assets among the various segments of the population, it is also necessary to evaluate the relative *value* that these assets represent in relation to that of overall individual estates.

The popularity of certain types of assets (notably bonds, investments in productive forms of capital, deposits, or real estate) did not change drastically between the two years of reference (Table 4.1). They attracted the same number of wealth holders. In contrast, the sharp increase in the number of participants in the stock market was paralleled by an even more dramatic decline in the relative salience of mortgages and prom-

The Composition of the Estate

Table 4.1. Composition of the Estates of Decedents in 1920 and 1944

	Percentage Owning		Percentage of the Estate			
			1920		1944	
	1920	1944	Sample	Universe	Sample	Universe
Real estate	89.0	80.7	38.6	24.7	25.1	15.2
Life insurance	17.8	45.6	0.9	3.1	10.0	17.0
State bonds	11.8	14.0	1.1	3.3	0.8	5.1
Federal bonds	74.6	91.1	4.1	4.4	7.9	8.4
Private bonds	30.5	34.2	6.7	7.2	3.8	4.4
Stocks	68.6	80.7	24.9	31.3	23.5	39.5
Nonfarm assets	17.8	26.3	2.0		4.6	
Mortgages	47.4	34.2	10.0	{ 12.9	6.2	{ 3.6
Promissory notes	44.9	27.2	2.7		2.0	
Deposits	80.5	85.9	6.2		10.3	
Cash	27.1	30.7	0.1		0.7	
Others	—	—	2.7	13.1	5.1	6.8
TOTAL			100.0	100.0	100.0	100.0
Number of cases	118	114	n-a		n-a	
Average value	n-a	n-a	99.104		99.187	

issory notes. These changes reflect the growth of anonymous impersonal capitalist structures during the entire period. Meanwhile, the spectacular diffusion of life insurance policies during the period raises an important question as to the strategies of insurance companies. To the extent that the samples used here represent the lower end of the wealth continuum, does the increase in the number of life insurance policy holders suggest that, as an innovation, this type of investment trickled down from richer individuals who adopted it at an earlier date? Does this evolution reflect a democratization of the market and hence an increase in the number of policy holders? Or rather, is it a shift in the tastes of distinct segments of the population?

At the same time, shifts in the values of these assets evoke a somewhat different picture. The decline in the value of realty is more spectacular than the fall of its popularity. In a symmetrical manner, the growth of the value of life insurance policies present in individual estates is far below what could be anticipated from the rise of its popularity. Alternatively, the growing popularity of private stocks or private bonds has still been associated with a relative decline in the amount of dollars invested in them. Convergences in the evolutions of estates for both the subsample and the full population of small estates in the IRS file suggest that the democratization of wealth has more than one meaning. An increase in the number of participants in a particular market does not say anything about the distribution of their respective investments.

The Diversity of the Composition of Estates

Individual investors must choose whether to concentrate or alternatively to diversity their investments. Within a maximal range of eleven distinct types of investments (real estate, stocks, state bonds, federal bonds, private bonds, private stocks, nonfarm assets, mortgages, promissory notes, deposits, and life insurance), the 1920 decedents participated as an average in 4.83 of these types against 4.77 for their 1944 counterparts (Table 4.2).

Socioeconomic factors account for a larger part of the variance of the corresponding distributions in the case of the 1944 as opposed to the 1920 decedents. In this sense, the social variability of individual investments became more structured with the passage of time. Moreover, the determinants of this structure also became more numerous. For both cohorts, every additional unit of estate broadened the range of individual investments. For the second cohort, however, this range also shrank with age. Under conditions of collective hardship like a depression, retirement obliges individuals to withdraw from a number of markets in order to have cash more readily available on the eve of the liquidation of their estates.

Finally, for the cohort of 1944, the variability of estates also became a reverse function of the urbanization level of the state where individual decedents were residing. The higher this level, the more specialized are its social networks and the more difficult it was to obtain the information necessary to enter a large number of markets. To summarize, there seems to have been a tightening up of the socioeconomic and modernizing (urban) forces that have shaped the range of investments made by decedents between 1920 and 1944.

However, this type of analysis may be misleading since it unduly treats all types of assets as being equivalent. The next task is then to ascertain how investors treat time in their evaluation of the risks they are taking. Under certain conditions, time is the most salient component of the risks taken by individuals, since investors assume that their debtors will have no difficulty reimbursing what they have borrowed. In their eyes, the real value of the capital they have committed or of the income

Table 4.2. Diversity of Assets in the Estate: Regression[a]

Independent variable	1920	1944
Age		−.039**
Estate size	.009*	−.006
State income		
Occupation		
National origin		
Number of children		
Gender		
Unmarried daughters		
Urbanization		
State's urbanization		−.026
State's legal status (a)		
Region		
Mobility		
R^2_1	.053	.131
R^2_2	.046	.037
R^2_3	.020	.041
Mean	4.83	4.77
N	100	109

[a] Notes on independent variables:
Gender: men have been coded 0, women 1.

Estate size, the values of the regression coefficients are counted by reference to units of thousand dollars. For instance, a coefficient of 15.914 indicates that for every one thousand dollars, there is a change of 15.914 units of the dependent variable.

National origin: German-Americans are coded 0, Irish-Americans 1.

Occupation is scored 1 when the respondent is a businessman (everybody else being coded as 0). However, for the equations concerning realty, it is the farmers who are coded 1. For those concerning bonds and the number of secondary stocks, it is executives who are coded 1.

Legal status of the State, community property is coded 1 for the equations concerning notes, but the separation of conjugal estates is coded 1 in all other cases.

The absence of a coefficient indicates that the relevant t is below 1.80 for a two tails test. The absence of a star after a coefficient indicates that the t is between 1.80 and 1.96,
* means that the coefficient is significant at the .05 level
** means that the coefficient is significant at the .01 level

Loglikelihood 1, 2, and 3 represent the outcome of the three logistic regressions testing the relative explanatory power of the three models pertaining to socio-economic factors, familial structures, and modernising experiences as determinants of the choices made by respondents as to *whether* to own a particular type of capital.

R^2_1, R^2_2, and R^2_3 represent the outcome of the three regressions testing the relative explanatory power of the variables included in the same models as determinants of the choices made by respondents with regard to the *value* of a particular type of capital accumulated, or to the *number* of titles owned.

The Ns vary with each equation, depending on the number of missing values.

they may claim over the years should remain the same over the years. Thus, they want to be rewarded in terms of opportunity costs.

Under other conditions, individuals capitalize on the likelihood that the returns to their investments will undergo some changes that will enhance their profits substantially. This second population wants to be rewarded for the risks taken rather than for the alternative investments forgone. In the first case, individuals are likely to invest in bonds, deposits, and promissory notes. In the second one, they are more prone to invest in stocks, life insurance certificates, and eventually in nonfarm assets (equipment) or in real estate. Thus, there should be marked contrasts in the profile of those decedents who hold each one of the two clusters of assets.

Among the estates processed in 1920, individuals were most likely to own both life insurance and stock, but ownership of the two types of investment became independent of one another for the 1944 cohort. Further, there were also shifts in the attraction exerted by various types of bonds. Members of the earliest cohort were likely to own both private and federal bonds, but not necessarily state bonds. Among their 1944 counterparts, the possession of bonds only pertains to corporate and state bonds. In other words, the psychology of investing in fixed-income securities evolved between the two dates of reference.

Similarly, to the extent that nonfarm assets, mortgages, and promissory notes on the one hand, and stock, bonds, and deposits on the other are not negotiated with the same ease, they should attract differing types of populations. There is, however, no significant difference between the characteristics of the populations who hold and do not hold the first form of capital. In contrast, there are significant contrasts in the profile of those who hold and do not hold corporate securities, and the determinants of these contrasts are different for the two cohorts. In the case of the 1920 population, as already suggested, ownership of corporate securities refers primarily to the possession of both private and federal bonds. Among the 1944 population, the same ownership of corporate securities evokes possession of both bonds and stocks in the private sector. In other words, the social definitions of financial risks and their guarantees has changed during the period as a result of the succession of depressions undergone by the relevant money markets. The fact that such definitions are increasingly focused on the public or private profile of the borrower rather than on the conditions of the loan reflects a parallel shift in the decisions taken by investors.

To conclude, the structure of the assets accumulated became selectively more diversified with the passage of time between 1920 and 1944. Distinctions between income-producing real and symbolic types of assets ceased to differentiate various populations of decedents. In con-

The Diversity of the Composition of Estates

trast, the choices of the two cohorts compared here are inspired by distinct definitions of the risks involved.[13]

The Contribution of Real Estate

As already noted, land is the oldest major form of valuable. As such, it represents a type of asset owned by the overwhelming majority of decedents included in the sample. Yet, its popularity has declined over the years. German- and Irish-American small estate holders are even more conservative than the general population of decedents with an estate smaller than $200,000. In that population, only one-third of the 1920 cohort owned real estate as opposed to less than one-fifth of their 1944 counterparts. In other words, the greater the differentiation of assets available to individuals, the smaller becomes the share of realty in their estates.

The distinction between those who did and did not hold this type of asset declined from the earlier to the later cohort. This decline is probably the result of the growing heterogeneity of the market, which serves simultaneously residential, agricultural, and speculative functions and attracts therefore an increasingly diverse population (Table 4.3).

Further, the determinants of ownership of real estate vary across cohorts. For the 1920 decedents, this type of ownership depended on the relative opportunities of the environment rather than on individual socioeconomic or cultural characteristics. More typical of the residents of poor states where there were few alternative investment opportunities, this type of ownership prevailed also among the residents of the states where the segregation of the estates of conjugal partners was limited.

Among the 1944 decedents, the possession of real estate tended to characterize individuals who had many children alive at the time of their death. Thus, the requirements of ownership of human and nonhuman forms of capital are not always mutually exclusive. Individuals seem to acquire additional pieces of land because they have a sufficient number of sons and daughters able to cultivate them.

For those decedents who were in the realty market, the variance of the distribution of the value of their investments remained stable between 1920 and 1944. In both cases, socioeconomic factors account for the largest part of the variance (Table 4.4). In both cases, the value of realty increased with the number of lots acquired by decedents and with the size of their overall estate.[14] In both cases, this value was also higher for farmers than for the remaining segments of the population at large. Since in 1944, this value also increased with age and became significantly higher for men, the passage of time marks a more complex in-

Table 4.3. Decedents' Participation in Various Markets: Logit Analysis[a]

Independent variable	Realty		Mortgage		Promissory notes		Nonfarm assets	
	1920	1944	1920	1944	1920	1944	1920	1944
Age								−.056**
Estate size								
Occupation							1.895**	
State income	−.004**		.001			−.001		−.002*
Family size		.280	−.178					
National origin								
Gender							−1.692**	−1.784*
Unmarried daughters						−.920		
State's legal status	−1.655*							
Urbanization					−1.905**	−1.351		−1.289*
State's urbanization	−.090**				.039**			−.068**
Mobility								−1.598*
Region								
Log-likelihood₁	96.44	53.24	3.62	18.40	2.42	30.04	58.74	37.56
Percent placed	93.0	80.7	55.2	66.9	54.0	74.3	85.0	77.9
Log-likelihood₂	91.28	52.44	4.4	15.96	29.44	1.94	64.36	44.98
Percent placed	88.9	80.7	60.2	65.8	73.7	54.2	82.2	77.2
Log-likelihood₃	108.46	50.62	0.96	16.48	25.08	27.14	59.74	49.16
Percent placed	88.9	81.1	56.8	66.0	72.8	71.7	82.2	80.2

[a] See footnotes to Table 4.2.

terplay of variables.[15] Economic growth maximizes the complexity of choices.

The Contribution of Nonfarm Assets

Entrepreneurship requires individuals to invest in forms of capital other than land, more specifically, in the machinery needed for producing or selling goods. With the declining importance of the corresponding type of enterprise, it becomes increasingly difficult to distinguish

The Diversity of the Composition of Estates 109

Table 4.3. (Continued)

Independent variable	Life Insurance 1920	Life Insurance 1944	Federal bonds 1920	Federal bonds 1944	Private bonds 1920	Private bonds 1944	Stocks 1920	Stocks 1944
Age		−.042		−.055*				
Estate size				.007	.009*	.009*	.014*	
Occupation						−2.314*		
State income				−.002				
Family size				−.240			−.192	−.244
National origin	2.241**							
Gender	−3.229**	−1.617**			−.819	1.518		−1.865
Unmarried daughters					−1.648			
State's legal status								
Urbanization								
State's urbanization								
Mobility								
Region								
Log-likelihood$_1$	51.12	12.06	31.22	16.04	19.46	23.86	23.90	50.52
Percent placed	82.0	67.9	68.0	68.9	68.0	70.6	67.0	81.68
Log-likelihood$_2$	90.42	17.68	28.34	9.06	39.42	31.94	29.12	53.14
Percent placed	84.74	66.7	71.2	64.0	72.8	75.4	72.8	80.7
Log-likelihood$_3$	55.84	3.06	27.68	3.26	32.00	16.6	27.76	50.42
Percent placed	82.2	60.3	72.0	58.5	73.7	66.0	67.8	81.1

those who own this type of asset from those who do not. Further, to the extent that this form of capital behaves like the realty attached to agricultural enterprises and is a major source of income, it is gender related. In both cohorts, men were more likely than women to own this type of asset and this has probably always been the case (Table 4.3). Originally, this type of ownership also distinguished businessmen from the remaining segments of the population and it tended to be more typical of decedents residing in small communities.

With the progress of the economy, ownership of nonfarm assets evolved to prevail in 1944 among the decedents residing in the least developed states, that is, in those states with few alternative economic

Table 4.4. Value of Assets Held by Decedents: Regression[a]

Independent Variable	Nonfarm assets		Deposits		Realty		Notes		Federal bonds	
	1920	1944	1920	1944	1920	1944	1920	1944	1920	1944
Age			−.288			688.7*				
Estate size				.117**	.261**	.244**				.095**
State income					25.074**	25.761**				
Occupation										
Number of units			2.498**	3.038**	5.816**	3.774**	.614*	.963*		
Estate diversity										
State's legal status	20.545							13.396*		
National origin		−3.862								
Family size								−10.741*		
Gender						−14.519**				
Unmarried daughters										
Urbanization	30.310**						6.148*			7.814*
State's urbanization			.278**							
Region	−6.343*									
Mobility		−16.945								
R_1^2	.014	.069	.219	.345	.292	.320	.014	.166	.046	.137
R_2^2	.185	.120	.015	.026	.018	.028	.009	.145	.012	.051
R_3^2	.352	.015	.100	.035	.026	.051	.061	.166	.007	.063
Mean	21	30	98	95	105	92	53	31	85	54
N	11,353	17,324	11,932	7,622	43,096	30,861	5,987	7,908	7,984	9,188

[a] See footnotes to Table 4.2.
[b] The results presented here pertain to the number of *high quality* titles. For an analysis of the changes produced by the substitution of *secondary* titles to the variable used in the table, see endnote 17, p. 216.

Table 4.4. (Cont.) Regression of the Value of Assets for Decedents Who Own Them

Independent Variable	Life Insurance		Stocks		Bonds		Mortgages	
	1920	1944	1920	1944	1920	1944	1920	1944
Age		−741.4*				603.6*		
Estate size	.040	.238**	.511**	.177*	.187*	.168**		
State income		19.067*						
Occupation								
Number of units[b]			2128*	1488*	1061**	1748**	1435**	1135**
Number of children								
Gender[a]								
State's legal status[a]						14.332*		
National origin[a]	−5801**							
Unmarried daughters								
Urbanization								
State's urbanization	−84.736**							
Region								
Mobility								
R_1^2	.127	.426	.591	.189	.401	.347	.378	.082
R_2^2	.428	.080	.030	.032	.104	.087	.073	.090
R_3^2	.174	.036	.040	.035	.064	.095	.055	.094
Mean	21	49	81	92	36	39	56	39
N	5,037	22,012	36,013	35,450	21,743	11,060	20,672	17,913

[a] See footnotes to Table 4.2.
[b] The results presented here pertain to the number of *high quality* titles. For an analysis of the changes produced by the substitution of *secondary* titles to the variable used in the table, see endnote 17, p. 216.

opportunities. In other words, the survival of family-owned business has been selective. The same developmental processes also explain why this type of ownership becomes a negative function of age. Driven away from the market by economic growth, the aging businessmen of the second cohort retired increasingly frequently and were increasingly likely to sell their equipment long before dying.

Given the small scale of the activities typical of nonfarm assets, the value of the relevant investments depends initially on the opportunities offered by the environment rather than on the characteristics of individual investors. For the 1920 cohort, this value was higher for the residents of larger urban centers and for the residents of the states that fully segregate the estates of conjugal partners. This value was also lower in the southern and thus the least urbanized part of the United States. In short, in 1920, successful entrepreneurs who could accumulate a substantial amount of working capital were not randomly distributed throughout the country. They were most visible in the least complex zones of the nation.

In 1944, the determinants of success were much less powerful (Table 4.4). The accumulation of nonfarm assets varied as a reverse function of family size, confirming that the presence of children often impedes the mobilization of the resources necessary for making additional investments. This accumulation was also more significant for individuals who did not experienced any large-scale geographic mobility between their birth and their death.[16] Commercial success often requires stable social networks.

The Contribution of Stocks

Among all decedents owning less than $200,000, the proportion of those holding stock declined from 25 percent for the 1920 cohort to 19 percent for their 1944 counterparts. The German- and Irish-American subsamples departed markedly from this pattern. No matter which of the three modes of explanation (socioeconomic, cultural, or modern factors), the analysis is focused on, the distinction between individuals who died with and without stocks is clearer for the 1944 than the 1920 cohort. Since I will show that *objective* conditions for being successful in the stock market and hence for making money were more salient in 1920, one can argue that this salience has been instrumental in structuring further the "democratization" of the market for the second cohort. In addition, the depression enhanced the risks attached to the stock market and this could not but enhance the visibility of the distinction between those participating in the market and those staying out.

For the 1920 cohort, participation in the stock market increased with the size of the estate. For their 1944 counterparts, this participation was also more typical of male than of female decedents. For both cohorts, however, the presence of numerous children discouraged entry into the stock market.

As already noted, the distribution of the value of the stock owned by individuals at the time of their death is more clearly structured for the 1920 than the 1944 population. Thus, the number of quality stock certificates held by individuals became less significant determinant of this value between the two dates of the period of reference (Table 4.4).

For theoretical as well as empirical reasons, the contribution of the number of certificates held by decedents to the value of the stocks they owned is not tautological. Theoretically, it makes as much sense to place one's resources in one blue chip company as to spread the risks across the board. The question is then to ascertain whether the profiles of individuals who acquire a varying quantity of first- and second-quality stocks differ from one another. Empirically, variations in the number of primary or secondary stocks owned follow distinct patterns. Originally, to hold a large number of *secondary* stocks was typical of executives, of men, and of decedents with the most diversified estates. In contrast, the individuals who purchased a large number of *high-quality* stocks tended to be German-Americans, to have fewer children, and to live in states with high urbanization rates. Thus, the distribution of the risks imputed to various stocks was structured clearly.

With the evolution of the market, the meaning attached to the possession of a large number of high-quality stocks has changed. In 1944, this possession highlighted the increasing desire of reducing the risks taken. To be sure, those decedents who had the most high-quality stocks were those with the most diversified estates and those originating from the eastern seaboard, and hence, those who could take risks because they were knowledgeable; but they were also more often women than men and they were more likely to have unmarried daughters. As such, they were not supposed to take risks.

Independently of these contrasts, the number of titles held is a significant determinant of the overall value of the stock present in estates when the titles are first quality, but this is not so when such titles are negotiated in secondary marketplaces. Not only is the proportion of the variance accounted for lower in this second case, but the lack of significance of the coefficient attached to this variable is made even more glaring by the jump of the coefficient attached to estate size. In other words, it is not only the number of stocks held that made a difference, but also the quality of the markets where these stocks were negotiated.[17]

The Contribution of Life Insurance

Both the presence of life insurance in an estate and its value should enable us to pinpoint more precisely *when* Americans changed their definitions of familial obligations to translate them into specific monetary terms. In other words, when did life insurance become just another variety of investment among others rather than a form of familial obligation?

There was a marked increase in the number of decedents holding life insurance policies from 1920 to 1944, the increase being almost twofold for the general population of small estate holders (the relative number of decedents with this asset shot from 28 to over 53 percent), but even more spectacular for the Irish- and German-Americans.

Yet the distinction between those who did and those who did not hold such policies is statistically clearer for the earlier than the later cohort. Further, factors accounting for the distinction differ for the two populations. Ownership of life insurance was more of a male characteristic for the 1920 than for the 1944 cohort. This ownership was also initially more frequent among the Irish-Americans than the German-Americans, probably because of the distinct beliefs concerning the participation of the state in insurance schemes in the two cultures. Alternatively, for the 1944 cohort, ownership of insurance policies was typical of younger decedents, and it is difficult to determine whether the effect of age in this regard still reflects early phases in the diffusion of a *new* type of investment in the population, or the tightening of the links between particular phases of the life cycle and distinct types of investment.[18]

As in the case of other investments, the passage of time implies a greater complexity in the socioeconomic determinants of the sums invested in life insurance (Table 4.4). Not only was there a sharp increase in the influence of estate size, but in addition the value of insurance policies was higher among younger decedents and among businessmen than among other categories of the population at large. Alternatively, the passage of time is associated with a decline in the significance of cultural or "modernizing" variables. For example, in contrast to the 1920 decedents, who put more money in their insurance policies when they resided in the least urbanized states, and hence in states with close-knit social networks, their 1944 counterparts took decisions regarding insurance independently of their environment.

Similarly, there was a decline in the influence of national origin on the functioning of the insurance market. Among the 1920 decedents, the Irish-Americans were more likely to enter the insurance market, while

The Diversity of the Composition of Estates

their German-American contemporaries invested more money in it. In 1944, the two populations were alike on that score.

To conclude, the logics governing whether to own insurance policies and how much to invest in it seem to involve parallel processes. Initially governed by ethnic and geographic factors, the market seems to have been dominated by particularist forces. It is only subsequently that the value of the investments to be made becomes a challenge defined in more "rational" terms.

The Contribution of Bonds

As already noted, the risks attached to the purchase of bonds differ from those associated with the possession of stock certificates. In the first case, investors assume that time is inert; in the second, they assume discontinuities in the value of the capital invested or in the returns it might yield. Yet there are differing types of bonds. As federal bonds are safer than corporate or state bonds, the decision to enter a particular market should involve distinct motivations.

In the case of the 1920 population, the presence of both a large number of children and of unmarried daughters discouraged ownership of corporate bonds, which were still considered to be risky investments. Alternatively, as ownership of federal bonds was deemed to be both safe and patriotic, it was randomly distributed throughout the wealth distribution. For the second cohort, however, ownership of federal bonds became more structured, typical of younger decedents, and of wealthy individuals living in states with a low level of economic development. At the same time, occupation turns out to be a significant predictor of ownership of corporate bonds, executives minimizing their participation in a market that became safer and attracted women rather than men (Table 4.3).[19]

With the passage of time, it becomes easier to account for the variance of the distribution of the monies invested in federal bonds. The very fact that decedents who invested most in such a market were those with unmarried daughters represents another sign that the low risks involved rendered this specific market more attractive. There were similar changes in the views held about corporate bonds. Whereas the sums invested in this type of security kept depending on socio-economic factors, and notably on estate size and the number of units purchased, they also became determined by more particularist motivations. The sums invested in this type of asset by the 1944 cohort increased with age: older individuals preferred to invest in assets that could easily be redeemed

Table 4.5. Number of Titles Held by Decedents: Regression[a]

Independent Variable	Secondary stocks		Quality stocks		Bonds	
	1920	1944	1920	1944	1920	1944
Age						
Estate size						
State income						
Occupation	13.951*					
Estate diversity	1.504*	0.999*		1.176*		
National origin			−5.213			−4.771
Family size			−1.987*			−1.379
Gender	−4.380*			5.499*		
Unmarried daughters				5.252		
Urbanization						
State's urbanization			0.207**			
Region				5.402	−8.691	
Mobility				−6.112*		
R_1^2	.143	.003	.019	.076	.028	.052
R_2^2	.045	.055	.123	.059	.024	.142
R_3^2	.023	.014	.140	.044	.004	.053
Mean	5.23	4.93	6.28	9.56	8.38	6.08
N	64	75	25	52	37	48

[a] See footnotes to Table 4.2.

and transformed in cash. The same stress placed on liquidity explains also why investments in bonds were higher among residents of states where conjugal estates were kept totally separate. This minimized the risks of seeing investments diverted toward beneficiaries deemed unworthy.

The importance of analogous particularist factors is also evident in the distribution of the number of titles held by individuals (Table 4.5).[20] To be sure, the number of titles held by the 1944 decedents present in the bond market varies as a reverse function of their family size, and hence as a function of their capacity to mobilize additional resources. But since this number is also greater for German- than for Irish-Americans, one can infer that national groups hold distinct time orientations. More specifically, German-Americans seem more prone to trust the cumulative properties of economic development and disregard the likelihood of downswings in the cycle.

The Diversity of the Composition of Estates

Table 4.5. (Continued)

Independent Variable	Deposits		Mortgage certificates		Promissory notes	
	1920	1944	1920	1944	1920	1944
Age						
Estate size	−15.914**					
State income						
Occupation						
Estate diversity						
National origin					−2.017*	
Family size					.774*	
Gender		1.082				
Unmarried daughters						
Urbanization	−1.073*		5.132*			
States urbanization	.044**	.040				
Region		1.512				7.568
Mobility						
R_1^2	.110	.024	.070	.021	.022	.054
R_2^2	.001	.072	.065	.059	.187	.090
R_3^2	.080	.095	.013	.098	.067	.117
Mean	2.86	2.90	6.14	5.22	3.93	4.41
N	95	91	56	36	53	31

The Contribution of Mortgages and Promissory Notes

During earlier stages of capitalist development in the United States, wealth holders were often engaged in long-term ventures related to their immediate surroundings. The bonds established between lenders and borrowers could last longer than their respective lives, because they were not easily transferred.

Mortgage and promissory notes represent two forms of wealth that are slow to die. Almost half of the 1920 decedents held mortgage certificates and about 40 percent of them owned promissory notes. In 1944, the corresponding figures were significantly lower, but they still reached 31 and 24 percent, respectively. In both cases, mortgage certificates or notes were often offered to relatives and neighbors, or to individuals with the same national background as the decedents themselves.[21] Thus, the relatively high incidence of this type of investment during early stages of development suggests that capitalism does not always require or cause the weakening of critical community bonds.

Instead, the declining popularity of this type of asset seems to result from ideological rather than structural forces. It is difficult otherwise to explain why the contribution of the number of certificates to the sums invested declined over time in the case of the safer mortgages but increased in the case of the more insecure promissory notes (Table 4.4). From 1920 to 1944, the significance of the number of borrowers as a predictor of the sums invested in this type of assets became more marked, which suggests that particularism helped decedents to select the individuals to whom they lent money.

Finally, the positive contributions of both national origin and family size to the number of notes held by the 1920 decedents (Table 4.5) as well as the positive contribution of national origin to the value of these notes for the 1944 cohort (Table 4.4) highlight the rational aspects of the cultural nature of the choices made by individuals in their lending policies. The findings confirm the effectiveness of the selective persistence of German-American communal solidarity in various regions of the country. The same solidarity explains also why the value of promissory notes is higher for decedents with unmarried daughters or for decedents residing in states bound by the rule of community property. In order to be both effective and numerous, notes require trust within and among familial groups.[22]

The Contribution of Deposits

Because of the flexibility they offer, deposits have become more popular investments over the years. Because of their increased popularity, the differential profile of decedents who held and did not hold money-making accounts changed between the two cohorts. In 1920, holders of deposits were fewer in the South than in other parts of the country. In 1944, these holders were concentrated in small towns but they also tended also to have larger estates.

The logic governing the value of deposits is somewhat different. To be sure, estate size contributed, as expected, to increasing the sums deposited in banks and saving and loan associations. Similarly, the value of these deposits also grew with the number of institutions where they were sheltered, and the corresponding relationship became more marked over time. Yet, among the 1920 decedents, holding deposits characterized decedents with a limited urban experience, while the value of their deposits was a function of the urbanization rate of the state of residence and hence of the extent to which the multiplicity of networks maximizes competition among banking institutions.

Last, while the value of deposits depends on the number of institutions involved, this number itself varies originally as a reverse function of estate size. In other words, it was originally the holders of small estates who split the risks attached to this type of account by using the services of as large a number of institutions as possible. Prevailing later on among female rather than male decedents, the choice of this strategy was also geographically selective. Most frequent among the residents of the states with a high urbanization rate, it was initially atypical of the eastern seaboard, to become in 1944, most visible among the residents of southern regions.

The Contribution of Personal Property

From the very beginning, Americans have been on the go. Tocqueville noted that Americans hardly finished the house they were building with their retirement in mind that they sold it to indulge in new dreams (as quoted by Glendon 1987:117). Similarly, today, many Americans sell the homes they own during their active lives to raise the cash necessary to pay for the care provided to them by the retirement communities in which they end their lives. Not only does this move entail the abandonment of many items of personal property, but it also makes it necessary for the elderly to be very selective in the objects they retain.

In the sample examined here, the most important item recorded is the automobile (usually a Pierce Arrow or a Duesenberg), whose number per capita shot from .23 for the cohort of 1920 to .44 for the cohort of 1944.[23] Alternatively, one is struck by the absence of any valuable piece of furniture. The items listed are cheap and regrouped into undifferentiated lots (which confirms the lack of interest they could stir). Inventories of personal property were rarely conducted room by room and only identified a few visual artifacts. Collectors of objects d'art were few and they acquired their pieces by the same and uniform logic. In the two instances out of well over one hundred returns of top wealth holders where the presence of art collections was established (one in the Midwest, the other on the West Coast), decedents had purchased relatively recent European painters (Delacroix, Isabey, Diaz, Corot, Dupre, Jongkind, Daubigny, and Rousseau). In these two instances, the inventories highlighted the segmentation of the art markets of the period. Thus, the value of the Delacroix owned in one case was estimated at $7, whereas the Delacroix purchased by the second decedent was valued at $7,200. Similarly, the one Diaz owned by the first collector was estimated at $25, but the second was evaluated at $2,200.[24] In the sample of smaller estates included in the present study, the only decedent with an art collection was a painter, and his collection can be considered as equivalent to the business equipment of innkeepers or farmers. In other words, it should be viewed in utilitarian rather than esthetic terms.

Between these two extremes, the majority of decedents owned carpets and rugs, jewelry, and furs, thus items that could be transported easily.[25] Individuals with jewelry owned three kinds of valuables: at the lower end of the scale, jewelry refers to small items in gold, such as a pocket watch, in the middle, the term refers to silverware; at the upper end, it evokes the presence of diamonds in simple or elaborated forms (studs).

The differentiation between those who owned jewelry and those who did not is statistically significant for both cohorts (the number of decedents with jewelry went down from 36 to 21 percent from 1920 to 1944). The likelihood of ownership is uniformly greater for female than male decedents, which confirms the symbolic rather than instrumental value of this particular item, even though for both populations the likelihood of ownership is independent of the presence of daughters in the family. Furthermore, the likelihood of this type of ownership has something to do with social change. For the 1920 population, it was highest among the residents of highly urbanized areas and in 1944, among those of the eastern seaboard. In this sense, it continued to be typical of urban and mobile cultures.

Conclusions

The perpetuation of the treasuries acquired by individuals across generations is the result of two distinct logics. On the one hand, this perpetuation is contingent on the materialist logic that governs the specific markets in which the valuables accumulated are negotiated. On the other, it depends on the cultural logic that corresponds to the sociodemographic profile of the decedents and to the experience they have acquired as a result of their gender, their age, their familial life, or their national origin, but also to the collective features of their immediate environment. Individual choices never take place *in vacuo*. They represent a constant resolution of the tensions that oppose individual and collective dreams or aspirations to one another.

The Materialist Logic of Wealth Accumulation

Assets differ in terms of their popularity as well as of the sums they attract. The structures of the distributions of specific investments follow three distinct patterns. Certain markets, like realty, are stable in terms of the relative number of their participants or their characteristics, of the sums invested, and of their determinants. For example, the effects of estate size on the amount of money invested in realty have been alike for the two cohorts.

Other markets are governed by diverging dynamics. Thus, since specific assets (for example, working capital or nonfarm assets) were on their way out due to the declining importance of familial businesses, the overall salience of their determinants kept decreasing between 1920 and 1944. Both the value of the log-likelihoods and of the overall variance accounted for declined between the two cohorts, even though their determinants remained the same over the years. Nonfarm assets were and remain a preserve of male decedents living in small towns.

Alternatively, the dynamics underlying other types of assets were more complex. At one end of the continuum, the increasing popularity of life insurance policies was associated with a systematic erosion of the distinction between those who did and those who did not participate in the relevant market; the erosion was accompanied by the strengthening of the socioeconomic determinants of the monies involved, but by a concomitant decline in the significance of cultural predictors. At the other end of the continuum, the declining popularity of mortgage certificates was paralleled not only by a parallel strengthening of the distinction between those who did and did not hold such certificates, but also by the erosion of the socioeconomic determinants of the values involved. In short, the progress of the first market and the demise of the second one help identify who participates and for how much.

The Cultural Logic of Wealth Accumulation

Regardless of the role played by resources in the decisions to enter or stay in a particular market and to invest specific amounts in it, differences in the role resources play both across markets and over time highlight the importance of the interpretations that individuals elaborate of their surroundings. Thus, the depression sharpened the differential approaches of men and women toward financial risks. Women have become more likely to invest in bonds, men in stocks. As another example, German- and Irish-American decedents have adopted at differing periods of time diverging "tastes" toward life insurance programs or toward lending money to relatives or to neighbors.

However, analyses of risks and returns are always contingent on the context in which individuals operate. Thus, the decisions to enter or stay in a market and how much to invest are often dependent on the level of economic activities of the state where decedents reside and hence on the alternative forms of investments available to them. As another example, such decisions are also contingent on the urbanization level of their surroundings and hence on the complexity of the social networks operating around them. Finally, these decisions depend also on the legal profile of the state of residence. Indeed, decedents appreciate the long-term consequences of their decisions on what they will leave to their spouses or their offspring.

To summarize, the presence of significant shifts between 1920 and 1944 in the presence of specific assets in individual estates, in their values, and in their determinants underlines the need to specify further the level at which the reproductive processes inherent in inheritance operate. Such processes are interpretive rather than mechanical whenever or wherever individuals must constantly monitor their immediate environments in order to choose the alternative mechanisms that offer them the best chances to maintain their relative position in the social structure. For example, they must constantly assess the conditions under which material and human forms of capital are complementary or mutually exclusive. Thus, while the presence of many children stimulates the acquisition of immediately productive investments (e.g., land for farmers), such a presence discourages the formation of other forms of capital wherever or whenever the forms of wealth accumulated are more immediately dependent on a corporate economy and hence on stocks and bonds. When farming parents miss the exact time when the nature of their occupation changes, they turn their children from assets into liabilities. Because of such a shift, parents and children lose the edge in their chances to survive.

After having sketched the material and social conditions under which both the amount and the form of the wealth accumulated reproduce across adjacent generations, it becomes possible to ascertain how these two sets of conditions affect both the instruments used by decedents to transfer their estate to their surviving relatives and the form of the bequests present in their wills.

5

Testacy and the Limits of Free Wills

In Chapter 1, I alluded to Maine's (1954) metaphor of inheritance as a transfer of the decedent's legal "clothing." In traditional societies, this transfer and the ensuing continuity of generations are shaped by customs that leave few initiatives to individuals. These customs specify the sequential order in which heirs are to be chosen as a function of their age and their gender, but above all, as a function of the segment of lineage and the generation to which they belong. In such a context, there is little improvisation, since there are few references to the specific psychological qualities expected from heirs.

Alternatively, the progress of individualism that the American Revolution symbolizes has been conducive to the diversification of legal instruments of transfer (wills, trusts, donations). With such instruments, decedents are now endowed with a greater variety of means of control over the destination of their individual assets. They enjoy additional degrees of freedom with regard to what they give to whom, how, and when. Individualism, however, does not only broaden the range of choices available, but it also changes the central tendencies of testators' distributions. It marks the triumph of achievement over ascription during the early stages of development of a capitalist society, but later it also evokes the victory of an ideology of impulses over an ideology of delayed gratification.[1] Not only is this evolution marked by a decline in the overall amount of bequests made by testators, but there should be also a greater variability in both the amount and the form of such bequests.

Historically, the progress of individualism has entailed a concomitant increase in the number of decedents who write wills across all segments of the population. At first, individualism was an ideology elaborated for the exclusive benefit of white males; women were not empowered to dispose of their assets, which were returned to their families of origin upon their deaths, retained by their surviving spouses, or automatically passed on to their male children. Later, when underprivileged ethnic groups and social classes themselves learned to invoke individualistic ideologies for their own purposes, they learned how to imitate established elites and to rely on wills as instruments of transfer. Intestacy, and thus the application of state laws to the definition of estates and their distribution, became a residual category. Today, the law can only be invoked in the absence of a will and is used for those marginal segments of the population who did not bother to organize their own death.

As long as individualistic ideologies stressed the role of achievement in the definition of the self, wills retained a religious overtone. The notion of testament, which currently survives as the English adjective *testamentary*, evokes the need for decedents to make a final public statement about their deeds and misdeeds. Even today, as wills remain the ultimate public material symbol of commitment to a metaphysical view of the self, they retain an exemplary quality. Correspondingly, decedents often bequeath money to churches in order to finance the performance of yearly memorial services.

For the most part, however, the original function of wills has declined under the influence of new forms of individualism. As soon as the experience of private feelings and preferences became socially acceptable, the ensuing secularization transformed wills into legal instruments that empower their authors to overcome the seemingly temporary character of human passions. American wills are no longer bound by the enduring habits of their hearts. Some wills overtly exclude relatives, others ignore them. As the agenda of the most recent forms of individualism is to overcome the divisive and destructive effects of time, many of these wills are used to legitimize and "freeze" passions of the fleeting moment. In writing wills, individuals have therefore two concerns. Anxious to include as well as exclude significant others from their riches, they are also keen to perpetuate their own rank ordering of relatives and friends beyond their death.

Insofar as the capitalist ideology to which these two concerns correspond posits simultaneously the formal equality of all individuals and the need to pay attention to their identity and to their unequal achievements or life chance, the following analysis seeks to chart the simultaneous erosion and accentuation of social disparities in the use of instruments of transfers.

Death and Time

Since gaining control over time becomes the ultimate function of heirship, the progress of individualism should be paralleled by increased variations in the timing of the corresponding transfers. At one end of the range of attitudes toward time, claims about the right to change one's

Death and Time

preferences and to reject any limitations in the pursuit of one's feelings should be associated with the parallel growth of gifts *inter vivos* at the expense of wills. Whenever or wherever individualism condones the experience of the current moment, gifts are often taxed at a lower rate than bequests *mortis causa*. Yet the legitimation of the present at the expense of the future is only partial. For example, when estate planners note that many informal cohabiters (i.e., homosexual couples) now prefer drawing wills rather than making donations, they point out the dual requirements of legitimation. In order to be legitimated, feelings must be expressed publically, but they must also give the impression of being enduring (Black 1987).

At the opposite end of the same range, trusts mark two other facets of individualism in a capitalist world. On the one hand, they enable decedents to survive their deaths and control the lives of their survivors.[2] On the other hand, the ensuing freezing of the resources constituting the trust fund gives them a fiscal immunity. In allowing individual decedents to minimize the taxes they should have paid otherwise, trusts symbolize the preeminence of the private realm over the public sphere.

In the light of the growing diversity of testators, their heirs, and their assets, the purpose of this chapter is to identify interindividual differences in the use of the various legal instruments of transfer (gifts *inter vivos*, wills, trusts) as ways to overcome the divisive and destructive effects of time. More specifically, the purpose of the chapter is to examine how the effective use of these instruments varies not only with the economic and demographic characteristics of individual decedents, but also with the profile of their potential heirs, the culture of all these actors, and finally the dominant socioeconomic features of the larger society.

Yet these instruments not only help overcome the divisive effects of time, but they also facilitate the classification of things and people. In the same way that Marx saw the notion of exploitation as pertaining to relations involving both nature and human beings, legal instruments of transfer highlight complementarities in the bonds that decedents weave with their material and their social environments, more specifically, with their assets and with their survivors.

In view of the interaction between the dispositions of American law, the norms of the reference groups of most testators, and the idiosyncratic character of the choices they make, the rank orderings of time, things, and people are not necessarily systematically interdependent (Berkner 1976). For instance, whenever wills refer to cars and sewing machines on the one hand, and to sons and daughters on the other, they may or may not posit as a rule that cars should go to sons, sewing machines to daughters. Similarly, when testators make bequests contingent on certain events in the lives of their beneficiaries (graduations, marriages, divorces, returns to the familial homestead), the conditions they impose may be particularistic: some of these conditions may exclusively affect the lives of daughters, and others may concern exclusively sons.

Thus sociological analyses of transfers require the identification of the "natural history" of the three ranking systems used by decedents (time, things, and people) and their interaction. For this reason, this chapter is focused on the conditions under which decedents use testacy for specifying the temporary or the ultimate destination of key items of personal property (e.g., jewels, clocks, silverware), of particular lots of real estate, or of specific stocks. In this sense, it is focused on how changes in the functions of testacy reflect the evolution of the forms of wealth and hence of the economy.

Finally, to the extent that testacy is also about ordering social relations, the purpose of the chapter is not only to identify the determinants of the choices of executors of wills or trusts, but also to ascertain how decedents use wills to depart from the number of beneficiaries spelled out by the law.

What Is Known about Testacy in the United States

In the United States as elsewhere, testacy reflects the desire to depart from existing norms. This desire is embedded in local contexts, since the laws governing the definition of individual estates and those spelling out the rank order of eligible heirs vary across states.

The frequency of testacy should be greater among the residents of the states with an ideological orientation that goes against the libertarianism of the official American ethos. Hence, wills should be more frequent in community property states (Louisiana, Arizona, California, Idaho, Nevada, New Mexico, Texas, and Washington), where laws presuppose a coordination of conjugal feelings and assets that is probably at variance with the specifically American forms of individualism. However, existing data do not confirm this assumption (Fellows, Simon, and Rau 1978).

At the same time, testacy may reflect the desire to confirm the validity of the models of familial relations that prevail in the decedents' cultures of origin, as these are symbolized by the norms governing transfers *mortis causa*. Thus, the incidence of wills should vary with the national origin of decedents.

Findings on the effects of cultural variations in this regard are spotty. Although for both historical and theoretical reasons, religion should be a significant determinant of heirship practices, the literature is mute as to the differences it makes on testacy. At the same time, the distributions of testacy are proven to vary both by occupation and national origin.

Yankee and German-American farmers of Illinois differ from one another in this regard. In the recent past, three-quarters of German-American farmers died testate against only 43 percent of their Yankee counterparts. Further, while the incidence of testacy remains relatively stable among the German-Americans, it has tripled among the Yankees from 21 percent for those who died before 1901 to 67 percent for those who passed away after 1960. Since the Yankees moved more recently and in a more individualistic way than their German-American neighbors, it looks as if their commitment to testacy represents a coordinated challenge to the rules prevailing in the immediate environment (Carroll and Salamon 1988). Indeed, while mobility jeopardizes the perpetuation of religious and familial models, the corresponding threat is not necessarily irreversible.

Insofar as wills emphasize the meaning that distinct cultures give to economic pursuits, it is not surprising to note that distinct national groups use testacy for different ends. The Irish-American farmers settled in Illinois, for instance, seek to perpetuate the higher status accorded to one of the sons (usually the oldest). In addition, like their counterparts in the old country, they wait as long as they can before passing the land to the heir. Only one-fourth of Irish-American farmers received land before they were 25 years of age against two-thirds of their German-American counterparts (Salamon 1980). Alternatively, over one-half of the same Irish-American farmers got their land from strangers, against only 15 percent of their German-American counterparts. Further, the effects of the economic cycle are culture specific: Irish-American commitment to impartibility seems to be independent of the economic cycle. In contrast, the vagaries of the same cycle induce variations in the German-American commitment to equality among children. The declining stress placed on equality from the earliest (prior to 1901) to the latest (post-1960) cohorts of German-American decedents confirms that heirship practices may vary with the availability of land (Cole and Wolf 1975).

Yet the persistence of the influence of national origin on testacy is contingent on the awareness that individuals have of the differences opposing American law to their own traditions. To the extent that testacy requires individuals to evaluate the costs and benefits attached to each legal model, the likelihood of testacy should increase with educational attainment. In 1977, no less than 60 percent of individuals with a graduate school education had drawn wills as against 37 percent of those who had not finished high school. Similarly, in the sample of New Englanders interviewed by Rossi and Rossi (1990), educational attainment is a significant determinant of the likelihood that respondents have written a will, even when other variables are taken into account.[3]

Thus, the contribution of schooling to testacy is twofold. It enhances income, savings, and the ability to transfer, but it also accentuates commitment to individualistic ideologies. The role of education as a facilitator of individual intentions is not new. Among the first cohorts of German immigrants in the United States at the end of the eighteenth century, those who knew English relied more often than others on specific items of the local law to perpetuate German models of transfers *mortis causa* (Roeber 1987). In this sense, education is as much past as future oriented. Enhancing awareness of new opportunities, schooling also enables individuals to identify the strategies that will allow them to perpetuate the practices of the past to which they are attached.

To conclude, while the various cultures to which individuals belong affect both their resources and their orientations, the two relevant effects are not always cumulative. A low educational attainment often reduces individual estates, but does not necessarily prevent testators from perpetuating the practices they cherish, which may be deemed obsolete by the rest of the population. Alternatively, the distributions of the various instruments of transfer should not always be more clearly patterned for educated respondents who use schooling for implementing the values to which their culture (national origin, religious background, etc.) commits them. This happens because people are often caught between modern and traditional ideologies. In the sample of New Englanders studied by Rossi and Rossi (1990), both educational attainment and the number of objects already inherited increase the likelihood of testacy. In other words, schooling enables individuals to choose the components of their cultural heritage they want to reproduce.

Against this general background, testacy depends on two distinct and interdependent logics. On the one hand, the incidence of wills depends on the stakes that the estate of decedents represents. On the other, the drawing of wills is also contingent on the demographic profile of the same decedents.

The Stakes as Determinants of Testacy

Testacy is determined by the amount of assets accumulated by individuals. Whether the relevant data pertain to a priori reported intentions or to a posteriori material observations, whether the same data concern geographically circumscribed communities or nationwide random samples, they all indicate a strong relationship between estate size (the amount of wealth accumulated) and testacy. For instance, in 1977, only 15 percent of individuals with a net worth less than $13,000 reported having drawn a will, against 69 percent of those with a net worth over $100,000.

The positive relationship between estate size and testacy is seemingly invariant in space or time. In Cleveland, wills are more numerous among decedents with the largest estates. The estates of individuals who died testate averaged $35,160, those of individuals who died intestate averaged only $6,694. Earlier, the corresponding figures were, respectively, $41,885 and $7,920 for Illinois and they were $66,954 and $9,954 in the case of Washington (Price 1975; Sussman, Cates, and Smith 1970).

Over time, wills became more numerous as a result of economic development. Thus, the relative number of wills among the decedents of Bucks County, Pennsylvania, a community that has kept the relevant records for a long time, remained stable prior to the early phases of industrialization before climbing from 62 percent in 1893 to 92 percent in 1979 (Shammas, Salmon, and Dahlin 1987). However, far from being linear, this long-term increase of testacy is adversely influenced by downswings in the economic cycle. In Wisconsin, for instance, the incidence of testacy declined sharply, from 61 to 39 percent between 1929 and 1944 as a result of the Great Depression (Ward and Beuscher 1950).

Finally, in the same way that income is only a moderate predictor of net worth, because of the distinct time dimensions within which these two variables evolve, the relationship between testacy and income is modest, albeit significant. In 1977, only 38 percent of those individuals with an income under $8,000 reported having drawn a will, as opposed to 65 percent of those with an income over $25,000 (Fellows, Simon, and Rau 1978).

To conclude, the effects of estate size are powerful enough to mask other possible forces, notably those associated with its composition. To return to the case of Bucks County, even though the share of realty in probated wealth has declined from 56 to 28 percent between the beginning of the eighteenth century and 1979, the incidence of testacy has kept growing. In this sense, testacy seems to be independent of how much realty people have.

Alternatively, however, those who hold exclusively life insurance policies do not need a will, since their beneficiaries are designated once for all on the certificates purchased. This makes the logics of life insurance and of wills independent and complementary. This, however, has not always been the case. As we shall see, since both the writing of a will and the purchase of life insurance policies were originally signs of modern forms of individualism, these logics were mutually reinforcing. Testators confirmed the beneficiaries of their policies in their wills. Today, however, men purchase life insurance early in their life cycles in order to fulfill their conjugal and parental obligations. Yet the structure of the distribution of this type of investment is less determinate than that of testacy, not only because it has become quasi-universal (Rossi and Rossi 1990), but also because as men get older, many forgo insurance to diversify their investments.

The Effects of Occupation

The strength of the relationship between estate size and testacy also contributes to masking the intrinsic effects of occupation. Distinct occupational pursuits do not engender the same knowledge of various assets. They also entail specific risks. For instance, the negative effects of the depression on the incidence of testacy have been selective. The relative number of wills dropped more sharply among the self-employed and proprietors than farmers. In relative terms, the losses of the latter were probably more moderate, because land tends to be more depression-proof.

The influence of occupation is also more direct. Distinct occupations do not foster convergent views of the future. The amount and the form of their investments differ accordingly. Further, as various jobholders also differ from one another in terms of the capital they borrow, the conditions of the loans they contract, or the help they might obtain from their relatives, the decisions they take with regard to transfers *mortis causa* are subject to distinct challenges from third parties. Finally, professionals and wage earners do not subscribe to the same fiscal principles. All self-employed individuals enjoy more leeway to spread their gains and expenses in ways that are advantageous to them. In short, the various American occupational groups learn to face distinct financial and legal risks.

The Effects of Age

Even though the distribution of testacy corresponds to a life cycle effect, this effect is not necessarily cumulative. On the one hand, the imminence of death accentuates the urgency of introducing order in one's life. On the other hand, the influence of aging is also a by-product of estate size. Enhanced by occupational seniority, income and savings diminish with retirement. During earlier periods, the relationship between age and testacy was correspondingly curvilinear. Prior to Social Security legislation, decedents were more concerned with the growing expenses of the last years of their life than with their commitment to survivors. They wanted above all to cover their needs and their final payments. Especially in a society devoted to self-reliance, what might happen to their unused reserves did not matter that much to them.

Beyond the Social Security legislation, however, with the growing number of pensions, retirees began to experience the dilemmas common to more fortunate populations as to what to do with their estate *after* their death. Correspondingly, the relationship between age and testacy became tighter for the post– than for the pre–Social Security period.

Today, the frequency of wills increases systematically with age (Dunham 1963). In 1977, only 8 percent of those individuals less than 25 years of age reported having drawn a will against no less than 61 percent of those between 45 and 54 years old and 85 percent among those over 65 years old (Fellows, Simon, and Rau 1978). More recently, Rossi and Rossi (1990) have confirmed the major contribution of age in this regard, even when other variables are taken into account.

The Effects of Gender

Gender differences in the distribution of testacy reflect historically and culturally relative disparities in the economic and the legal status of American men and women. In economic terms, the lower incidence of wills among females is a by-product of their lower participation in the labor force. This has prevented them from gaining the same opportunities as men for accumulating savings (Dunham, 1963). However, with the combination of economic and ideological changes, overall differences between men and women have continued to decline. In Bucks County, for example, decedents with probated estates represented no less than 66 percent of male, but only 40 percent of female decedents between 1891 and 1893. In contrast, the relevant figures for 1979 were 59 percent in both cases (Shammas, Salmon, and Dahlin 1987).

Increases in the number and the size of the estates held by women have reduced gender differences in the distribution of wills. Women who have accumulated wealth have become as likely as their male counterparts to die testate. For the male population, the incidence of probated wills in Bucks County has hardly changed from 30 percent for the male population deceased between 1891 and 1893 to 34 percent of their counterparts deceased in 1979. But for women, the relevant figures shot up from only 19 percent for the first period to 38 percent for the second one (Shammas, Salmon, and Dahlin 1987; Brittain 1978).

As a result of current convergences in the economic status of men and women, three other determinants of the differential frequency with which the two genders draw wills become more evident. (1) First, the economic gains achieved by women reduce gender difference as far as the middle part of the distribution of estates by size is concerned, but they are without effect for the top part. Among the wealthiest segments of the population, testacy remains more frequent among men than women. Females transfer only money; males often transfer both money and power. Money can be split; power cannot. (2) Second, since women enjoy a longer life expectancy, they are expected to bear the responsibility to take the ultimate decisions concerning the transfer of familial assets to the next generation. The ideological changes that underline the preeminence of conjugal over parental bonds cannot but reinforce such a responsibility. (3) Finally, gains in the domestic status of women are not coterminous with their status in the larger society. Thus, recurrent stereotypes as to their legal "irresponsibility" induces many of them to plan their estates in order to avoid future challenges and protect their heirs.

Convergences in the economic status of men and women are associated with parallel declines in the timing of their respective wills. As long as the distinction that people make between instrumental and emotional functions followed gender lines, the time interval separating the date of the will from the death of decedents was longer for men than for women. In Ontario, for instance, no less than 51 percent of the male decedents during the 1960–1962 period wrote their wills more than five years prior to their deaths, as against only 37 percent of female decedents. With the continuous economic progress of women during the subsequent period, the relevant gender differences have disappeared. For those decedents who died in 1974–1976, the corresponding figures were 48 and 49 percent, respectively (Kubat, Porter, and Landa n.d.).

The Effects of Matrimonial Status

Matrimonial status influences whether individuals write wills. Testacy is more typical of married than of unmarried decedents, whether unmarried refers to single or to divorced individuals. While widowhood increases the likelihood that decedents have written a will, the relevant differences are currently much sharper for men than for women.

As with regard to occupation, age, and gender, the matrimonial status of decedents is masked by the influence of estate size. For this reason, the effects of matrimonial status are gender specific. Among the women of a recent past, "spinsters" and widows were often more likely than married or divorced women to draw wills. As the former participated more frequently in the labor market, they were also more often able to accumulate savings and create their own estates.

Among married women, the decision to draw wills depends on the history of their marriages. Whenever they have children, almost three-quarters of them die with a will when they are widows as against only one-third of their counterparts who die prior to their spouses.[4] Clearly, these distinctions are historically relative. Since modern no-fault divorce has little negative effect on male wealth, the successive spouses and children of the corresponding population of men are more prone to challenge their bequests. This likelihood makes it imperative for men who marry more than once to draw wills. By contrast, since modern divorce depletes the estates of women, it should make divorced women most unlikely to draw a will.[5]

The effects of matrimonial mobility on the testamentary practices of men and women also present analogous properties. In both cases, the incidence of testacy is greater among decedents with than without children. In 1977, only 11 percent of childless individuals indicated they had a will against one-third of those with at least some minor children and three-quarters of those with adult children. However, testacy seems to be discouraged by both childlessness and a large progeny (Rossi and Rossi 1990). The presence of numerous children exert strong financial pressures on individual estates. These pressures are indeed sufficiently strong to override the frequent desire that parents of large families have to distinguish children from one another and provide each of them with distinct bequests.

The Role of Testacy in 1920 and 1944

As this overview of testacy suggests, legal instruments of transfer enable human beings to triumph over the constraints that time imposes on their designs. From this perspective, wills do not represent the first or the last step in the gratuitous transfers that individuals are willing to make in favor of selected beneficiaries. Domestic transfers begin with prenuptial agreements that enable future conjugal partners to identify the assets over which they intend to retain exclusive control or that they intend to share. Rare in the United States, prenuptial agreements are nevertheless becoming more frequent with the rising rate of divorce. While the estate tax returns analyzed here do not provide any information on such agreements, they still throw light on joint-property arrangements, and hence on the subsequent mechanisms of transfers used by spouses.

Similarly, returns also shed some light on gifts *inter vivos*. As already suggested, the meaning of transfers before death varies across cultures. In many traditional contexts, the extent to which the elderly relinquish valuable assets into the hands of their heirs depends on the domestic authority they are able to retain. For example, Irish farmers pass the farm down to one of their sons because they will keep their bedroom, will be fed, and will retain some informal influence over the daily routines of the farm. In more modern contexts, gifts *inter vivos* symbolize both the socioeconomic independence of parents (notably as a result of retirement programs, which lower their financial worries) and the enhanced vulnerability of some or all of their children, (notably as a result of inflationary tuition fees, rising mortgage rates, or increases in the down payments required for the purchase of a home).

Against this background, the next step of the analysis concerns the distribution, the functions, and the timing of transfers within the family. Indeed, the meaning and functions of these transfers should also depend on the time interval between the elaboration of the document and the death of the decedent.

Joint Property

Even though American sociologists and demographers have been prolific in their descriptions of the domestic division of feelings, practices, and powers between spouses, they have been surprisingly more discreet about the material bases of such interactions. For example, studies of variations in the tenancy of bank accounts and a fortiori of other forms of capital are both rare and recent. These studies suggest that joint tenancy reflects in part the commitment of each partner to the notion of couple, and in part environmental factors such as the legal status of their state of residence or the relative vulnerability of each spouse to legal pursuits (Treas, 1988).

Until fairly recently, conjugal partners tended to keep their assets apart, even those acquired during the duration of the marriage. Yet the segregation of estates between husbands and wives is often functionally limited and only concerns certain assets. As far as realty is concerned, for instance, the percentage of deeds in which Bucks County buyers included both conjugal partners skyrocketed from 0.4 percent in 1890 to 70 percent in 1980 (Shammas, Salmon, and Dahlin 1987). The same trend toward community property is evident in the two cohorts examined here. Thus, 43 percent of the 1944 decedents were joint tenants over parts or the totality of their assets as opposed to none of those who died in 1920.[6] For the 1944 cohort, joint tenancy prevailed among male decedents (the correlation is .255) and among the holders of life insurance policies (the zero-order correlation is .295).

Since joint tenancy symbolizes a modern American life-style, its likelihood is significantly typical of couples with fewer children and of those with unmarried daughters (Table 5.1). In this sense, the underlying modern concern over the future is typical of families that have limited their progeny to individualize the care they give to each child.

Table 5.1. Likelihood of Joint Tenancy in 1944 (Full Population and Married Men)

Variables	Coefficients	
	Full population	Men
Constant	1.325	.002
Number of children	−.293*	−.009
Presence of unmarried daughters	.960*	.764
Possession of life insurance	.983*	1.692*
Estate size[a]	−.009*	−.003
Gender[b]	−1.211*	—
Age	—	.002
Log-likelihood	27.02*	17.26
χ^2 with 6 d.f. (< .005)	18.55	18.55
N	114	54

[a] Expressed in thousands of dollars.
[b] Men are coded 0, women are coded 1.
* Significant at the .005 level.

As an innovation, joint tenancy also depends on the material bases of domestic life, more specifically, on the size and the composition of the wealth accumulated. It is more typical of small estates whose holders are less tradition oriented than their richer counterparts. The very fact that this arrangement also prevails among couples that have acquired life insurance policies to ensure the comfort of the surviving spouse confirms that it is a symbol of a modern family style.

The same material bases of familial life also account for the higher incidence of joint tenancy among husbands than wives. A low involvement in the labor market reduces female sensitivity to the practice. Further, to the extent that joint tenancy prevails among the younger components of the population, it is less typical of female than of male decedents. In the sample, young wives had, indeed, older husbands who were themselves unlikely to push toward this particular innovation.

When one eliminates female decedents from the analysis, possession of a life insurance policy remains the only significant determinant of joint tenancy. Since the underlying decision is independent of age, national origin, or residence, it seems to have become a universal American concern.

The Role of Gifts *Inter Vivos*

Estate tax returns offer only a selective view of the extent to which transfers based on familial loyalties precede death. This view is selective because of the temporal and functional limitations that characterize the fiscal definition of this particular type of transfer. In order to be taxable as a part of the estate, and thus to be recorded, donations (or gifts *inter vivos*) must have been made within five years prior to the testator's death. In addition, they must have been inspired by the awareness of the imminent character of this event. Only the donations that are suspected of satisfying the two conditions are recorded.

Despite these limitations, gifts *inter vivos* are significant indicators of the forms taken by solidarity among relatives. On the one hand, the frequency of these gifts should decline wherever and whenever mobility constantly undermines the control of elders. On the other hand, the same frequency may also increase with individualism and with the growing belief that feelings as much as obligations serve as criteria legitimating this type of transfer. Shifts in the ideological definitions of familial bonds were sufficient between 1920 and 1944 to make the practice of gifts *inter vivos* more widespread. Their incidence doubled from 11 to 25 percent of the estates considered in 1920 and 1944, respectively.

These gifts symbolize variations in both the objects of decedents' affections and the needs of individual children. In either of the two cohorts of decedents, about 70 percent of the individuals who made gifts *inter vivos* discriminated among their descendants. In the majority of cases, the resulting inequality confirmed the equivocations underlying gender differentiation. Some families used gifts *inter vivos* to help male children start their businesses, others to help daughters, married or unmarried, with the purchase of their first homes.

However, gifts *inter vivos*, which were originally governed by conservative principles governing the search for efficiency, have become more symbolic of a child-oriented society. Prevailing originally among male testators, the practice became independent of the testator's gender in 1944 (the relevant zero-order correlation drops from .248 to only .034). Similarly, it was less a privilege of the testator's age for the second than the first cohort (the correlation declines from .277 to .107). Alternatively, the likelihood of gifts *inter vivos* was clearly related to family size. The greater the number of children, the more likely it was that some of them would experience needs and the more likely it was that these needs would be covered with the help of parents (the relevant zero-order correlations increase from .216 to .319 between the two cohorts).

The diffusion of the innovation nevertheless follows culturally selective paths. Thus, gifts *inter vivos* became slightly more salient among populations living in large urban centers (the zero-order correlations increase from .023 to .161). They became more typical of German- than of Irish-American decedents (the zero-order correlations shoot from .007 to .202). The growing contrast may reflect the differential evolution of both the standards of life and the cohesiveness of the two ethnic groups. Either a lack of resources or the persistence of their traditions induced many Irish-American decedents to retain the typical Irish practice of keeping heirs on their toes as long as possible.

When one examines jointly the determinants of the likelihood of gifts *inter vivos*, the practice seems to have become more socially differentiated in 1944 than in 1920. Family size, which was the only significant contributor for the first cohort, operates in conjunction with national origin or urbanization for the 1944 decedents. In this latter case, the practice prevailed among large families that were German-American or lived in major urban centers. Yet the effects of an urban residence are more robust than those of national origin: the inclusion of other critical variables such as estate size or composition, or rules governing the division of community property hardly affects the statistical significance of the first variable, but completely masks the explanatory power of the second (Table 5.2).

The Incidence of Wills

For the whole population of estate tax returns, the incidence of wills increased between 1920 and 1944 from 72 to 84 percent.[7] This secular

Table 5.2. Likelihood of Gifts *Inter Vivos*

	Coefficients			
	Model A		Model B	
Variables	1920	1944	1920	1944
Constant	−3.009	−2.649	−1.181	−1.780
National origin	.270	−.635	.004	−.930*
Family size	.219*	.421*	—	—
Family composition	—	—	1.054	1.718*
Percentage of estate invested in real estate	—	—	−.726	−.390
Intestate segregation of conjugal estates	—	—	.504	−.470
Urbanization	.316	1.040*	—	—
Percentage correctly placed	88.4	88.5	78.9	74.5
Log-likelihood	81.94	92.84	47.54	41.80
χ^2 with 3 d.f.	12.84	12.84	—	—
χ^2 with 4 d.f. ($p < .005$)	—	—	14.86	14.86
N	113	113	114	106

increase confirms the trends observed on other samples. It reflects both the rising educational level of the American population and the effect of economic development on individual resources. Indeed, both cultural and economic capital induce people to pay more attention to the destination of their estate.

Even though the gap closed between 1920 and 1944, testacy remained typical of female than male decedents with small estates (74 versus 69 percent in 1920; 83 versus 81 percent in 1944). Such differences reflect the longer life expectancy of women and the responsibility they have to transfer familial assets to the next generation. It probably also reflects their fear of seeing their decisions challenged.

The incidence of wills also increased with age. Individuals of the first cohort who died testate were 68.1 years old against 64.5 for their counterparts who died intestate. The corresponding figures were 69.7 and 65.0 for the 1944 cohort. But while the effects of aging were alike for the male segments of the two cohorts, they became more marked over the years as far as women were concerned.

When one controls for national origin, the relationship between age and testacy declined over the years. For Irish- and German-American decedents, the relevant zero-order correlation dropped from .240 to .078 between 1920 and 1944. This decline may reflect the erosion of the differential status assigned to age in these two cultures and/or the superimposition of an American ideology that minimizes the relevance of this particular factor for this type of decision. But the same decline may also result from convergences in the economic constraints and opportunities experienced by the entire adult population of the two nationalities.

Despite the ceiling imposed on the wealth of the sample used here, testacy remained positively related to estate size (Table 5.3). This was true for both the entire population of decedents with less than $200,000 and for the subsample of Irish- and German-Americans. In both cases, however, the zero-order correlation between estate size and testacy increases slightly from the first to the second cohort. Even though those decedents with the least resources are said to be more concerned about controlling the distribution of their assets (Goody 1976), the use of appropriate legal documents still varies as a direct function of wealth.

Testacy also depended on the composition of the estate. The number of will writers increases with the diversity of the forms of wealth accumulated. But this number also depends on the specific type of asset owned by decedents. Thus, testacy was less frequent among those who owned realty than those who did not, but more likely among those who owned stocks or life insurance policies, even though the contrasts declined from the first to the second cohort. When Rossi and Rossi (1990) note that one acquires life insurance at a young age to meet one's re-

Table 5.3. Differences ($) in the Value of Individual Estates and Individual Forms of Capital by the Filing Status of Decedents with Less Than $200,000.

	1920		1944	
	Testate	Intestate	Testate	Intestate
Realty				
Full sample	44,294	47,220	33,054	33,805
N	2,269	976	2,079	513
Irish/German	40,880	45,754	31,414	47,008
N	71	12	71	11
Stocks				
Full sample	30,832	24,415	37,408	26,104
N	1,884	662	2,202	429
Irish/German	39,831	37,599	29,914	27,189
N	51	7	75	5
Insurance				
Full sample	12,389	11,605	21,769	17,578
N	2,086	800	5,857	1,222
Irish/German	4,795	—	22,714	9,512
N	17	0	44	4
Estate size				
Full sample	92,960	85,223	99,613	89,872
N	7,017	2,960	11,542	2,499
Irish/German	96,150	86,638	103,333	78,122
N	79	12	90	11

sponsibilities toward one's dependents and that one does not need a will at this point since insurance policies designate beneficiaries, the observation is time-bound. Earlier in the century, both the writing of a will and the purchase of life insurance policies symbolized reinforcing forms of individualism.

Further, the sums invested in a type of asset are as significant predictors of testacy as the mere possession of this type of asset. Thus, not only are individuals who own realty less likely to die testate, but in addition those who die with a will have invested less money than their counterparts who died without. The skews introduced in the Irish- and German-American sample do not modify the direction of the relationships observed. Yet, while the relevant correlations remain relatively stable across cohorts when one considers the full population, they increase from $-.167$ to $-.303$ between 1920 and 1944 for the subsample comprised of Irish- and German-American decedents.

The opposite is true for the owners of stocks or of life insurance policies, both in the full population of small estates and in the German- and Irish-American subsamples. The greater the investments in either one of these types of assets, the greater the chances there was a will.[8]

Over the years, the incidence of testacy also became more tightly related to the composition of familial groups. In other words, the progress of "child centrism" rendered parents increasingly sensitive to what they perceived to be the diverging aspirations or needs of their sons and daughters. Correspondingly, the correlation between the presence of both sons and daughters in familial groups and testacy shoots from −.028 to .301 between 1920 and 1944.

Finally, the distribution of wills originally varied across regions. Since the 1920 decedents were more prone to testacy when they resided in a state where the properties of spouses were kept integrated, the legal individualism symbolized by wills seem to have been initially more typical of regions where laws required conjugal partners to cooperate with one another. In this sense, this study confirms the views of Maine (1951), who, in other contexts, saw testacy as an attempt to depart from prevailing practices. In 1944, however, a uniform legal culture had sufficiently spread throughout the nation to make wills uniformly appealing.

Of all the determinants of testacy evoked in the preceding lines, only those that pertain to the composition of the progeny and to the importance of realty remain significant when added to others in order to assess the overall likelihood of testacy. And this is true only for the second cohort. In other words, as time passed, testacy became most typical of families with both sons and daughters, on the one hand, and with an estate in which realty occupied a minor part, on the other.

Time Interval between Testacy and Death

As already suggested, the date of wills is perhaps as important as testacy per se as an indicator of the individual attempts to control the divisive and erosive effects of time.[9] The earlier a will is written, the greater the commitment of its author to rational estate planning. With the increasing incidence of testacy over time, early wills become relatively less frequent. The average time interval between the dates of will and of death only declined from a little bit over eight years for the 1920 population to less than six years for the 1944 group. However, the variances of the two distributions are quite large. Both cohorts include decedents who planned their estate more than a quarter of a century before dying.

With the growing popularity of testacy, the determinants of the distinction between early and late wills became less significant. More typical of women than of men for the 1920 cohort, the question of gender became insignificant for their 1944 counterparts (the zero-order correlation dropping from .220 to .099). Relatively more frequent among certain occupations (notably farmers and executives) for the first cohort, early wills ceased to differentiate any occupational category in the case of the 1944 population. But the progressive erosion of the social determinants of early wills implied a parallel tightening of the linkage between physical aging and the date of wills (the zero-order correlation went a notch higher, from .104 for the first cohort to .156 for the second one).

Alternatively, however, the growing popularity of testacy is also associated with a corresponding increase in the influence of the estate's composition on the timing of wills. Because of the additional importance that individuals with limited resources attached to the rational management of their estate, early wills became relatively more typical of small fortunes (the relevant zero-order correlations are $-.065$ and $-.102$, respectively). For the same reason, early wills were also increasingly typical of wealth holders who had not diversified their estate (the relevant zero-order correlation between the date of wills and the number of distinct types of assets held by testators increases slightly, from $-.130$ for 1920 to $-.169$ for 1944).

Finally, the differential influence of the owning of distinct assets on the timing of wills also varies across periods. As long as early wills symbolize a modern form of rationality, they prevail among those decedents who have invested a large proportion of their estate in "modern" assets. As a result, zero-order correlations between the date of wills and the relative percentage of the estate invested in life insurance reaches .243 for 1920 before declining to .049 in 1944. The diffusion of life insurance across all social groups means that decedents were increasingly aware of the rule of the game and no longer felt the need to link the possession of insurance certificates to a will. The two became temporally independent of one another. Alternatively, during the same period, zero-order correlations between the dates of wills and the relative percentage of the estate invested in realty increase from .100 to .267, respectively. In other words, shifts in the use of realty rendered their owners increasingly keen on controlling the ultimate transfer of this form of capital earlier in their lifetimes.

The combination of various independent variables only accounts for 7 percent of the variance in the distribution of the dates at which wills were written for the 1920 population and significantly less for their counterparts who passed away in 1944. In the case of the first population, early wills prevailed among women residing in states with high urbanization rates, and hence with relatively dense social networks. In contrast, there was no significant individual contributing factor to the relative date of wills among the 1944 decedents.

The Incidence of Trusts

Since the purpose of trusts is to impose an enduring control on the behaviors of survivors, they offer a striking contrast with gifts *inter vivos*. Despite such contrasts, these two mechanisms of transfers serve analogous functions. They both reduce the fiscal burden faced by benefactors.

Trusts not only specify which behaviors should be subsidized and which should be punished, since they identify the conditions under which beneficiaries may or may not gain access to the capital earmarked for them. But they also specify the period during which the decedent retains relevant control. Some trusts are supposed to last a specified portion of the beneficiaries' lives, others to span several generations.

In the case of both the 1920 and 1944 subsamples, two-thirds of decedents who died testate added a trust to their wills. In most of the cases, these trusts were set up in order to ensure the education of one or several children or even grandchildren. In other instances, their purpose was to attend to the needs of a disabled son or daughter. Even though the distribution of trusts remained stable across the two cohorts, their social determinants and functions evolved.

Insofar as the original concern of the authors of trusts often was to rationalize the uncertainties of the future, trust agreements were still written long before the testator's death (even though the correlation declines from .308 to .124 between the first and second cohorts). Trusts were typical of larger estates, despite a slight drop of the relevant zero-order correlation from .160 to .125 between the first and second cohorts). Independent of local legal traditions, the use of trusts was also initially related to the composition and to a smaller extent to the size of familial groups. Thus, zero-order correlations between the existence of a trust on the one hand and the presence of both daughters and sons on the other decline from .309 to .031 between the two cohorts. Similarly, the correlation between the first variable and family size declines from .149 to .072 during the same period of time.

To conclude, when combined with any other variable, both the presence of sons and daughters in the family and the time interval between the writing of the will and the actual death of the decedent contributed significantly to the likelihood of a trust. This, however, was true of the first cohort only. In other words, since trusts originally represented "rational" mechanisms designed to reduce the specific uncertainties that testators attach to the gender differentiation of their offspring, it is originally easier to distinguish those who use this particular instrument from those who do not. Alternatively, if the passage of time has made it more difficult to predict the likelihood of trusts, it is because of the increased diversity of their social and psychological functions as well as of their forms.

Testacy and the Control of Time

Throughout this chapter, I have suggested that all transfers *mortis causa* seek to alleviate the divisive effects of time. To the extent that time is both a treasure and a means of social control, the authors of trusts or of wills frequently impose time conditions on the bequests they make.

Some of these conditions are social and refer to educational attainment, marriage, or remarriage. In other words, decedents indicate explicitly that the form or the amount of the bequest will be modified as a result of a change in the matrimonial or educational status of the beneficiary. For example, wives or daughters-in-law are to lose their bequests or to see the income they received transformed into a flat one-time single payment if they remarry. In another example, sons or daughters get access to the principal of the bequests made in their favor only when they graduate from school.

Other conditions are "natural" and evoke the death or the aging process of the beneficiary or of a third party. For example, bequests in favor of children may be made contingent on the death of the surviving spouse. They may also be contingent on the coming of age of the descendant chosen as a beneficiary. The requirements imposed on sons and daughters in this regard differ from one another. Some parents believe that sons should get access to the principal of a trust made in their favor at an earlier date than daughters. As others take the opposite view, the differential definition of maturity by gender clearly varies across American subcultures.[10]

Time conditions partially lost their salience between 1920 and 1944. No less than 57 percent of the decedents who wrote wills in 1920 introduced such conditions in their bequests, against only 42 percent of their 1944 counterparts. The nature of these time conditions changed between the two dates as well. Only 38 percent of these conditions were "social" in 1920 as opposed to 71 percent in 1944. In short, transfers became increasingly contingent on what passes for achievement in the eyes of testators.

Shifts in the presence of time conditions in wills or trusts changed their meanings. Originally imposed by decedents residing in small communities (the zero-order correlation is .211), the practice became independent of the decedents' environment in 1944 (the coefficient is .050). Further, such conditions became increasingly typical of small families (with zero-order correlations increasing from −.016 to −.199 between 1920 and 1944). Alternatively, however, zero-order correlations between the presence of such a time condition and of *both* sons and daughters evolved from .144 for the 1920 cohort to −.127 for the 1944 population. Finally, the imposition of time conditions is increasingly contingent on the profile of the estate and of the environment. Thus, the correlation between this imposition and the number of types of assets accumulated jumped from .023 for 1920 to .144 for 1944.

To conclude, shifts in the popularity of time conditions among testators between 1920 and 1944 are associated with changes in the overall structure of the determinants of the underlying choices. In contrast to 1920, where no combination of factors accounts for the distinction between those decedents who imposed time conditions on their heirs and those who did not, the likelihood of the presence of time conditions in wills among the 1944 decedents is clearly related to their gender (it was a practice of male testators), to their matrimonial status (decedents who died first were more likely to impose time conditions than widows or widowers), and to the presence of corporate securities in the estate (Table 5.3).

Instruments of Transfers as Instruments of Ordering Things and People

Wills are not only about controlling time or about preventing or facilitating the perpetuation of specific beliefs or practices. They are also about ordering relations with things and people. This makes it necessary to ascertain the extent to which decedents use their wills to specify who gets what. Historically, wills have confirmed the legitimacy of assigning familial mementos such as bibles or clocks to male or female children. Indeed, certain things symbolize the patterns of division of tasks by gender. Jewels, silverware, and pots and pans are "feminine"; cars, clocks, and business equipment, "masculine" (Gotman 1988)."[11] Gifts of real estate are more difficult to define in this regard because sometimes they are dwelling units, and sometimes productive forms of capital.

The passage of time marks shifts in the importance that testators attach to particular types of assets. Specific references to personal property (jewels, paintings, or cars) increased markedly between 1920 and 1944, from 23 to 34 percent. Alternatively, references to the destination of specific pieces of realty declined from 30 to 22 percent, references to specific stocks or bonds remaining equally rare in both subsamples. In one instance, the testator passed down stock of the familial company to the one child who worked there. In another instance, the testator sought to achieve equality in the definition of individual bequests by assigning different stocks and bonds to each child.[12]

Originally, variations in types of bequests by types of assets characterized wills written shortly prior to the testator's death. Before dying, testators "froze" the relationships they had elaborated between the hierarchies of objects and of potential beneficiaries. With the progress of the abstract society and the resulting loosening of the links deemed to exist between objects and heirs, zero-order correlation between the timing of the will and bequests of personal property, declines from .236 to .109 between the two cohorts; for bequests involving realty, it drops from .278 to .176.

However, bequests of personal property and of realty follow distinct logics and reflect differing images of familial roles. In contrast to bequests of personal property that were independent of the decedent's age, gifts of realty characterized older decedents (even though the correlation declines from .335 to .105 between 1920 and 1944). In contrast to the first type of bequests, which were also independent of the decedents' gender, bequests of realty became more typical of male testators (the relevant coefficients increased from .060 to .191 between 1920 and 1944). Finally, while bequests involving personal property became negatively related to the number of children of the decedent (the correlation evolves from .062 to −.140), bequests involving realty were and remained typical of large families (the correlation moved from .162 to .178 between 1920 and 1944). In short, variations in types of bequests symbolize differing visions of what familial bonds are about. Thus, bequests of land evoke increasingly instrumental definitions of the family.

To conclude, divergences in the logics governing distinct types of bequests are made evident when one combines their determinants. Such combinations do not yield any significant results as far as the bequests pertaining to personal property made in 1920 are concerned. For 1944, however, self-employment is the most robust predictor of such bequests: self-employed testators (mostly men) were more likely to display this particular form of generosity than any one else in the general population, regardless of the other variables introduced in the equation. Conversely, while the bequests of realty characterized the 1920 decedents who wrote late wills and had a large proportion of their estate invested in realty, the distinction between those who made and did not make such bequests became indeterminate for the 1944 population.

The Ordering Of Social Relations

Instruments of transfer organize the testator's social relations in three distinct ways. First, the selection of executors constitutes an indicator of which survivor is most frequently believed to "hold things together" and to minimize conflicts among heirs. For instance, the conditions under which sons or sons-in-law are perceived to be more likely to maintain domestic harmony than the surviving spouse or the daughter(s) are not necessarily alike. Second, since wills and trusts enable decedents to depart from the familial model imposed on them by the laws of the state where they reside, there are variations in the conditions under which testators add to or subtract from the number and type of beneficiaries defined by the laws concerning intestate successions. Third and last, wills and trusts provide some indication of the differential generosity that testators display toward their immediate relatives and members of the extended kin group, or between these two groups considered jointly and strangers.[13]

The Choice of Executors

In the European societies from which many American immigrants originate, the notions of transfer *mortis causa* and intergenerational transfers are coterminous. Originally, American sons faced the same expectations as their European counterparts and were often asked to act in *loco parentis*, more specifically, to execute the will drawn by the parent who passed away first. Alternatively, the choice of one's spouse as exclusive or joint executor can be construed as a sign of conjugal solidarity, of the growing salience of the peer group, and, as such, of modernity.

In order to assess accurately the evolution of the decisions made by decedents along these lines, it is necessary to limit the analysis to situations where testators were obliged to choose. For instance, the selection of sons or daughters as exclusive or joint executor can only be assessed in the context of families with both sons and daughters. Similarly, the choice of a spouse can only be tested in the case of families with children.

The passage of time marks the decline of patriarchy in a number of ways. The relative number of decedents choosing sons rather than daughters to execute their wills has declined from 34 to 25 percent between the first and the second cohort, while the proportion of decedents preferring daughters to sons increased from 4 to 25 percent. At the same time, the partial demise of patriarchy does not necessarily imply a parallel growth of "horizontal" at the expense of "vertical" bonds. Decedents preferred their spouses to their children in 47 percent of the cases in 1920 and in 43 percent of the cases in 1944.[14]

The timing of the will is one of the most significant determinants of the selection of an executor (Table 5.4). In 1920, the decedents who drew their wills early, a long time before their death, tended to appoint their sons (the relevant coefficient is .344) and to a smaller extent, their surviving spouses (the relevant coefficient is .112). In contrast, late wills, that is, wills written shortly before death, implied the appointment of a stranger (the correlation is .126) and to a smaller extent of a daughter (the correlation is .091).[15]

Even though the results are statistically nonsignificant, they all run in the expected direction. The instrumentalist ideology that prevailed at the time induced the authors of early wills to make the stereotypic choices of the son or of the spouse as executors. In contrast, the choices made by the authors of late wills revealed the continuously contradictory effects of the aging process. Today as yesterday, as the process exacerbates emotional needs, it leads to the selection of daughters. Today as yesterday, as the process accentuates the complexity of the wealth held by individuals, it facilitates the selection of bankers or lawyers.

To the extent that modernization widens the range of options available to both testators and heirs, the passage of time implies a sharp decline in the links between the timing of the will and the selection of executors as a function of their gender. Alternatively, to the extent that modernization is also conducive to a strengthening of the notion of peer group, the passage of time marks the persistence of the relationship between early wills and the selection of the surviving spouse as executor (.170).[16] For the same reason, the negative correlation between the selection of the surviving spouse and the number of children declines from $-.446$ to $-.125$ between 1920 and 1944. The first cohort affirmed the strength of horizontal solidarity only when vertical bonds were not available, but for their 1944 counterparts, conjugal relations began to prevail over intergenerational dependance under any circumstance.

Finally, the relative erosion of the ideological and legal facets of patriarchy during the period was paralleled by a strengthening of the bonds between mothers and daughters.[17] Mothers of the second cohort were not only *less* likely than their 1920 counterparts to choose their sons as executors (the correlation declines from .152 to .038 between 1920 and 1944). They were also *more* likely to select a daughter (the correlation increases from .111 to .226 between the two dates). In short, as the end of patriarchy required the emergence of a counterforce, it also marked the emergence of a stronger solidarity between mothers and daughters.

Combinations of factors throw additional light on the interaction between the progress of conjugal solidarity and the erosion of patriarchy.

Table 5.4. Zero-Order Correlations between Choices of Executors and Selected Independent Variables

	Son		Spouse		Stranger	
Variable	1920	1944	1920	1944	1920	1944
Age	.216	.342	−.133	−.479	−.169	.053
Gender[a]	.152	.030	.030	.230	−.043	−.052
Number of children	−.180	.257	−.208	−.132	−.308	−.034
Estate size	−.104	.199	.095	.218	.055	−.231
Estate Diversity	−.170	.258	.155	.226	.092	−.058
Ethnicity	−.164	−.021	−.155	.099	.027	.122
Farming[b]	.483	.253	.090	−.096	−.149	−.158
Executive[b]	—	−.193	—	−.302	—	−.071
Self-employed[b]	−.193	−.068	.029	.112	—	.273
Life insurance	−.066	−.314	−.076	.345	−.124	−.025
Realty	.187	.211	−.146	−.027	.012	−.183
Corporate securities	−.174	.027	.200	−.084	.046	.188
Community property states	−.055	.006	.170	−.007	−.013	−.024
Separation of estates states	−.153	.066	.111	.249	.097	−.113
Date of wills	.344	−.137	.112	.171	−.126	.027
N^c	39	70	66	90	66	90

[a] For gender, correlations are positive when female behaviors prevail.
[b] Occupation concerns only male decedents. Hence, the numbers vary.
[c] The N differ for the selection of sons, of spouses, and of strangers. For the first selection, decedents must have both sons and daughters. For the last two, they must have children of either gender.

Not only was the likelihood of the selection of the spouse greater for the 1944 than for the 1920 cohort, but in addition the number of significant determinants of such a selection increased between the two dates (Table 5.5). For the first cohort, this choice prevailed only among all young men and women without unmarried daughters. For the second cohort, the choice prevailed among young men who had an unmarried daughter. In other words, the continuing presence of age in the two equations suggests that the selection of the surviving spouse is both a by-product of the decedent's position in the life cycle and a response to the forces of change. The differential role of unmarried (and most probably young) daughters in the two equations suggests that the growth of conjugal solidarity is a function of child-centered forms of familial life.

Nevertheless, the determinants of the decline of patriarchy are not necessarily cumulative or consistent. Initially, the selection of sons as executors prevailed among the holders of small estates. Initially, the same selection was also related to occupational status, notably farming (the zero-order correlation is .483).[18] Despite a decline in the influence of farming on the choice of sons between 1920 and 1944 (the zero-order correlation between farming and the choice of a son as executor drops to .253), the selection of sons as executors was still most typical of the wealthiest farmers for the 1944 cohort of decedents (Table 5.6). In this sense, there was reversal over time in the linkage between patriarchy and social stratification. This type of conservatism climbed the social ladder between 1920 and 1944.

To conclude these remarks on the selection of executors, it is noteworthy that the demise of patriarchy was not immediately accompanied by the increased use of professionals. In either of the two cohorts examined

Table 5.5. Selection of the Surviving Spouse as Executor: Logit Regression

Variables	Coefficients	
	1920	1944
Constant	7.734	9.556
Age	−.106*	−.131*
Gender	.103	−1.271*
Unmarried daughter	−1.329*	1.239*
Intestate equality	.756	−.608
Log-likelihood	12.02	35.60
Percentage correctly placed	73.5	78.9
χ^2 with 4 d.f. ($p < .005$)	14.86	14.86
N	64	90

* Significant at the .05 level.

Table 5.6. Choice of Sons as Executors by Male Decedents: Logit Regression

	Coefficients					
	Model A		Model B		Model C	
Variables	1920	1944	1920[b]	1944	1920	1944
Constant	.50	−3.73	—	−3.46	−.51	−3.19
Estate size (thousands)	−.02	.01*	—	.02*	−.02*	.01*
Intestate separation of estates	−.06	.79	—	1.11	−.10	.61
Occupation[a]	1.65	1.82*	—	−10.77	−9.59	.85
Log-likelihood	17.48	23.98	—	29.40	18.70	21.21
Percentage correctly placed	78.4	72.2	—	77.8	75.7	77.8
χ^2 with 3 d.f. ($p < .005$)	12.84	12.84		12.84	12.84	12.84
N	37	54		54	37	54

[a] Each model considers three occupations by turns: Model A refers to farmers, model B to executives, and model C to businessmen.
[b] The equation for executives in 1920 cannot be run because of multicollinearity.
* Significant at the .05 level.

here, only a little over 12 percent of decedents with a will asked a bank or a lawyer to execute the will. The choice of a stranger had relatively little to do with familial circumstances. It was independent of the decedents' age and gender, or even more important, of the gender of their offspring. Originally less likely in the case of families with many children, this choice became more closely related to the decedents' economic status. Thus, the likelihood that decedents of the 1944 cohort appointed strangers as executors was greater for those individuals who had small estates, who had the largest part of their investments in corporate securities, and who resided in states with a high urbanization level and hence, with dense networks of communication (Table 5.7). In other words, estate planning seems to have prevailed first among decedents who, having made modern forms of investment, appreciated the risks associated with the modesty of their resources because of the easier comparisons they could make between their own status and that of other segments of the population.

The Individualization of Bequests

In both 1920 and 1944, the presence of children reinforced the bonds that estators wove with their extended kin as well as with friends or

Table 5.7. Choice of a Banker or a Lawyer as Executor: Logit Regression

Variable	Coefficients	
	1920	1944
Constant	−1.124	−5.600
Percentage of estate in negotiable assets	−.067	2.709*
Estate size (thousands)	.002	−.027*
Family composition	−1.197	.846
State urbanization	.002	.065*
Percentage correctly placed	83.3	88.9
Log-likelihood	35.06	70.12
χ^2 with 4 d.f. ($p < .005$)	14.86	14.86
N	66	90

* Significant at the .05 level.

religious and cultural organizations. About 18 percent of those 1920 decedents who died testate and had two children mentioned their siblings in their wills either as an executor or as a beneficiary, as against 15 percent of their 1944 counterparts. About one-fourth of the same decedents mentioned their grandchildren, to whom they gave either a flat sum of money or the income of a trust. As beneficiaries of a trust, these grandchildren may have been given the share of their deceased parent or they may also have been treated as substitutes for their live mothers or fathers for fiscal reasons. Last, 9 percent of the wills present in the two cohorts of decedents with two children mentioned sons-in-law (eventually as executors) and 12 percent referred to daughters-in-law.[19]

The presence of children did not inhibit bequests made in favor of friends, churches, and organizations, and 10 percent of the wills of decedents with two children contained provisions that go beyond the boundaries of familial solidarity. In three cases, wills made explicit references to servants or professional associates, and in one case, to a former spouse, to remind us that the significance of free will entails constant individual negotiations of the tensions between the "ascriptive" and the "dispensable" components of familial obligations (Odendahl 1990).

The Number of Beneficiaries

The nuclearization of the American family involves a decline in the number of heirs. This number declined from 6.56 cohort to 4.04 between the 1920 and the 1944 cohorts of decedents. This decline and the underlying nuclearization were nevertheless selective. Even when the analysis deals with the smallest estates, the intuition of Pierre Bourdieu (1972), who links financial and familial capital to one another in the French context, also applies to the American scene.[20] Those decedents with additional financial means used wills to add rather than subtract heirs and relatives (Table 5.8).

There are, however, differences in the choices made by the overall populations of small estate holders and the subsamples of German- and Irish-American decedents. In the first case, the extent to which the addition of heirs prevailed among the elderly and the female components of the population became less marked between 1920 and 1944.[21] In other words, this addition became less symbolic of traditional values. In the case of the smaller subsample, however, this addition, which was a trademark of executives in 1920, became a characteristic of the 1944

Table 5.8. Multiple Regression of the Number of Beneficiaries Listed in Estate Tax Returns for 1920 and 1944

Variable	1920	1944
Age	.150*	.029
Estate size		
Occupation[a]	15.078*	3.656*
State income		
Assets[b]		
Gender		−1.048*
National origin		
Testacy	3.474*	
Unmarried daughters		
Intestate equality		−1.047*
Community property		
Urbanization		−.796
State urbanization		
Region		
Mobility		
R_1^2	.145	.294
R_2^2	.062	.089
R_3^2	.007	.013
N	118	114
Mean	6.84	4.30

[a] *Occupation* refers to executives for 1920 and to farmers for 1944.

[b] *Assets* refers to stocks for 1920 and realty for 1944.

farmers. In other words, it became more symbolic of a traditional value system.

In the case of the overall population of small estate holders, the addition of heirs that characterized those 1920 decedents with the smallest investments in life insurance policies became independent of the composition of the wealth of their 1944 counterparts. Alternatively, in the case of the subsample of German- and Irish-American decedents, the addition of heirs became a function of the legal status of the state of residence. This addition prevailed among those who lived in states where intestacy laws posit equality in the share of the spouses.

To conclude, while the addition of heirs symbolizes the linkage existing between economic and symbolic forms of capital, the form of this linkage varies over time and its concrete manifestations depend on the collective social background against which it is developed. In other words, the meaning of the linkage cannot be the same for distinct national groups or for the residents of differing legal systems.

Conclusions

However relative, changes in the instruments of transfer used by decedents and the determinants of their choices reflect the intervention of structural rather than cultural factors. Both the size and the composition of the estate, notably the relative importance of realty or of stocks in the estate or even the diversity of the assets accumulated, are better predictors of the selection of the instruments of transfers than the national origin of decedents or the legal constraints of their state of residence.

Further, declines in the influence of age or of gender between the two cohorts of decedents suggest a democratization in the use of these instruments. And as this democratization increases the number of degrees of freedom enjoyed by testators, the determinants of individual choices become more complex. In some instances, this complexity implies a greater number of factors operating jointly, but in other cases, a larger indeterminacy due to the fact that the data do not tap the relevant variables.

This democratization, however, is not cut from one cloth. To be sure, processes of change imply the erosion of certain social or psychological cleavages. Yet, the corresponding decline is not uniform. Thus, men become more prone than women to manipulate time conditions in the bequests they make in favor of their children or grandchildren. Men stand out more visibly in individualizing their bequests of realty. As another example, certain practices that were initially widespread across all estates become the trademarks of the upper or the lower segment of the estates sampled here, which constitutes a first indication of which part of the existing system of stratification is most vulnerable to the corrosive effects of change. Alternatively, the passage of time also heightens the salience of cleavages that were initially hardly apparent (like the effect of estate size), and it also fosters the emergence of new social alignments (like the overt solidarity between mothers and daughters).

To conclude, the analysis confirms the selective nature of the push-and-pull forces at work in the transformation of the instruments chosen by individuals to transfer their estate. The same conflicting forces should be operating in the way they actually transfer their estates.

6

Bequests and Inequality between and within Families

Analyses of transfers *mortis causa* in America pose both methodological and theoretical dilemmas. In methodological terms, the sacred nature imputed to ownership makes its study problematic on three counts. First, as this sacred nature renders heirship practices private and hence secret, the pertinent data are spotty and biased. Second, the motivations of testators have to be assessed at the right time. Wills and mere intentions are not comparable. Nor are the successive versions of the same will comparable. Third, since many Americans see the very existence of beneficiaries as being inconsistent with the ideal of self-reliance, the ensuing contradictions between the status assigned to testators and to heirs entail a marked asymmetry in the study of intergenerational bonds. On the whole, scholars have studied the motivations of testators rather than those of beneficiaries (Adams 1980; Behrman, Pollak, and Taubman 1982; Becker and Tomes 1976; Williamson and Lindert 1980). Further, those few researchers who examine what people *report* to have ever received from relatives or friends are faced with two equally damaging inferences (Jencks 1979; Tomes 1988). Either respondents lie about the inconsequential nature of what they have received, and this casts doubt on the validity of social surveys, or the low value of the bequests received by individuals undermines the myth of the United States as the land of opportunity. If so few people have anything to pass down to their children, social stratification proves to have been and to continue to be steeper and less reversible than is often argued.

In theoretical terms, the issue is to ascertain the relative freedom enjoyed by testators. Are the motivations that govern the selection of heirs randomly distributed, or is their distribution systematic? The issue is also to ascertain in what sense their determinants are universal, and in what sense they are culture and time bound. They are universal insofar as inheritance is inspired by what some anthropologists call "inclusive fitness" and thus by the propensity for individuals to maximize the reproduction of their genes within a population (Smith, Kish, and Crawford 1987). Thus, patterns of inheritance facilitate the material and symbolic perpetuation of the testators' familial groups, especially whenever and wherever there are few relevant cultural prescriptions and proscriptions. In such cases, the "manner of splitting property is a manner of splitting people" (Goody 1976:5). In such cases, it can be said that "by acting on things, inheritance affects persons, while by acting on persons, it has an effect on things" (Tocqueville 1961:46). Correspondingly, the rank ordering of assets and that of heirs are closely intertwined.

However, transfers *mortis causa* are also culture and time bound. For instance, as the functions of realty have evolved from the exploitation of land to the sheltering of close relatives, there have been parallel changes in the identity of beneficiaries: the unmarried female heir of the family home succeeds to the male inheritor of the family farm. Correspondingly, the challenge confronting analysts is to choose a method that enables them to identify the extent to which changes in heirship practices reflect parallel changes in the relative weights of slowly evolving legitimizing forces, on the one hand, and of immediate criteria of rationality, on the other. In this sense, the challenge is to identify in what sense the free will sought in testacy becomes more or less of an illusion.

The Testators' Dilemmas

Inheritance may be explained in terms of the pleasure of giving (Ryan 1984:98; Lichtman 1982; Hyde 1983). This pleasure, however, may have two opposite sets of motivations. People write wills either to appropriate prevailing norms for their own moral benefit, or to depart from such norms and assert their independence. The pleasures derived from conforming overtly with the prevailing ideology differ from those derived from exercising one's power and free will.

Further this distinction disregards the specific content of the dominant orientations of the larger society. Testators' choices do not take place *in vacuo*.

In contrast to what neoclassical economists like Becker (1981) or rationalist sociologists like Coleman (1990) would like us to believe, testators' choices do not take place *in vacuo*. Rather, they are shaped by both collective and individual forces. Informed by the history of the material and cultural environments in which testators have grown up and/or live at the time they draw their wills, these choices are also influenced by the amount and the nature of the assets accumulated by individual decedents as well as by the ideology prevailing in their reference groups (religion, national origin, social class, age and gender). As the underlying economic and cultural forms of capital follow distinct dynamics and evolve at differing rates and in independent directions, there are ensuing inter- and intra- individual variations in heirship motivations. Not only do differing categories of decedents adopt differing strategies, but their choices evolve also over their life-times, notably in response to the changing status of their eligible beneficiaries. These choices enter three analytically distinct categories: the search for efficiency, the quest for ascriptive equality, and the commitment to the norm of reciprocity.

Heirship motivations are located on three separate axes. First, each weighs differentially the role of testators and of their beneficiaries in the structures of their familial groups. In the search for efficiency, the choices of testators are inspired by their own conceptions of the transfers most beneficial to their own estate and to their own kin. In the quest for ascriptive equality, these choices are informed by the perceived needs or aspirations of survivors. Finally, the norm of reciprocity places bequests in a succession of material and symbolic exchanges that bind decedents and beneficiaries to one another over the full duration of their respective life cycles.

Second, the norm of ascriptive equality originates from a collectivist tradition, which posits the chronological and logical preeminence of societal consciousness over individual self-interest (Comte 1848; Levi Strauss 1957,1958). The norm emphasizes "a culturally shared prescription of one sided generosity" (Gouldner 1960:164). In general, as the authors of the collectivist tradition tend to describe societies where market economy plays at best a marginal role in shaping social interaction, they are inclined to assume that the logic underlying transfers *mortis causa* or other forms of gifts and the logic governing the commercial transaction of commodities are successive and cannot co-exist (Carrier 1991). As already noted, Durkheim (1957), for example, was convinced that this particular form of intergenerational solidarity was doomed by the modernization of social structures. Conversely, both the search for efficiency and the commitment to the norm of reciprocity posit the logical and chronological salience of self-interest in relation to the common good. (Homans 1961; Blau 1964; Ekeh 1974). While the stress they place on self-interest leads these social scientists to assume that inheritance and other forms of gifts are absent of industrialized capitalist societies, they are also inclined to view the last two heirship strategies as more frequent than the quest for ascriptive equality in modern America.

The third and last axis concerns the time orientations specific to these motivations (Greenhouse 1989). The search for efficiency is future oriented since it underlines the returns that testators anticipate obtaining from their investments. In contrast, the quest for ascriptive equality is primarily past oriented, insofar as the choices involved are shaped by the need to do things the right way and by the legitimizing quality of precedents. Finally, the norm of reciprocity involves an equal emphasis on both the past and the future. The choices of testators are guided by both their memory and their anticipation of the favors received as well as by the marks of generosity they have displayed or will display themselves.

In the United States as elsewhere, the distributions of these three motivations and the underlying strategies depend on the degrees of freedom provided to decedents by the complexity of economic structures, the wealth they have accumulated individually, and the ideological forces to which they are exposed. But the greater the diversity of the sources of wealth and the more contradictory the ideological stances pertaining to intergenerational links, the looser the determinants of the choices available and the more diverse the heirship strategies that decedents adopt as a function of their social position. This is what makes the study of inheritance in the United States so exciting. While state and federal laws define heirship solutions that differ from the norms mandated by the religious, national, or social traditions represented in the United States, the ensuing discrepancies between general and particularistic successional models are further accentuated by the freedom that individuals enjoy in their interpretations of the relevant prescriptions and proscriptions.

Heirship and the Search for Efficiency

Some testators consider their estates as investments that should yield optimal returns. This is the source of the notion of estate planning. The definitions of these returns vary, however. For many Americans, the purpose of planning is primarily to reduce the claims that privileged creditors such as the state can make against the assets accumulated. Their libertarianism induces them to distinguish between the state toward which they feel no obligation, and the community in favor of which they are willing to make gifts (Woods 1928; Barber 1983).

The major function of estate planning, however, is to ensure the perpetuation or even the growth of the wealth accumulated. The pursuit of this goal requires the selection of able heirs, and thus the identification of the qualities and shortcomings specific to each of them (Becker 1981). Their rank ordering parallels a similarly hierarchical classification of assets, the distribution of the estate being determined by the hierarchical position that decedents attribute to each heir. "Differences of persons [notably in terms of abilities] are made a basis of corresponding differences of treatment" (Hobhouse, as quoted by Hochschild 1981:52). In brief, the search for efficiency involves the identification of the heir deserving to manage the largest and/or most productive part of the estate.

Depending on structural and ideological factors that both emphasize the self-reliance and the rationality of enterprising testators, the search for efficiency leads to formal partibility and hence to *qualitative* disparities among bequests, or to impartibility and hence to *quantitative* differences in the shares assigned to various heirs (Habakkuk 1955). Under conditions of affluence, the search for efficiency induces testators to rely on the principles of division of labor operating in the community at large and divide their estates accordingly. For instance, the notion of "house" or of dynasty enables sufficiently wealthy and influential testators not only to endow a variety of economic, cultural, and social organizations, but to make the corresponding endowments contingent on the appointment of their own heirs to the executive boards of these organizations. Thus, the notion of dynasty does not only allow testators to identify and implement a coherent "private" policy in a variety of social arenas, but it also enables their beneficiaries to enjoy regular and comparable sources of income (Wyatt Brown 1982; Marcus 1983, 1989; Odendahl 1990). For this reason, dynasties prevail in communities with a specific elite structure, where the same few families have their fingers in a variety of pies.

Alternatively, while impartibility requires the diffusion of an ideology that extols self-reliance, it prevails whenever and wherever most forms of capital are income producing. More specifically, this practice is salient among the self-employed (farmers, artisans, traders, professionals, etc.) and during eras when self-employment characterizes the majority of the active population. In addition, testators choose this particular mode of transfer whenever they fear that the survival or the growth of their estate might be jeopardized by present or future forms of material or symbolic scarcity. Almost two centuries ago, an American minister of Connecticut was already admonishing his parishioners "to keep their estates in one hand" and Adam Smith saw all forms of partibility as inhibiting the concentration of capital (as quoted by Becker 1981). In short, impartibility prevails in communities characterized by a sharp segmentation of elites.

Insofar as the search for efficiency necessitates the identification of the strengths and weaknesses specific to each heir, it is necessary to identify the criteria that testators utilize for selecting who will benefit which part of their estate. Their choices may result from direct observations, but they are most often the by-products of collective classificatory schemes that involve gender, birth order, and matrimonial status. These classificatory schemes may then act as self-fulfilling prophecies, the effects imputed to birth order, for example, being the result of parents choosing the models of primogeniture or ultimogeniture, of the ensuing behaviors, and of the rationalizations they use to justify the differential amount of care they provide to each of their children (Adams 1972).

From early on, Americans have based their heirship practices on gender. Sons and daughters did not receive the same type or the same amount of bequests. During the colonial era, for instance, daughters received their shares of the estate in the form of a dowry, which excluded realty. The need to avoid jeopardizing the functioning of the familial group as an economic unit constituted the rationale invoked to justify differences in the forms of capital transferred to sons and to daughters and in the timing of the transfer itself. Continuing contrasts in the educational and occupational opportunities enjoyed by individuals as a function of their gender have induced many generations of decedents to expect the returns to the investments made in daughters to be lower than those attached to the investment made in sons. As a consequence, testators kept considering income-producing assets to be male properties. At a minimum, they used the principles of division of labor by gender operating in their families for dividing these forms of wealth. For example, the land would go to the sons, the houseware or the tools needed by a female craft to the daughters.

For analogous reasons, the distinction established among assets may be used to differentiate the shares transferred to the sons themselves as a function of their birth order. During the last century, for example, the first sons of farming families in Bohemia got the land, while daughters and late-born sons were provided with the amount of formal schooling necessary for ensuring their survival in the new urban environments created by industrialization. Even though the role of matrimonial status is less documented, one might suspect that testators do not view the singleness of their male and female adult children as a comparable indicator of their socioeconomic potential.

To conclude, as the search for efficiency characterizes familial groups that are critically involved in the production of income, one might wonder whether changes in the types of assets socially most valued or changes in the amount of capital required to run an economic organization efficiently foster parallel changes in individual heirship strategies. For instance, as already suggested, the accentuation of the "credentialing" functions assigned to higher education has been instrumental in raising the fees charged by exclusive universities (Hauser and Sewell 1985). But does the ensuing change in the costs of the most rewarding forms of human capital induce modern parents to be less egalitarian in the choices they make concerning the enrollments of their children in various types of colleges? Do they use primogeniture in the transfer of human capital in the same way their ancestors used it to pass down the farm and its equipment?

Heirship and the Quest for Ascriptive Equality

Commitment to equity and principles of ascriptive equality reflects the diffusion of the altruistic orientations symbolized in the expression *"Noblesse oblige"* among various segments of the American population. The practices corresponding to this strategy follow divergent paths. In some instances, the formal stress placed on equality requires all eligible heirs to receive uniformly the same bequests (Sabine 1956). Testators who follow this model disregard contrasts in the life chances and the incomes of their offspring (Behrman, Pollak, and Taubman 1982). In its most extreme forms, commitment to equality is such that testators require the executors of their wills to sell every component of the estate in order to standardize the form and the amount of what is to be distributed among beneficiaries. Money is the most efficient equalizing mechanism.

For other testators, the stress placed on ascriptive equality implies acknowledging the differential profiles of children and hence their identity (Boulding 1975; Hochchild 1981). They are then inclined to privilege those of their heirs who are at risk to prevent them from experiencing the social fall to which they may be condemned because of their physical, emotional, or cognitive shortcomings. Thus, parents may give the best part of the estate to their handicapped son or daughter. To the extent that spinsterhood was and remains stigmatized, they may also be partial toward the unmarried daughter (Rossi and Rossi 1990).

Whether in the United States or elsewhere, testators invoke the notion of legitimacy to overcome the dilemma between treating their children uniformly and taking their identity into account. As already noted, Weber (1968) observed that even though Polish and German peasants occupy the same environment, and hence share the same technical constraints and opportunities, they hold distinct definitions of what doing the right thing involves. A fortiori, divergences in the economic trajectory of the various religious, national, and social groups in the United States render their respective definitions of the "right thing to do" even more diverse, and hence more "irrational."

To conclude, the quest for ascriptive equality is likely to prevail whenever and wherever the family is a unit of consumption rather than of production. This quest should be the most frequent motivation of American testators because the enormous resources of the country facilitate the diffusion of an ideology which extolls generosity and emphasizes the role played by private structures as sources of individual support. Yet since the relative incidence of either one of the forms taken by this quest always depends on the ideology governing intergenerational bonds, commitment to the notion of identity should involve primarily the satisfaction of the differential needs experienced by the testators' children. Today, for example, insofar as the increased frequency of divorces jeopardizes the socioeconomic status of divorced women and their offspring, there should be growing differences in the timing and the size of transfers that parents make in favor of their daughters and their sons. The increasing number of divorced women seems to foster a selective renascence of the various forms of assistance that their parents are willing to extent in their favor or in favor of their offspring. In short, divorce may be conducive to a partial restoration of matrilineal bonds.

Heirship and the Norm of Reciprocity

From this perspective, inheritance may be viewed as the ultimate component of the chain of reciprocal services that testators and heirs offer one another during their lives.[1] The reciprocity of the corresponding bonds is relatively easy to document concretely as long as families are autonomous economic units.

Parents spend money, time, and energy raising their children in the hope that some of the children will survive the hazards of life to be able and willing to help them when they reach old age. Indeed, they expect to receive both financial and emotional assistance from their offspring during the last stages of their lives, especially in the absence of social welfare programs for the elderly.

To be sure, the notion of reciprocal services is not devoid of ambiguities. The stress placed on exchanges between adjacent generations is unequivocal as long as there is only one heir who meets the expectations of the testator. Conversely, the consequences become more problematic as soon as there is more than one child. Any increase in the number of children requires a division in the reciprocal services that the two adjacent generations expect from one another. Some parents divide what they expect from their offspring into interchangeable tasks, but others tailor their demands to the gender, the birth order, or the personality of each of these children.

Most significant, the investments that parents make in each of their children and the specific returns that they obtain from each of them are not necessarily commensurate. In parts of Africa, for instance, parents invest more in the schooling of some children, but receive more domestic help from others (Caldwell 1982). Such disparities highlight the fact that exchanges between adjacent generations are governed as much by the search for legitimacy as by the search for rationality and, for instance, as much by the differential expectations that parents develop toward their children as a function of their gender or their birth order.

The significance of the notion of legitimacy in this regard accounts for variations in the degree to which the actors involved perceive the successive exchanges as being parts of the same whole. For example, Americans may view their own financial contribution to their children's schooling in terms of parental responsibility rather than of inheritance. Even though the two realms may be governed by distinct sets of ethics, there is little research as to the limits within which they are perceived as overlapping. Yet the very fact that a number of economists and lawyers consider that, in the contemporary world, the payment of college tuition is symbolically equivalent to more traditional forms of bequests does not necessarily mean that parents themselves adopt this definition of the situation. As already noted, even though some economists and some parents view the financing of college education as a form of intergenerational transfers, significant third parties such as fiscal authorities consider that such a payment represents an ordinary expenditure rather than a gift.

Social definitions of the services expected vary according to religion, national origin, social class, and gender. However, the models of heirship practices transferred to Americans as part of their cultural heritage keep clashing with their reinterpretation of these models, as it is inspired both by the emerging national American culture and by their commitment to rationality, which induces them to emphasize the opportunities and constraints of the current moment. Correspondingly, the whole universe of intergenerational bonds is placed under the sign of sociological ambivalences, that is, of compromises between definitions of individual roles that are mutually exclusive (Merton and Barber 1963). The father's images prevailing in the Irish or the German tradition are not necessarily compatible with the American imagery of fatherhood, nor a fortiori with the exceptionalist ideology, which belittles any kind of intergenerational loyalty.

The form and the significance of the services that parents and children expect from one another also depend on the structural and ideological salience of the "welfare state." In structural terms, two adjacent generations are in solidarity with one another only as long as their significant needs are not attended by agencies outside the familial realm. The growth of public or private programs of social welfare, for instance, the diffusion of Social Security and other retirement benefits, has minimized the dependence of the elderly on their children. This is especially so since economic development also accentuates the physical and emotional distance between parents and children, which enhances the uncertainties surrounding the performance of reciprocal obligations within familial groups. Conversely, the salience of reciprocity is likely to increase with the rising costs of education and of housing, and/or during periods of economic downswing, especially for new immigrating groups that have not learned yet how to pull the appropriate strings.

In ideological terms, the stress placed upon self-help and familial responsibilities in the acquisition of human capital remains a recurrent theme of the American ethos. As this ethos also emphasizes a pragmatic version of individualism, the combination of all these orientations accounts for the continuing presence of reciprocity in the American social landscape.

Yet reciprocity takes forms that vary with the nature of the exchange practiced and the culture of the familial group. As far as education is concerned, there are continuing variations in the definitions that the parents of distinct social categories hold of their socializing responsibilities. Some parents view their responsibilities as ceasing the day when their children leave high school, but others would like to believe that their "job" is not completed until their offspring graduate from college. But as the recent inflation of educational prerequisites in the labor market induces many parents to adopt loftier educational goals and consider that they should also finance the graduate studies of their sons and daughters, they must choose which child they will support. Similarly, privileged families who have always made a point to send at least one child to the same prestigious university face the same type of decision. What was originally a privilege is becoming a necessity. With the lengthening and the accentuation of the financial dependence of children, the criteria used by parents for selecting which son or daughter they will send to a prestigious institution cannot but change.

The same cultural variations also characterize intergenerational relations pertaining to housing. Rising mortgage rates and/or increases in the down payments required have certainly raised the expectations of adult children with regard to what they might expect from their parents in terms of financial assistance. In some subcultures, the parents are expected to shelter their adult children who do not have enough resources to purchase their first home. In other subcultures, the primary parental obligation is more financial than material. It is to lend or give the money that is necessary for a down payment.

The Evidence

As already suggested, while heirship strategies are inspired by the interplay of cultural and material factors, such an interplay changes over time. Even though economic development has modified the nature and the number of both beneficiaries and bequests, the ensuing evolution of heirship practices is not necessarily consistent. As already suggested, societal change implies simultaneously the survival of archaic forms of wealth and models of inheritance, and the adoption of new practices that fit better the constraints and opportunities of the current immediate environment and are stimulated even further by the exceptionalist ideology.

As far as the persistence of archaisms is concerned, I have already alluded to the differential expectations of initial waves of Irish and Jewish immigrants to Boston (Thernstrom 1964, 1973). As the Irish wanted to buy a house as quickly as possible, they sent their oldest children to work in factories at an early age in order to accumulate the down payment required and secure the monthly mortgage payment. But in redeeming their mortgage, they freed their property from any lien, which enabled them to spend more for the formal training of their youngest children. The ensuing differential demands imposed on Irish children as a function of their birth order have probably been instrumental in creating parallel contrasts in the forms of inter- and intragenerational mobility experienced by each of them.[2]

In contrast, Jewish parents of the same period were sufficiently wary of the discrimination to which they had already been exposed to disregard the purchase of a home as an impediment to their mobility. Since they believed that the sedentary life that goes with home ownership would heighten their vulnerability to employers' pressures, they preferred to facilitate the acquisition of human capital by their children. In contrast to their Irish counterparts, Jewish immigrants were probably more often in a position to favor their oldest children, since the chances of their exhausting the savings accumulated for educational purposes probably increased over time.

Such ethnic differences are likely to persist in new forms. Contrasts between the Jews and the Irish of Boston during the past century are analogous to contemporary contrasts between Asian and Hispanic immigrants. Not only are there variations in the human capital effectively transferred by the parents of the two groups, but in addition, there are also variations in how much these two sets of parents are willing and able to pay for the schooling of their progeny.

Regardless of the persistence of these archaisms, modernization exerts a variety of effects on American familial life-styles:

(1) Modernization blurs descent lines to the profit of conjugal solidarity, and testators are increasingly prone to bequeath their entire estate to their surviving spouse. This evolution, however, is most typical of small estates. In 1965, the estates of Cleveland decedents who transferred the whole estate to their spouse were on average worth only $17,654 as opposed to $44,235 in the case of their less exclusive counterparts (Sussman, Cates, and Smith 1970). At the same time, this pattern is also the most popular since it characterizes 86 percent of all testators. The finding is not accidental; the incidence of this particular pattern increased markedly in Bucks County between the end of the nineteenth century and today. Yet, there are differences between the two genders in this regard. Spouses are still more frequently mentioned in the wills or the intentions of wills of male than female decedents (Rossi and Rossi 1990).

(2) The diffusion of egalitarian ideologies in the larger society is associated with a decline in the differential size of bequests. Historically, the relative percentage of estates biased in favor of sons decreased from 40 to 15 percent throughout the first part of the nineteenth century. During the same period, unigeniture declined from 15 to 5 percent (Newell 1986, Ditz 1986). Today, however, the extent of American testators' commitment to equality is not properly documented.[3] In Connecticut, a state that is significant in view of the neutral character of local estate taxation policies, the shares enjoyed by children of wealthy testators with more than one sibling are said to depart rarely from the norm defined in intestacy laws (Menchik 1980a,b, 1988; Shammas, Salmon, and Dahlin 1987). Yet the boundaries separating wealthy from poor people are not necessarily clear.

(3) Modernization accentuates the extent to which commitment to equality characterizes smaller families. The impact of family size became more marked during the period stretching from 1919 to 1944. In the case of the decedents of the post–World War II period, disparities between the number of children and the number of beneficiaries are *least* likely with only *two* children, and *most* likely in the case of their counterparts with *five* children or more.[4]

(4) Despite the progress of modernization, commitment to equality might not be gender neutral. To the extent that the function of inheritance is to reproduce familial groups, the likelihood of this reproduction is not the same for the sons and the daughters of various wealth classes. Since the sons of rich testators are more likely to marry and have children than their sisters, they should receive larger bequests. The opposite should be true for people located at the lower end of the wealth continuum. Since the principle of hypergamy makes the daughters of poor testators more likely to marry and bear children than their broth-

ers, they should receive larger bequests than the latter. Even though matrilineal forms of familial bonds are often judged inferior in the Western world, they still represent a desirable form of social reproduction. However partial the relevant data might be, they run in the expected direction. In Ontario, the holders of smaller estates bequeath twice as much to their female than their male children, but their counterparts owning the largest estates do the reverse and transfer 30 percent of their wealth to their sons, as opposed to only 15 percent to their daughters.[5] Gender also affects the form of bequests. In Bucks County, for instance, the incidence of trusts made in favor of some or all the male children doubled from 2.9 to 5.7 percent from the end of the eighteenth to the end of the nineteenth century, but the corresponding figures evolved even more sharply, from 3.5 to 8.3 percent, when one considers the trusts made in favor of one or all female children. Further, as contrasts between sons and daughters increase with the amount of wealth accumulated, trusts represent an innovation most likely to have started at the top of the social ladder (Shammas, Salmon, and Dahlin 1987).

(5) Modernization accentuates the differentiation of the bequests received by female children. In Bucks County, the incidence of differences between the shares enjoyed by individual daughters increased from 4 to 12 percent in the case of families without sons between the end of the nineteenth century and now. During the same period, this incidence declined from 12 to 2 percent in the case of families with only one male child, but the relevant figures went up from 8 to 19 percent in the case of families where there were at least two sons (Shammas, Salmon, and Dahlin 1987).

(6) Insofar as modernization accentuates the ideology of self-reliance, the ensuing nuclearization of the family implies an increase in the incidence of disinheritance. Usually, there is disinheritance whenever and wherever children are perceived to differ from one another in terms of their commitment to the norm of reciprocity. Aging parents tend to give their whole estate to the one child who attends to their ultimate needs (Sussman, Cates, and Smith, 1970:chapter V). As a corollary, there is a close relationship between the elimination of one or several heirs and the distance that separates them from the testator. In Cleveland, two-thirds of the children living out of state were disinherited against only 15 percent of their counterparts residing close to the testator. In other words, physical distance becomes symbolic of socioemotional distance.

(7) As modernization also fosters increased matrimonial mobility, it tends to create additional pressures on estates. While the requirements of legitimacy clash with those of feelings, decedents seem to be slightly more often inclined to favor spouses or legatees of the last marriage. Their inclinations depend, however, on the relative duration of their

successive marriages. The longer their last marriage, the more prone testators are to forget relatives from preceding unions. Most important, however, decedents who split their estates between current and past marriages have a larger estate than those who do not.

(8) As modernization leads to an accentuated differentiation of the types of assets accumulated, it also broadens variations in both the extent and the form of inequalities between bequests. Among wealthy testators, commitment to equality is greater among those whose estates consist of stocks and bonds rather than of real estate (Rubinstein 1980). Alternatively, both in Illinois and in Wisconsin, farmers continue to be inclined to give away the farm to one or several of their sons rather than to their daughters. Only 14 percent of the beneficiaries of Wisconsin farming decedents were females, even though one-third had male siblings. Alternatively, three-quarters of the beneficiaries were males, even though 83 percent of them had sisters (Tarver 1952). This partial survival of the differentiation of male and female heirs makes it necessary to ascertain not only how long archaic heirship practices persist in a changing environment, but also to identify more accurately the type of assets that trigger the corresponding change. For instance, testators with agricultural land do not necessarily behave in the same way as testators who had anticipated the expansion of industries or commercial organizations and have accumulated urban lots accordingly. Further, even a modern form of investment like life insurance does not seem to imply greater commitment to equality in the bequests made in favor of children. Among heirs under 40 years of age, single women are more likely than their counterparts who have ever been married or than men to be the beneficiaries of an insurance policy made by their parents (Rossi and Rossi 1990). Among older heirs, it is the unmarried males who enjoy this privilege.

(9) The last effect of modernization is to broaden the range of heirship strategies available to testators. For example, individual bequests may differ from one another in terms of (a) their amounts, (b) the direct or indirect nature of the transfer they involve, and (c) the duration of the trusts attached to them. Some parents are sufficiently convinced by the ideology of self-reliance to infer that inheritance might jeopardize the achievement motivations of those of their children who already participate in the labor force. Correspondingly, they prefer to create trusts in favor of such children and endow the others who do not work with a capital. Alternatively, however, since other parents consider that those of their children who do not work have not learned how to manage capital, they prefer to provide them with a fixed income in order to reduce the likelihood that they will experience downward mobility or will indulge in irresponsible forms of prodigality. Similarly, since parents

hold differing views as to when their male and female children reach maturity and can be expected to behave responsibly toward money, the trusts made in their favors may have differing durations.

In summary, whatever its forms and its targets (children or previous spouses), exclusiveness is likely to prevail among small estate holders, who cannot afford to be generous toward everybody. The influence of modernization on this exclusiveness is diverse. Insofar as modernization differentiates familial wealth, it broadens the degrees of freedom enjoyed by testators and enables them to introduce more subtle forms of discrimination in the bequests they make in favor of their children. But insofar as modernization also accentuates domestic constraints, notably because of rising expectations concerning familial life-style and of the growing number of successive matrimonial experiences, there is a relative pauperization of decedents. In turn, while this relative pauperization makes the inequality of bequests more likely, especially since children have increasingly diverse origins, it also reduces the variability of its forms.

Determinants of Inequality

As already noted, for both historical and ideological reasons, religion is likely to be the most significant determinant of heirship practices. Regardless of the dearth of relevant data, differences in the commitment of two American Protestant sects have been shown even today to influence the differential educational and economic treatments of sons and daughters (Salamon and Davis Brown 1988).

Also as noted, national origin continues to shape the patterns of intergenerational transfers of German- and Irish-American farmers.[6] The continuing importance of national origin in this regard raises three questions: First, is the persistence of these specific cross-cultural contrasts specific to Midwest farmers or can it be generalized to other regions and other types of self-employed individuals? Second, how long are these contrasts likely to persist and what are the long- or short-term forces most likely to blur or to erase them? For example, is the cleavage between impartibility and partibility as a practice likely to decline with the successive phases of the economic cycle, the impartible Irish-Americans becoming egalitarian with upswings in economic activity and the partible German-Americans becoming "unfair" when the economic going gets rough?[7] Third, even if the overall significance of national origin declines, are there still forms of intergenerational solidarity that are specific to newly arrived national groups, for example, the Vietnamese, the Korean (Cheung Moon Cho 1989), or the Hispanic immigrants?[8]

In contrast to social class, gender is known to affect the benefits accruing to children. The accentuated salience of horizontal over vertical bonds delays intergenerational transfers and maximizes the bequeathing power of American mothers, but it also exacerbates intragender solidarities or conflicts. These mothers seem to be more egalitarian in their orientations toward their sons than toward their daughters. More demanding of the latter, they take drastic sanctions against those who deviate too markedly from the norm. In both the Midwest and in the New York area, they do not hesitate to disinherit altogether those of their daughters who fail to perform the obligations expected from them (Rosenfeld 1974; Rossi and Rossi 1990). At the same time, American women also seem to be more generous and ecumenical than their male counterparts in their selection of heirs. More often than male testators they include their own siblings in their wills (Rossi and Rossi 1990:475). Last, the choices of female testators are inspired by whether they have earned the money or whether they have received the funds from their husband's estate. In the first case, they seem to be more creative than men in their bequeathing patterns. In the second one, they claim not to have a say as to the destination of the funds (Matthews 1991). The question is to determine whether the progress of feminist ideologies will accentuate the specificity of female heirship practices or reduce the differences that oppose men and women in this regard.

Finally, gender modifies the effects of birth order. In the case of sons, primogeniture means privileged access to the income-producing activities of the family; for daughters, it means a greater dowry. This, however, is not universal and the direction of the influence that gender exerts on primogeniture varies across cultures. It often evokes additional advantages for sons, but additional liabilities for daughters. In Taiwan, for instance, the stress placed on the efficiency of investments made in children means that first-born sons are expected to attend the best schools, while first-born daughters are supposed to go to work as early as possible in order to finance the formal schooling of their younger male siblings (Greenhalg 1985). There is no reason to expect the practice to be immediately abandoned by Taiwanese immigrants settled in America.

An Assessment of Inequalities among the 1920 and 1944 Decedents

The assessment of relative differences between bequests is problematic on three counts. Many analysts are tempted to compare such bequests with the provisions of the intestacy laws of the state where testators lived at the time of their deaths (Menchik 1980a,b; Ditz 1986;

Shammas, Salmon, and Dahlin 1987). Yet such comparisons are problematic in view of the variety of *forms* of inequality practiced by individual decedents. Second, the meaning of unequal bequests varies according to the local laws that govern the division of the assets acquired by spouses during their conjugal life. What looks like inequality may constitute a mere attempt to restore equity wherever the legal definition of the individual estates of conjugal partners does not correspond to the latter's perception of what is fair. Similarly, evaluations of disparities in the bequests made in favor of male and female heirs remain potentially misleading, as long as their respective birth order remains unknown, since the effects of gender may be contingent on the influence of birth order. In short, the notion of equity is beclouded by a variety of methodological issues.

The Relative Importance of Surviving Spouses

Decedents do not harbor comparable feelings toward their spouses and their descendants. Insofar as modernization implies the triumph of horizontal over vertical bonds, and the subsequent systematization of peer groups, an increasing number of testators use wills as much for ensuring the economic welfare of their surviving spouse as for transferring to their offspring the resources they have accumulated.

Decedents adopt three distinct strategies to cope with the conflicting obligations they have toward the two categories of relatives: At the most conservative end of the continuum, some testators continue to make no specific provision for the welfare of their surviving partners. For both 1920 and 1944, one fourth of wills contained no reference whatsoever to the surviving spouse.[9]

Alternatively, those testators who make explicit reference to their partners can be divided into two groups. Regardless of the year chosen, another one-fourth of the male decedents included in the sample bequeathed all the assets they accumulated or inherited to their widows and left nothing to their children. For both economic and demographic reasons, they were more numerous than women. They tended to have more resources; they also appreciated the likelihood that their wives would outlive them. Conversely, about 40 percent of the male testators included in the two cohorts adopted a more conservative strategy, which consisted in dividing their estates and in distinguishing those assets that should go to their wives (usually a house and the income of a trust built to cover household expenditures) from those assets that could be divided right away among children.

Whereas the majority of male testators wanted to ensure the welfare of their widows, they were also keen both to control the ultimate destination of their own estate and to limit the period of time during which the funds mobilized to help their widow remained frozen. Thus, many testators specified that the income of trusts was to be provided to widows until their death, but they still identified the final destination of the assets that made up the trust. Further, conjugal solidarity was not always limitless: five male testators in the sample indicated that if their widows remarried, the payment of a regular income would be discontinued in favor of a final flat sum.

On the whole, the overall preference given to the surviving spouse over children was more typical of male than of female decedents (the relevant correlations are .299 and .274 for 1920 and 1944) for both the economic and demographic reasons evoked in preceding paragraphs (Tables 6.1 and 6.2).

Five sets of factors highlight the pattern of diffusion of the innovation that this practice represents. First, the preeminence given to conjugal over intergenerational solidarity was innovative insofar as it was typical of younger men, especially those of the first cohort (correlations between age and preference given to surviving spouse declined from −.412 to −.155). Further, the practice was increasingly characteristic of early wills, that is, of decedents who planned their death by writing wills early in their life cycles (the correlation increased slightly from .137 to .200).

Second, the practice prevailed initially among testators living in states where the estates of the two spouses are most individualized and where

Table 6.1. Zero-Order Correlations between Conjugal Solidarity Measured in Terms of the Preeminence of the Bequest Made in Favor of the Surviving Spouse and Selected Independent Variables

	Men only		Total population	
State bonds	−.148	−.117	−.113	−.081
Federal bonds	−.133	−.138	.273	.343
Bonds	.076	.169	−.136	.211
Stocks	.392	.151	.173	−.006
Nonfarm assets	.304	−.011	−.157	.056
Mortgages	−.102	−.167	−.100	.176
Notes	−.077	−.206	−.201	−.105
Realty	−.368	−.117	−.077	−.177
Life insurance	.308	.248	.073	.051
Widow executor	.235	.350	—	—
Number of beneficiaries	−.249	−.218	−.209	−.260
N	39	55	41	61

Table 6.2. Zero-Order Correlations between Conjugal Solidarity Measured in Terms of the Preeminence of the Bequest Made in Favor of the Surviving Spouse and Selected Independent Variables

	1920	1944
Number of children	−.168	−.079
Estate size	.204	−.052
National origin	.074	.014
Gender	−.299	−.274
Separate property	.361	−.141
Community property	−.109	.094
Age	−.412	−.155
Intestate inequality	.191	−.080
Trust	−.032	−.233
Time interval between will and death	.117	−.189
Disparities in duration of income between children	−.076	.053
N	57	74

their respective shares (as they are defined by intestate laws) were unequal, before declining among 1944 testators. Correlations between the preference given to the surviving spouse and the separation of conjugal assets declined from .361 to −.014 between 1920 and 1944. In the same vein, the association between the first variable and the institutional inequality of conjugal shares dropped from .191 to −.080. In this sense, the findings reproduce the observations made by Maine for earlier societies. While the purpose of wills is often to depart from prevailing local norms, and in this case from economic individualism, their function changes with the emergence of a nationwide legal culture and the relevant shifts in the meaning of individualism.

Third, the preferential treatment accorded to the surviving spouse prevailed initially among families with fewer children (the relevant correlation declined from −.168 to −.079 between the two dates of reference), regardless of their gender. At the same time, the preference accorded to the widow went hand in hand with her appointment as executrix of the will (the correlation increased from .235 to .350 between 1920 and 1944). Not only this, but such a preference was also paralleled by a smaller number of beneficiaries (the relevant correlation decreased slightly from −.294 to −.218 between the two cohorts).

This array of observations confirms the multifaceted nature of the nuclearization of the family. As argued by William Goode (1963), this nuclearization involves simultaneously a smaller family size, a lowering of the loyalties owed to members of the extended family, and the growing salience of conjugal solidarity.[10]

Fourth, the preference given to the surviving spouse over the children prevailed initially among the wealthiest segments of the sample, to become generalized in 1944 to the full population (the correlation drops from .329 to −.038). Alternatively, to treat the wife's share in competition with the bequests reserved for children tended to become more typical of smaller estates (the correlation shifts from −.037 to −.110). Similarly, while the restrictions imposed on the bequests made in favor of the wife prevailed among the most diversified estates of 1920 (the correlation is .207), such a pattern became more typical of the 1944 decedents whose estate was homogeneous (the correlation between estate diversity and the offering of a limited bequest to the wife is −.205).

Fifth and last, the preference given to the widow varied with the type of asset accumulated.[11] In 1920, individuals whose wealth consisted primarily of stocks, insurance certificates, or nonfarm assets favored their wives over their children. Those whose wealth included mostly realty remained faithful to a patriarchal vision of familial loyalties and transferred their assets to their offspring. In between, the offering of restricted bequests to widows prevailed among those testators whose wealth comprised a large proportion of federal or state bonds but was conversely least typical of individuals who invested most of their wealth in stocks. In 1944, the effects of the type of asset owned were smaller and narrower. Those testators who had most of their wealth in life insurance continued to be the least patriarchal of all, in contrast to those whose wealth consisted primarily of risky promissory notes who did not offer anything to their wives.

Of all the material and symbolic factors that affect the choices made by decedents in this regard, the relative date of the will is the most robust predictor and hence the one most likely to persist when other variables are introduced in the equation. The preference given to the widow over the children does not seem to be a routine decision, but rather, the result of a long-term commitment to a modern form of marriage.

Inequality among Children: An Overview

Insofar as the modernization of familial groups minimizes intergenerational continuity, it also reduces inequalities in the bequests enjoyed by the testators' offspring. The percentage of testators making distinctions between their children in this regard dropped from 54 to 39 percent between 1920 and 1944. These distinctions, however, continued to increase significantly with the number of children and the diversity of their gender for the first cohort, but not for the second (Table 6.3).

Since the egalitarian treatment of children reflects modernizing influences, its determinants are somewhat symmetric to those of the diffusion of conjugal solidarity. Thus, the greater the resources that male testators bequeath to their widows, the more egalitarian becomes their

Table 6.3. Correlations between the Preferences Displayed by Testators in Favor of Sons or Daughters and Selected Independent Variables

Variable	Inequality against sons		Inequality against daughters	
	1920	1944	1920	1944
Realty	−.277	−.160	−.118	.137
Corporate securities	.105	.165	.096	−.223
Age	−.231	.291	.473	−.114
Gender	.080	.373	−.250	−.236
National origin	.122	.081	−.280	−.144
Urbanization	.243	.098	−.089	−.175
Intestate separation of estates	−.113	.385	.250	−.279
Intestate inequality	.194	.048	.026	.053
Family size	−.214	−.196	−.030	−.190
Farmers[a]	−.346	−.243	−.067	.058
Executives[a]	.000	.326	.000	−.033
Inequality of shares	−.294	.111	.000	.071
Inequality asset/income	.487	.099	−.129	.117
Timing of wills	−.240	−.007	.144	−.167
Number of beneficiaries	−.250	−.331	.357	.078
Gender of executor	−.114	−.364	−.103	−.300
Conjugal solidarity	.027	−.286	−.015	−.065
Trust	.199	.232	.129	−.008
Stocks	.166	.121	.077	−.201
Nonfarm assets	−.212	−.252	.408	.239
Bonds	.018	.220	.173	−.184
Mortgages	.324	−.200	−.087	.282
Notes	−.139	−.038	.319	−.065
Estate size	.230	.082	.045	.156
Estate diversity	.381	−.141	−.082	.149
Time conditions	.199	.010	−.300	−.018
N	25	30	25	30

[a] Correlations involving farmers or executives are computed for male decedents only. In both cases, the male population is divided between those who hold the occupation under consideration and are scored 1, and the remaining part of the population, coded 0.

treatment of their children. As a result, patriarchal stances lose their coherence over time. Originally, testators who provided their wives with a restricted bequest tended also to introduce disparities in the shares assigned to their respective children. In the case of the second cohort, however, the two distributions became independent, with the correlation declining from .210 for 1920 to .021 in 1944.

Inequalities among children are influenced by both the date at which wills have been written and the age of the testators. In the same way that early wills symbolized conjugal solidarity, they also symbolized commitment to equality among children. Yet, the effect of the date of wills evolved in diverging directions for these two variables. As already seen, while the correlation between the timing of wills and the first variable increased between 1920 and 1944, the correlation between the timing of will and the equality of the shares distributed to children declined from .499 to .188. In this sense, the lack of discrimination among children became less of an innovation. By the same token, the very fact that the differentiation of the bequests made in favor of children became increasingly typical of older testators suggests that it was in the process of becoming an archaism. The same social dynamics also explain why the treatment of children became independent of the local legal context. Prevailing initially among the residents of states that keep conjugal estates separate and therefore emphasize an individualistic domestic morality, this particular practice was more evenly spread geographically in the case of the second cohort.

Influenced by cultural factors, the egalitarian treatment of children is also rooted in the material bases of social life, and more specifically, in the size and the composition of estates. Even though the relevant differences are not statistically significant, they all run in the expected direction. For the 1920 cohort of decedents, equal treatment of children characterized the largest and the most differentiated estates, confirming the validity of the theoretical analyses made by Goody (1973, 1976) in another historical and geographic context. Similarly, this egalitarianism was least typical of estates consisting mostly of realty or promissory notes, but most typical of those individuals who had invested most heavily in bonds, mortgage certificates, and nonfarm assets. Yet, since these coefficients decline systematically between 1920 and 1944, one suspects that the direct impact of the fungible character of the assets considered or of the risks involved in their possession has diminished to become filtered through a number of ideological forces related to the cultural capital of testators.

Of all the determinants reviewed here, the combination of the relative date of the will and the absolute proportion of the estate invested in realty (i.e., including estates with no realty) is the most robust predictor of the overall equality of the bequests made in favor of children in the case of the first cohort. This confirms the assumptions developed earlier about the emergence of egalitarian definitions of intergenerational bonds. Initially, such definitions prevailed among decedents who planned ahead of time and invested in assets that are easily transformed into monetary terms. As such definitions became more common in 1944, their determinants became more complex, because more closely related to the symbolic capital of testators.

The Variety of Forms of Inequality

Inequalities in the bequests made in favor of children take five forms. First, a majority of testators (58 percent for the first cohort, 51 percent for the second) systematically drew unequal shares for their children.[12] A second group put a particular asset aside in favor of one particular child. Regardless of variations in the value of the asset involved, the incidence of this specific form of partial impartibility declined from 38 to 29 percent between 1920 and 1944. Even though a third group of testators affirmed their faith in the principle of "share and share alike" and hence of equality among children, they still invoked gifts or donations made earlier in favor of one particular child or the urgent needs of a specific son or daughter as reasons for limiting the application of the principle of partibility. This particular form of inequality increased slightly, from 41 to 46 percent from the 1920 to the 1944 cohort.

Other forms of inequality are more subtle. Thus, 32 percent and 29 percent of the wills drawn by the 1920 and 1944 cohort of decedents, respectively, included provisions that provided some children with full control over specific assets or a certain portion of the estate while endowing others with the income of the trust formed with the remainder of the estate or with assets designated to that effect. For these decedents, trusts were adapted to the needs and lacks of their beneficiaries.

Finally, 20 and 23 percent of the wills made by decedents in the two reference years differentiated children in terms of the duration of the trust established in their favor. To be sure, this type of differentiation reflects inconsistent motivations. Some testators felt that at 25 years of age, their sons were more mature than their daughters to take responsibility for their share of the estate and that the latter should wait until they reached their 30th birthday. Other testators, however, felt the other way and allowed their daughters to get full control of their share of the estate prior to their sons. In this sense, wills represent good indicators of the evolving differential definitions of the age at which men and women are defined as economically mature in distinct social groups.

These various forms of inequality are not mutually exclusive. Thus, changes in the distribution of their intercorrelations between 1920 and 1944 suggest changes in the global strategies used by testators to differentiate their children from one another (Table 6.3). In effect, wills served more complex functions for the second than the first cohort of decedents. In contrast to 1920 when the use of unequal shares precluded the use of a trust, this ceased to be the case in 1944, when decedents were more likely simultaneously to make uneven bequests in favor of some children and built a trust to provide income to others. More important, in 1944, the use of a trust serving only some children became positively associated with both the use of personalized gifts (partial impartibility) and the use of distinct time restrictions.

The Inequality of Bequests

The profiles of inequalities in the value of bequests made in favor of children vary a great deal. In their most extreme form, they involve the total disinheritance of one or several of the children.[13] For the full sample of 1944 decedents with estates less than $200,000, the relative number of cases where the number of beneficiaries was smaller than the number of children increased with sibship size. In other words, the more children there were, the more chances that at least one of them would be disinherited.[14]

Disinheritance reflects a number of inconsistent factors. In one case, it resulted from a somewhat cryptic motivation: "My daughter will understand" the testator wrote. In four cases, this disinheritance included the payment of a symbolic dollar.[15] Most of the time, disinheritance is partial. This makes it necessary to identify the specific assets involved in each bequest as well as to evaluate them as fiscal authorities define them.[16]

The incidence of simple inequalities in the size of bequests made in favor of children declined over time. For reasons already stated, this incidence increased with the age and the gender of the testator. Women were more discriminating than men in the case of the first cohort but became more egalitarian in the case of the second. Since the frequency of this inequality also increased with the number of children, the salience of their respective identity seems to vary paradoxically as a direct function of sibship size.

For both cohorts, this dramatic form in inequality prevailed among the smallest and least differentiated estates. It was most frequent among testators who had invested most of their wealth in realty or in promissory notes. Alternatively, it was most unusual among those who had invested in bonds. In this sense, this most brutal form of inequality is a reverse function of the marketability of the assets accumulated by decedents as well as of the risks involved. Put another way, the safer the investments made by testators, the more egalitarian they were in their intergenerational transfers.

Finally, depending on the profile of individual testators, the incidence of this form of inequality also varied with the legal characteristics of the state where decedents were residing at the time of their deaths. Originally, this form of inequality was more frequent among individuals living in states where the estates of conjugal partners are least differentiated and where spouses are entitled to comparable shares of each other's estate. Thus, once more, individuals used their wills primarily to deviate from existing norms.

Inequality Based on the Distinction between Unconditional Transfers and Trusts

Women were increasingly more likely than men to distinguish their children in terms of giving some of them full and immediate control over an asset while providing others with the income derived from a trust administered by a third party. This type of differentiation was also more frequent among the writers of late wills and among those who used trusts rather than regular wills, even though the relevant correlations decline between the two cohorts. The visibility of this form of inequality is also a function of the composition of the estate. Minimal among individuals for whom realty represented a high proportion of the estate, its incidence was maximal in the case of testators with the most diverse estates, and of those whose wealth included a relatively large share of federal bonds. Thus, the purchase of federal bonds and the differentiation of children between those who were entitled to receive income and those who had direct access to full rights of ownership reflect convergent systems of placing people and things in time. Both systems rely on a time in which the differential effects of income and of wealth, on the one hand, and of distinct rights and obligations, on the other, were held convergent, or at least analogous.

Beneficiaries and Victims of the Will

As already hinted at the beginning of this chapter, differences across bequests were sometimes based on the cumulative judgments that testators made about the vices and virtues of their individual sons and daughters. Most of the time, however, these differences reflect the intervention of ascription. American testators distinguished their children as a function of their gender. They harbored distinct expectations about both the public and private behaviors of their sons and their daughters. They expected the former to achieve in the professional world, but the latter both to marry a well-to-do partner and to return home to attend to the needs of their aging fathers or mothers.

Similarly, testators differentiated their children as a function of their birth order. Like their counterparts in other countries, American parents held specific expectations, notably with regard to the transfer of human capital. Unfortunately, the data do not give any indication about the birthdate of the heirs.

Finally, since parents had distinct ideas as to the economic threats faced by their married and unmarried daughters, they did not want to provide them with comparable bequests. Nor did they impose the same demands on these two types of daughters at the end of their own lives. Some parents considered their unmarried daughters as being fully available to attend to their own needs. Others seemed to view them as being innocent and, as such, irresponsible, or as being busy surviving and hence unable to help them.

Inequality Based on Gender

Gender-based inequalities are not stable. Among those families that had both sons and daughters, 53 percent of the 1920 testators who treated their children differentially discriminated against their sons and 21 percent against their daughters. For their 1944 counterparts, the relevant figures are 29 percent and almost 50 percent.[17]

Despite the persistence of patriarchy during the period, the most striking feature of this form of reproduction concerns the lack of symmetry between the determinants of the treatment of male and female children. One cannot differentiate the degree to which the *privileges* of sons have persisted from declines in the *injustices* experienced by daughters, or vice versa.

The Influence of the Testators' Social Status

Testators differed from one another on two distinct counts. Some of them were more sensitive than others to the gender of their children in deciding how much they would give to each. Among those who were most sensitive, some privileged their sons; others, their daughters. In the 1920 cohort, gender-based inequalities prevailed among the youngest testators (Tables 6.2 and 6.4). For the oldest segments of that cohort, this discrimination worked against daughters; for their youngest counterparts, it worked against sons. Alternatively, in the 1944 population, it was not only the oldest testators who were most likely to base the division of their estate on the gender of their children, but they were also the ones most prone to discriminate against their sons.

This shift probably reflects both the declining role of the family as a unit of production and the differential decline of intergenerational solidarity between sons and daughters. As sons were more mobile than daughters, they were also more likely to forget their roots. In other words, both parental expectations and the actual behaviors of their sons and their daughters changed during the period.

The evolution of correlations between the timing of wills and the use of the children's gender to define bequests confirms these shifts. Efficiency and instrumentality were still the rule in 1920. They represented an abstract ideology insofar as early wills were written at the expense of daughters. But the ideology was still binding, since gender-based disparities were most typical of the authors of late wills who discriminated most often against their sons to protest against the latter's poor achievement. Among 1944 testators, even though the date of wills ceased to affect the use of the children's gender as a determinant of bequests, there were signs that heirship motivations changed and served increasingly symbolic functions. Shifts in the assistance that parents expected to obtain from their sons and daughters in their declining years explain why those 1944 decedents who made their wills just before dying discriminated most often against their daughters.

Both the distinction between the instrumental and the symbolic functions assigned to bequests and the use of disparities based on the gender of children depended also on the gender of testators themselves. This use prevailed among male testators, who in 1920 as in 1944 discriminated against their daughters. Since in 1944, however, female testators also discriminated against their sons, there seems to have been a parallel undermining of existing forms of patriarchy.

Reliance on the gender of children as a source of differentiation of their shares characterized the 1920 large families, but not their 1944 counterparts. But in contrast to 1920 when discrimination against sons was most typical of smaller families, the same small families were in 1944 the indiscriminate loci of discrimination against either sons or daughter. In short, the two facets of the differential salience of children's gender in relation to their number evolved during the period.

Finally, gender-based disparities in bequests also depended on cultural factors. In 1920, they prevailed among urban testators, who discriminated against their sons more often than their rural counterparts, notably farmers. In 1944, such disparities were more frequent among

Table 6.4. Zero-Order Correlations Matrix between Various Forms of Inequality and Selected Independent Variables

	Overall inequality		Inequality of shares		Inequality based on			
					Gender		Matrimonial status	
	1920	1944	1920	1944	1920	1944	1920	1944
Estate size	−.177	−.065	−.175	−.212	−.294	−.189	−.193	−.012
Estate diversity	−.095	.045	−.132	−.195	−.224	.000	−.404	−.135
Corporate securities	−.118	−.043	−.225	−.080	−.343	−.148	−.440	−.443
Nonnegotiable assets	.095	.032	.241	.177	.264	.116	−.131	.362
Realty	.190	.025	.284	.338	.346	.206	−.011	.396
Life insurance	.128	−.166	.176	−.118	−.074	−.091	−.117	−.215
Number of children	.197	.109	.248	.112	.408	.030	.546	.168
Intestate equality	−.191	.080	−.079	−.120	−.297	−.078	−.191	−.271
Age	.019	.209	.396	.271	−.163	.239	.002	−.064
Gender	−.059	.017	.123	−.146	−.207	.001	−.222	−.055
Separate property states	.142	.016	.120	.103	−.037	.031	−.091	.316
Community property states	.000	−.041	−.232	.120	.117	.087	.316	.046
National origin	.142	−.064	−.026	.061	−.018	−.283	.055	−.100

182

Conjugal solidarity[a]	−.132	−.297	−.168	−.148	.010	−.112	−.191	−.047
State bonds	.184	.145	−.051	.247	−.052	.163	.051	.227
Federal bonds	.045	.049	−.223	−.140	.051	−.056	−.109	.412
Bonds	−.040	−.050	−.278	−.284	−.357	−.062	−.329	−.011
Stocks	−.368	−.076	−.140	−.129	−.266	−.144	−.335	−.483
Mortgages	−.216	−.017	−.305	−.219	−.216	−.094	−.087	−.134
Notes	.277	−.038	−.098	.362	.162	.151	−.003	−.186
Nonfarm assets	−.214	.112	.118	.057	−.013	.003	−.258	−.211
Inequality asset/income	.274	.381	−.260	−.093	.227	.254	.121	.598
Inequality bequests	.442	.557	—	.092	.181	.516	.204	.444
Presence of sons	.201	.059	−.083			—	.420	−.396
Time conditions in will	.333	−.069	−.071	−.184	.435	−.283	−.330	−.203
Time interval between will and death	−.499	−.188	−.104	−.238	−.196	−.036	−.074	−.144
Inequality based on time	.142	.236	.075	−.145	.158	.164	−.196	.443
Trust	.360	.049	.027	.349	.435	−.220	.247	.125
N	51	84	41	61	35	45	21	18

[a] Conjugal solidarity refers to the unconditional transfer of at least more than half of the estate to the surviving spouse. This is coded 1, all other testors getting 0.

German- than Irish-American testators, the former being also more likely to discriminate against their daughters.

The Influence of the Legal Environment

The instruments of transfer chosen and the overall profile of wills also throw a significant light on the evolving importance that successive cohorts of testators attached to the gender of their offspring. Thus, the exclusive use of trusts implied discrimination against sons rather than daughters in 1920 but not in 1944. Similarly, the distinction between the transfer of assets and the creation of trusts helped both cohorts to differentiate the bequests they made between their sons and their daughters, but only the first one did so at the expense of sons. Alternatively, the beneficial consequences that the preference that male testators displayed toward their wives presented for the equality of children were temporally and functionally limited. This preference benefited only the sons of the 1944 cohort. Finally, as expected, the very selection of sons or daughters as executors protected them and their siblings of the same gender against any discrimination. As the correlation gets sharper over the years, the title of executor seems to have become as much a privilege as a responsibility.

Both the use of the gender of children as a source of differentiation of bequests and its actual consequences for sons or daughters also varied with the legal orientations of the testators' immediate communities. In 1920, gender-based inequalities of bequests were less likely among testators living in states where intestacy laws posit the equality of the shares claimed by spouses. In this sense, testators used wills only to *confirm* the dispositions of intestacy laws and to generalize to their children the equality that the law imposed on them with regard to their surviving spouse.

The Influence of the Estate

Gender-based disparities among bequests were most frequent among the smallest and least diversified estates. However, changes in the domestic status of sons and daughters have fostered changes in the logics underlying their relative or total exclusion from the estate. For the 1920 cohort, those decedents who had large and diversified estates tended to discriminate most often against their sons. In 1944, the same holders of large and diversified estates indulged, although in a subdued form, in the rejection of daughters.

The importance of the use of gender as a differentiator of children's bequests also varied with the percentage that each type of asset represented in the estate. Regardless of the cohort considered, holders of an estate composed primarily of productive forms of capital were most unlikely to discriminate against their sons. Alternatively, if the daughters of 1944 testators with this kind of estate were more likely to have a smaller share than their brothers, they were less likely to suffer in this regard when stocks and bonds constituted the largest part of the estate. Finally, while risky investments (mostly mortgage certificates and promissory notes) influenced the discrimination made between sons and daughters, the relevant effect was time specific. Thus, whereas the importance of promissory notes in the estates of the 1920 decedents increased the likelihood of discrimination against daughters, the relevant differences disappeared for 1944. Since the effects of the importance of mortgage certificates evolved in the opposite direction and were significant only in 1944, social definitions of "risks" seem to have changed over time and with them, the views that testators held as to their effects on the relative generosity they should display toward their male and female children.

As a final observation, contrasts in the correlations between the number of beneficiaries and the discrimination operating against sons or against daughters highlight the differential influence of gender as a determinant of familial structures. Discrimination against sons implied fewer beneficiaries altogether and hence a shrinking of familial loyalties. As the corresponding correlation became more marked over time, the negative effect of the active rejection of a son on the size of familial networks became more visible. In contrast, as the discrimination operating originally against daughters was initially conducive to an increase in the number of beneficiaries, it underscored the marginal and substitutable character of the status traditionally assigned to daughters in domestic groups. The rejection of a daughter induced testators to find substitutes. But since the relevant correlation declines between 1920 and 1944, the higher status achieved by daughters during the period heightened their identity and reduced the degree to which they could be replaced.

Inequality Based on the Matrimonial Status of Daughters

Contrasts in the last names of female heirs recorded in wills or in estate tax returns make it possible to compare the bequests made in favor of married and unmarried daughters. Because of the relatively old age of the decedents, contrasts in these bequests have probably less to do with the differential age of the beneficiaries than with their matrimonial status. In any case, out of the 18 testators that had both married and unmarried daughters in 1920, 57 percent used the matrimonial status of their daughters as a criterion for distinguishing them from one another. Out of the 20 testators with similar characteristics in 1944, only 44 percent did so.

The declining incidence of the distinction across cohorts is associated with significant changes in its determinants. Initially typical of male testators and of large-sized families, it later became independent of these two variables. Similarly, most visible among the 1920 testators residing in the states treating the assets acquired by spouses as community property, the distinction became most visible among the 1944 testators residing in the states whose intestacy laws keep the estates of conjugal partners separate and do not allow husbands and wives to make comparable claims on each other's estate.

Finally, the effects of the size or the diversification of the estate on the distinction between married and unmarried daughters followed the same pattern as those observed on the distinction between sons and daughters. In both cases, these effects were less pronounced in 1944 than 1920. Yet, the relative incidence of stocks and life insurance certificates in the estate are more powerful predictors of the lack of distinction between married and unmarried daughters for 1944 than for 1920. This distinction also became more marked among testators whose wealth involved a large amount of federal or state bonds.

This inequality has changed forms over time. The distinction between married and unmarried daughters has become less and less contingent on the construction of a trust. Alternatively, disparities in the value of their respective shares have become greater and testators have learned to rely more often on the distinction between full ownership of assets and the creation of trusts, or on the differential length of time during which female heirs were entitled to an income.

To conclude, the diverging evolutions of the distinctions between sons and daughters, on the one hand, and between married and unmarried daughters, on the other, probably reflect the progress of individualism in American society. As ideology erodes the distinction between males and females, it accentuates the distinction between married and unmarried females. More generally, the progress of certain forms of equality leads to the creation of new patterns of differentiation. The notion of equality is therefore highly relative. One form of differentiation chases another.

Conclusions

Four major themes emerge from the preceding analyses. First, the ideology of equality has spread among an increasing large part of the

American population of decedents. Fewer testators make distinctions among their children in their wills. The diffusion of this egalitarianism is concomitant with the progress of conjugal solidarity. Primarily, modern decedents write wills in order to maintain the independence and the status of their surviving spouses. As a result, as we get closer to contemporary times, intergenerational transfers should become less frequent. They should occur only with the disappearance of the last parent.

Second, the differentiation of bequests made in favor of sons and of daughters correspond to two distinct logics. The preeminent status accorded to the former does not necessarily imply the corresponding demise of the latter. The demise of the link assumed to exist between malehood and the instrumental character imputed to transfers *mortis causa* is independent of the progress of the link deemed to exist between femalehood and the symbolic-expressive quality imputed to heirship. Further, to the extent that the differential status of sons and daughters declines over time, it is associated with the emergence of new forms of individualization, notably between married and unmarried daughters.

Third, distinctions among children take increasingly complex forms. Decedents keep learning how to make full use of wills and trusts to tailor the disposition of their wills to the needs, aspirations, and foibles of each of their children. Whereas trusts were initially written to deal with the totality of the estate, their functions became more differentiated and attuned to the qualities attributed to the children of the second generation of decedents.

Finally, while these distinctions depend on cultural factors and notably on the gender and the national origin of the decedents, they are also a function of the size, the diversity, and the composition of individual estates. Land, stocks, bonds, mortgage certificates, and promissory notes involve differing types of risks in terms of the value and the timing of their returns. Despite the lack of appropriate documentation, I would venture that there is a definite linkage between the subjective experience that testators have of these risks and the choices they make in order to transfer the relevant assets to their children as a function of the latter's gender or matrimonial status.

7
Inheritance of Yesterday, Inheritance of Today

Americans prefer liberty to equality. Because of their collective commitment to liberty, they also emphasize to the same degree privacy and the right to be left alone. But insofar as their emphasis on privacy and on individualism excuses the Horatio Algers of American society from any obligation toward their peers, predecessors, or successors, Americans also glorify secrecy.

Correspondingly, the ideologies that view individuals as a loose collection of unrelated atoms also, implicitly or explicitly, portray Americans as being keen *not* to know anything about one another. Even though Americans claim to know a great deal about the poor and minorities in society, they do not seem worried that they know very little about the powerful or about the ordinary people of Main Street, U.S.A. Inheritance offers a case in point. Thus, while some American economists are interested in inheritance, the disproportionate place occupied by the champions of neoclassical views in the specialty is a sure sign of the benign neglect of intellectuals for assessing the consequences of variations in the amount and the form of wealth accumulated by testators as well as by their predecessors on current patterns of bequeathing. In sociology, the evidence is even more telling. The most recent handbook of sociology of the family does not have any entry on current transfers *mortis causa* in this country (Sussman and Steinmetz 1987). In this sense, sociologists reproduce the dominant forms of ideology. They are typically American insofar as inheritance offends their belief in mobility and their desire to be liberated from the past.

However, this stance unduly ignores the power that comes from knowledge and the inequalities that differential knowledge creates among various social groups. The social distribution of secrecy and the ambivalence of the American ethos about the distribution of information or of knowledge, and hence of power, on the one hand, and of wealth, on the other, are not without consequences. They exacerbate the negative impact that the phantasms caused by ignorance, notably rumors, exert on social life.

Such a dramatic rejection of heirship in the realm of privacy causes the views of many Americans to be dominated by irrational considerations. Many of them believe that inheritance only concerns the wealthiest segments of the population. Many are also convinced that federal or state authorities violate the testators' intentions and divert their funds. These views are becoming critical in view of the sums at stake. The share that estates represent in the American gross national product is projected to increase from a current 4.3 to 6.5 percent for the first five years of the next century. The largest share of the $6.8 trillion involved will go to individuals who are currently between 34 and 48 years of age (Farnham 1990). But in what form? And what will be taken from them?

Given the significance of the underlying economic and social stakes, the purpose of the research reported here has been to dispel the myths surrounding inheritance and systematically to highlight the underlying beliefs, behaviors, and feelings behind the development of inheritance. More specifically, the purpose has been to remind Americans that in their quest for self-reliance and for modernity, many of them have lost track of the commitment of some of their ancestors to the concept of community and to the intercalary structures such as the family that facilitate the integration of the individual in the larger social fabric. One cannot simultaneously boast of being a nation of philanthropic testators and deny also being a nation of heirs.

Thus the research reported here is based on two complementary premises. Against the libertarian ideology, which views the individual as an independent atom, I posit the importance of social networks. Many studies of familial phenomena such as abortion or divorce fail to be informative because they focus exclusively on one individual at a time and ignore the complexity of the social interactions involved. For example, the issues surrounding abortion involve the woman, her parents (if she is a minor), her husband (if she is married), the fetus, the medical community, social welfare agencies, and thus taxpayers. In the same way, divorce is not the exclusive concern of one partner, as unfairly suggested by the expression "he/she got a divorce." Indeed, divorce involves the two spouses, their children, and also their extended kin, the legal community, and the agencies likely to pick up the pieces if the conflict causes personal tragedies. The difficulties of simultaneously examining the perspectives adopted by different categories of relatives involved are not sufficient to explain why American social scientists have neglected various forms of intergenerational solidarity, including inheritance. Researchers invoke these difficulties in order to mask their attachment to an atomistic view of the world. Even though the analysis reported here concerns primarily testators, the reader must remember that the processes of social or cultural reproduction at work in intergenerational transfers necessarily involve testators, their heirs, their other relatives, their lawyers, and the fiscal authorities.

Against the same libertarian ideology, which extols the significance of the present at the expense of both the past and the future, the present research also seeks to underline the dialectical influence of memories and anticipations on current behaviors. Indeed, inheritance symbolizes this very dialectic. While Tocqueville had seen the dangers of this libertarian ideology when he argued that "democracy makes men forget their ancestors and clouds their views of their descendants" (1969:548), at least three indices suggest that the ensuing amnesia does not tell the whole American story. As already suggested, the evidence suggests that Irish- and German-American farmers of the Midwest remain faithful to the familial ideals of their communities of origin. Such a faithfulness is not exceptional. Americans reacted negatively to George McGovern's campaign proposal to raise inheritance taxes because they interpreted it as a threat to the whole notion of familial continuity. In more general terms, Bellah and his coauthors (1985) warn us that a certain rhetoric makes Americans sound more isolated than they are in reality. When the exceptionalist ideology transmogrifies the vice of amnesia into a virtue, it is more a posture than a practice. In this sense, Americans are less individualistic and less indifferent to time than a certain rhetoric would have us believe. To cite Russell Baker, Americans, like other human beings, "carry the dead generation within [themselves] onto the future aboard [their] children. This keeps the people of the past alive long after [they have been] taken to the church yard" (1989:351).

Inheritance and Reproduction: The Overall View

Both the notions of community and time, which form the premises on which the research is based, highlight the importance of social or cultural reproduction, and hence the continuity of social relations. As I suggested in Chapter 2, the word *reproduction* is clearly multifaceted, having physical, social, cultural, and economic components. In physical terms, heirs succeed their parents: "She's the spitting image of her mother" symbolizes the genetic stability of familial groups.

In social terms, since inheritance specifies the conditions and limits within which "relatives" can expect a share of the decedent's estate, it symbolizes the relative stability of both the boundaries of familial groups and the relations of dominance operating within such groups. As an illustration, the choice of key familial roles, such as executors, affects patterns of preference in the amounts or the forms of bequests made by decedents. Thus, the choice of a female executor minimizes the likelihood that testators will discriminate against daughters in the will. As an another example, in revealing the differential role of sons- and daughters-in-law in familial groups, the selection of executors highlights the process by which gender modifies extended familism. Naturally, the changes in the visibility of familial boundaries that result from divorce, separation, or death are associated with shifts in the patterns of bequests. In 1977, 60 percent of decedents having experienced any form of matrimonial mobility were likely to make bequests outside the immediate family, against less than 20 percent of those who left an intact marriage (Torrey 1990).

In cultural terms, inheritance ensures the continuity of the symbolic capital specific to each family, and hence the perpetuation of memories, feelings, and values that shape the identity of kinsfolk. Testators do not randomly choose any form of inequality nor any symbol in order to distinguish their sons from their daughters or their unmarried from their married daughters. Instead, forms and symbols of inequality are systematically distributed as a function of the status of testators, as a result of their gender, their national origin, or their social class. For example, male decedents use trusts to differentiate the form of the bequests that go to their sons and to their daughters in the hope that this will enhance the likelihood they will conform to the behaviors expected of them. In the same vein, the transfer of the one jewel, chair, clock, painting, or item of silverware which counts to the one deserving son or daughter symbolizes perhaps the differential attachment of dying testators to a privileged child, but it symbolizes above all the continuity of familial values and the underlying link between the objects and the individuals that are both located at the core of familial mythologies (Carrier 1991).

Finally, in economic terms, inheritance concerns the intergenerational transfer of various forms of material resources that modify the processes of upward or downward mobility experienced by all Americans as a result of their own individual economic trajectories. Numerous testators divide their estate and use certain assets or certain sums to form a trust designed to protect one or more heirs from the economic downfall that accompanies significant physical or mental handicaps.

To sum up, insofar as inheritance symbolizes the continuity of social life, it commands the crossroads that link patterns of social stratification (differences among families) with familial relations (hierarchies of positions within families themselves).

This backdrop, however, does not give a sufficiently compelling picture of the place occupied by inheritance in contemporary American society. Such a place is overlooked not only because of the excessive importance attached to reproduction, but also because of the frequent failure to distinguish *mechanical* from *interpretive* forms of reproduction. Much too often, analysts sidestep this distinction. Much too often, they do not seek to ascertain whether the changes observed in the familial realm are reversible or not. To give just one example, it is easy to view divorce as breaking the integrity of familial bonds and to overlook the partial restoration of the relations between maternal grandparents and grandchildren that often results from this mobility.

Mechanical and Interpretive Forms of Inheritance

Mechanical reproduction involves a one-to-one correspondence between each element of the initial and the succeeding figure. As far as inheritance is concerned, mechanical reproduction obliges the heir literally to step into the shoes of the decedent and to mimic his or her power, activities, and responsibilities.

At the societal level, mechanical forms of inheritance and reproduction prevailed in feudal systems, where intergenerational transfers concerned the transmission not only of wealth but also of political or religious authority. Within modern societies, mechanical forms of inheritance continue to characterize all occupational groups in which heirs inherit not only the resources of the decedent, but also his or her instruments of production and eventually his or her residence. It would be wrong, however, to infer from differences in the practices of the two cohorts that they are independent and that the 1944 decedents ignored the dominant orientations and strategies of their predecessors.

Instead, these differences suggest more modestly that mechanical forms of reproduction have become marginal. In the analysis conducted here, the very fact that aging farmers stand further apart from the remaining part of the population with regard to the acquisition of certain types of assets (notably realty) or to the choice of heirs (for instance, in the preference they show for sons) offers a case in point. Yet this form of mechanical reproduction survived after 1944. Scandinavian-American farmers of Wisconsin and their German- or Irish-American counterparts in Illinois pass the farm (the land, the house, the equipment, etc.) to one or several of their sons. These forms also continue to characterize a narrow segment of the top financial elites, despite growing inconsistencies between familial traditions and the relevant components of corporate culture. As an illustration, An Wang, the builder of the computer empire, followed strictly Chinese rules when he chose his son as successor to run the business (Cohen 1990).[1]

To conclude, mechanical forms of reproduction are likely to persist in the case of all self-employed decedents who retain partial or total control over the hiring of their personnel. These forms involve all the occupational categories, ranging from small-town professionals (lawyers, medical doctors, architects) who continue to have their own personalized practice, to artisans or businessmen who retain their own enterprises.

Alternatively, interpretative forms of reproduction and inheritance allow a greater latitude to both testators and heirs in the pursuit of identical goals. Successive generations use a large range of means to enable heirs to keep the same status as that of the testator both within the family and in the larger society. To be sure, interpretive forms of inheritance and reproduction always involve transfers of money. But these transfers nevertheless allow the fulfillment of purposes that are alien to the testator's original life-style. For example, contemporary interpretive forms of inheritance involve the transformation of material into human forms of capital through the payment of college tuition fees (Langbein 1989). This transformation does not occur randomly. Not only does it intervene selectively among children, but in addition, the approximations inherent in the notion of "interpretive" allow some "fortunate few" to retain the same status as their ascendants or even to climb higher in the social hierarchy, but others to fall.

In contrast to mechanical forms of transfers that take place exclusively at the time of the death of the decedent, the timing of interpretive transfers is more flexible. It could not be otherwise in the case of societies or communities characterized by high rates of technological or social change. This is what Tocqueville (1969) seemed to have forgotten when he alluded to the demise of hereditary privileges as a specifically American phenomenon, demonstrating his proposition by observing that the children of the rich landowners of New York State became lawyers, merchants, or medical doctors in neighboring cities. Accustomed as he was to European feudal systems, the French traveler could not imagine a form of inheritance that would *not* be mechanical and would therefore be equivalent but not identical to the way initial testators used land as a source of power and money. Further, by ignoring the problem of determining which child entered an urban profession, Tocqueville sidestepped the issue of assessing the procedures chosen by testators to pass down their assets.

However, to reaffirm here the duality of forms of reproduction in the contemporary United States remains insufficient. Like many other dichotomies, the value of the distinction is heuristic and analytical rather than demonstrative. In the real world, the two forms of reproduction coexist and have a variety of shadings. For instance, parents who give the family enterprise to one child and provide others with a high-quality education follow both mechanical and interpretive models.

Further, it may be misleading to infer that there is no reproduction whatsoever from the observation that few heirship practices retained the same frequency of occurrence and the same determinants between 1920 and 1944. The economic and social upheavals that accompanied the two world wars and the depression may have shaken all the bases of existing social and cultural orders and rendered the models of behaviors and feelings handed down by previous generations moot and obsolete. At the same time, the impression of discontinuity between the behaviors of two adjacent generations may be caused by the difficulties of tracing the symbolic equivalences to which I have alluded. Indeed, the differential dynamics of the two cohorts of German- as opposed to Irish-American decedents studied here suggest that the outlooks of the two national groups do not necessarily converge to form a national familial culture. The diverse forms of adversity faced by specific groups induce them to restore or cling to old ways. The issue is to identify the underlying pattern of selective retention.

Whether the reproductive processes inherent in transfers *mortis causa* are mechanical or interpretive, the present analysis has enabled us to suggest that they depend on two distinct logics. The logic of assets differs in this regard from the logic of culture. On the whole, the former evolves more rapidly than the latter. Since the first logic is inspired by the prevailing traits of each specific asset imputed to the market, and hence to the short-term risks involved as well as the short-term profits anticipated, it should discourage mechanical forms of reproduction, or at least diminish their image.

The Logic of Assets: The Evidence

Assets exert three distinct types of effects on the practices pertaining to the accumulation and the transfer of wealth. First, some of the effects of estate size in this regard seem to be universal, but others depend on the context. Estate size enhances the degrees of freedom enjoyed by individuals with regard to the assets they can accumulate. It affects the number of markets in which decedents place their savings; it also affects the number of titles they can hold within each category. Estate size also seems to multiply patterns of egalitarian bequeathing while, conversely, the poorest segments of the decedents' population differentiate the bequests they make in favor of their children as a function of the latter's gender or matrimonial status. In this sense, the analysis confirms the views of Jack Goody on the social functions of inheritance. Both in relative and absolute terms, scarcity makes it more difficult to be egalitarian. It accentuates in proportion the dramatic nature of individual choices.

Yet the effects of estate size do not necessarily remain constant over time. Their evolution is evident when one assesses the innovative or conservative character of the provisions present in wills. For example, even though the use of banks or of lawyers seems modern, their services were most often used by the most modest segments of the second cohort of decedents who were most likely to "innovate" in their choices of executors and to reach out for experts of family boundaries. Alternatively, ownership of a large estate does not necessarily induce individuals to be innovative in their choices of instruments or in their conceptions of the loyalty they owe their surviving spouses or their children. Thus, the patriarchy-inspired selection of a son as an executor typified holders of small estates in 1920, but the owners of large resources in 1944. In other words, it is not always the same American social groups that aspire to perpetuate a particular traditional pattern. The underlying reproductive processes are not always located in the same part of the social hierarchy. Sometimes conservatism prevails at the top of the wealth or the income distribution; sometimes it remains popular in its lower parts. Like the distinction between local and cosmopolitan, the meaning and the appeal of the distinction between tradition and progress vary across groups and over time.

Second, the variety of assets accumulated has two implications for the reproduction of wealth across generations. On the one hand, the greater the variety of types of assets one holds, the more diverse the risks taken within a single type of these assets and, for instance, the greater the number of distinct stock certificates owned at the time of death. In other words, the amount of money accumulated increases with the diversity of the risks taken both across and within categories of assets. On the other hand, the variety of forms of capital accumulated conditions the extent of the quantitative and qualitative disparities in the bequests made in favor of children. The less diversified the estate, the greater the likelihood of differences in the form or the amount of the bequests made in favor of sons and daughters.

Third and most significant, the specific nature of the risks attached to distinct types of assets not only reflects the profile of their owners, but also affects the heirship strategies they adopt. At one end of the continuum, not only does the popularity of realty and its average relative contribution to the overall size of the estate size remain relatively constant over time, but the same stability characterizes as well the determinants of the relevant distributions. At the same time, interindividual variations in the relative size of realty holdings affect the instruments of transfer chosen, the dispositions included in these instruments, the number of bequests, the relative commitment to equality toward children, and the form of the disparities across bequests.

In contrast, both the popularity and the relative contribution of life insurance to overall estate size changed considerably between the two reference years, as have their respective determinants. Originally conditioned by the cultural capital of decedents (notably their national origin and the level of urbanization of their state of residence), the popularity and the relative size of this particular type of asset became influenced by the decedents' socioeconomic status (their age, their occupation, and the size of their estate) in 1944. But the relative value of insurance also determines a number of key behaviors between spouses, notably whether they have adopted a system of joint tenancy in the management of their wealth and, equally important, whether they tend to favor one another rather than their offspring in their wills. In the same vein, the ownership of life insurance does not imply the equal treatment of heirs. Testators who have accumulated life insurance annuities tend to transfer them to their unmarried sons (Rossi and Rossi 1990:467).

To summarize, the logic of assets is both quantitative and qualitative. How much people have and what they have govern in part the instruments that individuals retain for transferring their estate, the extent to which they differentiate what they consider to be their obligations or their favors toward their spouses as opposed to their children, among the latter, toward their sons as opposed to their daughters, and among the latter, toward their unmarried as opposed to their married female children. The importance of the distinction between realty and corporate assets is not new. Social historians have contrasted the "landed gentry," unlikely to treat their children equally, with the barons of industrial or commercial empires, who were more prone to share their estate in equal parts.

In demonstrating that the form of the wealth accumulated is as important a determinant of social behavior as its amount, I have shown the importance of variations in the relative importance of the safety and the risks attached to distinct types of assets. These distinctions are likely to persist in their original or in equivalent forms, as long as parents remain able to differentiate the needs or the abilities of their individual children.

The Logic of Culture: The Evidence

It is, however, quite appealing to counterargue that assets have no intrinsic qualities and cannot shape the variety of successive decisions that concern both the accumulation and the transfer of wealth (Thompson 1979). Instead, it is tempting to assert that the notions of markets and risks are all social constructs that vary with the position of their respective actors in the social structure.

To elaborate the point even further, emphasizing the extent to which interrelations between the instruments chosen by decedents, the targets, and the forms of their preferences represent a unified whole is to epitomize the *human* origin of the coherence of inheritance systems. But to see this coherence as a by-product of culture raises the question of identifying the social sources of legitimation operating in the United States. On what bases do people identify the right thing to do with regard to their immediate relatives? Even though both gender and age operate within larger settings (national origin, religion, and social class), the first two factors contribute nevertheless on their own to organizing relations with familial groups. As long as men and women are deemed to react differently to the various markets and as long as they are supposed to feel differently toward their children, they are unlikely to adopt analogous patterns of wealth accumulation or distribution. The same holds true of age. As expectations concerning major expenditures vary with the life cycle, the old and the young will not invest in the same fields. Nor will they invest for the same reasons. Nor will they entertain the same notions about their eligible heirs.

But even though individuals carry within themselves the specific sets of expectations that go with their age, their gender, and their national origin, they constantly compare such expectations with the benchmarks of the cultures of their fellow citizens, as those are expressed through larger social networks. The study confirms in this regard the importance of the size of the communities where testators reside. It also confirms the significance of the prescriptions and proscriptions embodied by the intestacy laws of such communities. Indeed, the major source of variations in actual heirship practices lies not only in the gap between state laws and the informal heirship culture of the groups to which testators belong, but also in the differential knowledge that these testators have of such a gap as well as the opposite conclusions they derive from such knowledge.

The Role of Gender. Even now, men and women do not occupy symmetric positions in the social structure. The two genders own unequal amounts of money and accumulate different types of wealth for three distinct reasons. As their respective levels of participation in the labor force differ from one another, the origin of their respective wealth is not the same. Wages and salaries are less significant sources of wealth for women, even though the relevant differences keep declining. In addition, up to now, women have not been expected to take the same risks as men. For this reason, the male and female decedents of the two cohorts have not accumulated the same kinds of assets. Some of these assets are said to be "feminine" because they are supposed to correspond to typically "safe" motivations and can be negotiated easily. Finally, since men and women do not enjoy the same life expectancy and are not supposed to share a comparable level of legal knowledge, they do not use the same instruments of transfer.

Gender differences in patterns of wealth accumulation are associated with parallel gender contrasts in patterns of wealth distribution. Supposedly, male testators should be concerned with decisions pertaining to disinheritance or at least with the imposition of their own personal preferences. Indeed, male testators do not hesitate to make unequal bequests among their children. In contrast, their female counterparts more frequently underline connections between generations and relatives (Gilligan 1982:5). In this sense, men are more inclined to create, women to preserve. The strategies of women are more subtle, as they modulate trusts to differentiate their sons and daughters by providing access to the principal of a bequest in the case of some children, but by allowing others only to enjoy the income of a trust constituted to that end.

Yet difference between male and female testators may be culture and time bound. Thus, as long as husbands participate more extensively in the labor force, they are also more likely to protect the interests of their widows, but as they do so, they are also more likely to be egalitarian toward their children, and particularly to cease discriminating against one or several of their sons. Alternatively, female testators themselves became increasingly prone to discriminate against their sons between 1920 and 1944, and during the same period, the likelihood of their choosing sons as executors declined in proportion. With the passage of time, there are increasingly numerous signs of a stronger intergenerational female solidarity.

Correspondingly, the gains or the losses experienced by male or female beneficiaries are not symmetric or simultaneous. Indeed, the growth of female solidarity did not prevent the second cohort of men from faithfully reproducing the discriminatory practices of their predecessors against their daughters. As another example, the use of trusts as instruments of discrimination against sons has increased between 1920 and 1944, but it has been increasingly rarely used for discriminating against daughters. Similarly, while discrimination against sons was increasingly more often paralleled by the undermining of extended familism and by a concomittant decline in the number of beneficiaries, discrimination against daughters no longer implied a rise in this number, which suggests that the substitutable quality imputed symbolically to females has declined proportionately.

However, since the findings presented here are already 45 years old, the issue is to determine whether convergences between the status of male and female testators or of male and female beneficiaries have become more or less pronounced with the passage of time. The question is also to identify the time lag separating such convergences from changes in the material structure of social life and to ascertain whether these convergences are irreversible. As already seen, insofar as rising divorce rates alter the socioeconomic trajectories of men and women, they modify accordingly what fathers and mothers expect from their adult sons and daughters.

The Role of Age. In an ever-changing environment, age exerts conflicting influence on the behaviors that concern the accumulation of wealth. Insofar as aging maximizes financial vulnerability, older individuals invest increasingly in assets that are more easily negotiable. This vulnerability, however, is not uniform across all social categories. At one end of the continuum of the distribution of assets, occupational seniority enables older farmers to accumulate more land than their younger counterparts. In this case, aging accentuates mechanical forms of reproduction. At the opposite end of the same distribution, the acquisition of life insurance is negatively related to age, but the reproductive processes at work are initially interpretive rather than mechanical. Since insurance was still a risky investment in 1920, it was most likely to attract young individuals keen to use new means in order to fulfill the same social obligations as their parents and help their children maintain analogous social positions. It reflected a cohort effect. With the passage of time, however, the meaning of the relationship between this asset and age has changed. Today, ownership of life insurance epitomizes the exercise of parental responsibility. As such, it goes with a particular phase of the domestic life cycle and represents a mechanical form of reproduction (Rossi and Rossi 1990).

The effects of age on heirship practices are similarly divergent within or across cohorts. On the one hand, among the testators stated here, aging means a greater commitment to conservative values; it means the selection of more beneficiaries and the selection of a male executor (usually a son). At the other end of the age continuum, younger decedents were most likely to introduce time dimensions in their wills because they were able to see the implementation of their demands during their lifetimes. Both behaviors represent mechanical forms of reproduction.

In contrast to these invariant effects, however, other influences of age are also relative to each period. For example, in contrast to 1920 when it was the youngest testators who discriminated most between sons and daughters (most often against the latter), it was their oldest counterparts who most often made such distinctions in 1944, usually at the expense of their sons. Thus, the relationship between aging processes and patriarchy evolved between the earliest and the latest generation of testators to remind us of the significance of the cohort effect identified in general terms by Ryder (1965).

Since the passage of time has been associated with the generalization of retirement programs and the lowering of the financial constraints imposed upon the elderly, most estates have become larger. But with longer life expectancies, the passage of time has also been accompanied by a greater dependence of the elderly on their adult children as well as on their peer groups. Indeed, they have become more easily alienated, with a concomitant greater selectivity toward the recipients of their generosity. The question is to ascertain how these conflicting changes affect the socioeconomic status of the current elderly population and how the underlying change has modified relations between current generations throughout their respective life cycles.

The Role of National Origin. As anticipated, national origin has proven to be a critical component of the reproductive processes at work in inheritance. German- and Irish-Americans adopted differing strategies with regard to the accumulation of wealth, because their orientations toward risks were not alike. More Irish-Americans may purchase life insurance policies, but their German-American counterparts invested more money in this type of capital. Similarly, German-Americans were likely to be more active in the bonds market and, for the 1944 cohort, in the promissory note markets. While the second cohort of German-American decedents was also more likely to indulge in gifts *inter vivos*, they were also more prone to distinguish between their sons and their daughters, usually at the expense of the latter. In brief, there are signs, as predicted, that the two national groups did not hold the same views of their bonds with objects and with relatives.

Yet, to the extent that contrasts between the two groups are selective, the conditions under which national origin continues to facilitate the reproduction of familial arrangements and intrafamilial inequality remain uncertain. Contrasts in the heirship practices of differing nationalities may be masked whenever they have not experienced the same rates of intermarriage over time and/or whenever there are sharp differences in the history of their migrations to the United States, notably with regard to the length of their American experience.[2] To get a better bearing on the importance of national origin as a continuous source of legitimacy in the United States, it would be necessary to introduce a greater number of controls to remove those "noises" that blur the effects of the models of behavior typical of the countries from which most Americans originated.

To conclude, since the persistence of national origin is both selective and relative, it is necessary to ascertain how long it takes for intergenerational transfers to be influenced by an emerging American domestic culture; to assess whether the corresponding shifts are irreversible, and to identify the sequential order in which various national groups forgo the models that regulate all the practices related to death and inheritance rituals to acquire an authentically American repertoire of corresponding beliefs and behaviors.

The Role of Legal Culture. Individual strategies concerning the acquisition or the transmission of assets are contingent not only on the sociodemographic profile of individual decedents, but also on the networks of constraints and opportunities offered by the laws of the state where they reside. In other words, individuals do not articulate their cultural repertoire *in vacuo*, but rather in response to the specific institutional forces that amplify or dampen their own aspirations.

Whether the law keeps the estates of conjugal partners separate or enters them in a common entity used to determine both whether decedents would accumulate specific assets and the sums they would place in the corresponding markets. In other words, individuals make their investments with a look to the future and specifically to the legal imbroglios that their investments might produce. Similarly, whether this law posits equality between conjugal partners or discriminates against the wife used to affect the number of beneficiaries listed in the will and the differentiation that decedents established between their sons and daughters or between their married and unmarried daughters.

However, the effects of these two types of law are not constant over time. For example, the intestate separation of conjugal estates operated against daughters in the case of the 1920 testators, but against sons in the case of the 1944 cohort. In other words, as parental concerns toward their sons and their daughters evolve differentially, they do not make the same use of the laws. There are changes in the extent to which they view such laws as threats to their aspirations or, alternatively, as tools facilitating their implementation.

With the passage of time, more specifically, with the growth of the American legal culture as well as with the legal rationalization of conjugal relations, notably as a result of prenuptial agreements, it remains necessary to ascertain how long the contents of wills and bequests will continue to reveal regional trends and to ascertain the sequential order in which the "Americanization" of heirship practices will occur.

The Relativity of the Results

Like many other studies that claim to be indicative rather than demonstrative, the present analysis suffers from two major limitations. The first one reflects problems of internal validity, insofar as the data do not say as much as they should on the concept of reproduction, which is claimed to be the cornerstone of the entire exercise. The other one mirrors problems of external validity, insofar as it is difficult to determine the conditions under which the results reported here can be generalized to a more contemporary American setting.

Problems of Internal Validity

To emphasize the continuity of patterns of familial identity and of social stratification as these result from inheritance is to raise four questions about the data used here: (1) First, this continuity involves a succession of decisions and uncontrollable events in the lives of decedents on which IRS files remain mute. For example, the history of the acquisitions and sales of various forms of capital would give a more accurate sense of the reasons accounting for the final composition of the estate. Remarks about the popularity of differing types of assets and their values would be more compelling if one had the facts about the moves made by wealth holders in and out of the various categories of assets.

(2) Similarly, the history of the vital statistics of all children would throw some light on the testators' decisions. For example, preferences expressed at the time of the last will may be only the "second bests," coming after the earlier death or disappearance of the first choice.[3] The fact of the matter is that whereas it has been possible to differentiate children in terms of their gender or, in the case of daughters, of their matrimonial status, the data do not say anything about the birth order of children. This lack is unfortunate for three reasons. The cognitive and emotional attributes imputed to children and thus, their life chances are often believed to vary with their rank in the family. Furthermore, parents differ in the demands they impose on their offspring. Even though first-born children may complain about the favoritism displayed toward their younger siblings, the literature suggests they receive more attention and achieve more than those children who come after them. Finally, as parental resources increase with occupational seniority, late-born children are more likely to benefit from the additional attention of their fathers or their mothers. In short, especially when sibship order is associated with the knowledge of the time interval separating births from one another, it is a significant component of modern inheritance for both

structural and cultural reasons. In structural terms, it mirrors the changing amount of economic or social resources that parents mobilize in favor of their successive children. In cultural terms, birth order may be a "survival" of less complex communities and eras, in which case it acts as a source of legitimation. As remarrying gives a new twist to the notion of primogeniture, it reminds all of us of the continuing presence of significant archaisms in social life (Gouldner 1960).

(3) Third, social or cultural reproduction and the enduring nature of social life evoke not only the stability of social arrangements, but also the recurrence of conflicts. The success of the Oedipal myth results from the repetitive nature of intergenerational tensions. Thus, the reproductive processes attached to transfers *mortis causa* also concern the perpetuation of domestic conflicts. Insofar as inheritance awakens latent interpersonal feuds or creates them, it causes and mirrors ambivalences (Rosenfeld 1991). Thus, testators may decide to disinherit totally or partially some of their children, either out of a pique caused by the prodigality of a son or the promiscuity of a daughter, or in order to restore justice among all the children. In one of the wills included in the sample, as already noted the testator accompanied a bequest of one dollar in favor of one daughter with the notation, "She will understand." The cryptic nature of this remark, which can be construed as an ultimate form of insult or of an exclusive bond, underlines the recurrent nature of evasiveness in intergenerational bonds.

Quarrels among siblings are as important components of the reproductive processes inherent in transfers *mortis causa* as the choices that decedents make with regard to the accumulation or the transfer of wealth (Rosenfeld 1982; Schoenblum 1987). These quarrels are in part determined by structural factors, and they are said to be more frequent in the case of small estates. But as they are also in part culture bound, they tend to reproduce themselves, and it is said that inheritance feuds are more typical of some families than of others. The Montagues and the Capulets did not only live in Shakespeare's imagination. In contrast to impartible societies where heirs tend to band together and express animosity toward their testators, their counterparts living in partible social systems are more likely to have feuds with one another (Titus, Rosenblatt, and Anderson 1979). The authority of the oldest generation is more evident in the first than the second case. While death uniformly causes a critical "havoc" in domestic relations, the forms of the ensuing turmoil vary nevertheless across cultures and over time. Since in the United States challenges to wills often breed quarrels among siblings, one can infer that American culture is partible. But to the extent that American siblings are often keen to moderate the effects of the inequalities imposed by their parents and to give to the "black sheep" the one asset (e.g., car, furniture, jewel) he or she always wanted to have, one can also infer that American culture is impartible (Sussman, Cates, and Smith 1970). These two observations underline the need to explore further the dynamics governing the objective and subjective facets of the tensions between partibility and impartibility in the current American context.

Last, the references made to reproduction make sense only insofar as transfers cause shifts in the patterns of investments and consumption of the beneficiaries. In other words, reproduction refers also to the extent to which bequests confirm or modify the socioeconomic rank ordering of children within families and the corresponding differences between families. The next step of the research presented here would therefore consist in linking the records of estate tax payers to the income tax records of their beneficiaries in order to ascertain how the latter have made use of the windfall to which they have been entitled.

To summarize, the study confirms from a new angle a number of observations that anthropologists, historians, and economists have already formulated about the implications of estate size or estate composition, gender differentiation, and national origin on transfers *mortis causa*, both prior and subsequent to 1920 and 1944. The results, I hope, are sufficiently provoking to stimulate more systematic and contemporary analyses.

Problems of External Validity

The choice of the small sample used here reflects the desire to test the notion of wealth class and to assess the homogeneity of the behaviors of individuals sharing the same amount of money. Concentrating on small estates made it possible to emphasize the impact of other factors such as age, national origin, or gender and examine how these various "cultures" introduce variations in the practices of individuals who have the same resources.

But this strategy also raises questions about the homogeneity of the entire wealth continuum. When the analyses suggest that holders of larger estates (albeit below $200,000) adopt specific strategies concerning the accumulation or the distribution of assets, one must ask whether the results would remain similar if the data had included smaller as well as larger estates than those present in the current sample. For now, the contrast between "more" and "less" only pertains to the actual range of the estate values used in the context of the study and hence to estates between $40,000 and $200,000. The findings presented here say nothing about the median effect of estate size.

Second, the study deals with a comparison between two adjacent cohorts. In the same way that one can challenge the narrow range of financial space that has been explored here, one can also argue that the two cohorts chosen here are not representative of a sufficiently broad range of years. One cannot be sure that the years between 1920 and 1990 represent a homogeneous period. Since one can suspect that the increase in divorce and phenomena like surrogate mothering generates new inheritance strategies, the conclusions of the study are more indicative than demonstrative. They primarily help define the grammar of this type of research, that is, the kind of variables that must be taken into account.

Thus, at the end of this sociological journey, the lessons offered concern not only the world "out there," but also the tools used by the profession to explore and understand it. Sociology cannot claim to be a science as long as it does not seek to improve the score and make it more compelling the next time around (Gouldner 1976; Cicourel 1974).

Policy Implications

The growing importance of transfers *mortis causa* in American wealth makes it essential for the various categories of actors involved (heirs, testators, lawyers, IRS) to develop a common analytical framework. In contrast to current cohorts of Americans who are tempted to equate legitimacy with efficiency, one suspects that efficiency is unlikely to be the exclusive determinant of the capitalist accumulation of wealth and heirship practices as long as the tensions opposing public and private spheres of interaction retain their current forms.

In this sense, the purpose of the book has been to delineate empirically the motives governing the choice of the forms of capital accumulated by two cohorts of decedents, the instruments of transfer they retained, and the extent as well as the form of differentiation they selected in their patterns of bequeathing. This purpose has been to show that such choices do not take place *in vacuo* but rather in a legal context that must be constantly reassessed.[4] Despite their protests to the contrary (they are firm believers in the reality of free markets), the Horatio Algers constantly learn how to pull the appropriate strings.

To conclude, the only contribution of this book (but it is not a trivial matter) is to help current cohorts of individuals involved in transfers *mortis causa* appreciate the challenges that the shifts from an entrepreneurial and self-reliant to a consumption-oriented society represent for the survival of the American family and the bonds woven between generations. This appreciation requires Americans to reintroduce in their worldviews the notions of time and of social bonds that mainstream sociology has helped eradicate for so long. Americans are not exclusively the amnesic lonely crowd depicted by social scientists. Only some of them are, but then, only at some points of their lives, and only in certain social arenas. I have attempted here to pinpoint the relevant contingencies, and to show in what sense the presence of the past makes ideas, feelings, and symbols evolve more slowly than is often believed.

Notes

Chapter 1

1. The myth of the tabula rasa (the belief cherished by libertarian ideologists of child rearing), that infants are born free of any parental imprint, is popular for the same reasons. The popularity of the myth explains the ambivalent reactions of the American public toward Alexander Mitscherlich (1969). Indeed, his book hits hard at the ahistoricity of so many American ideologies. Of course, the allusion to the book's title should not be taken literally: the notion of "father" evokes the authority of the past; it involves, therefore, both parents.
2. Textbooks on the sociology of the family are mute on the issue of inheritance in modern America (for example, Sussman and Steinmetz 1987). It should be added that at least one reviewer of the National Science Foundation has used the silence of most authors to reject the funding of a research proposal concerning the inheritance practice of Korean immigrants in America as being trivial.
3. For an example of this stress placed on luck in explaining monetary success, see Christopher Jencks (1979).
4. In this regard, one can only deplore the benign neglect of Theodore Caplow and his associates (1982) of the heirship practices of Middletown. To pay attention to the Christmas gifts of friends and relatives and to disregard more significant but more dramatic forms of inter- and intragenerational solidarity suggests a blind faith in the opportunities for mobility offered by the American social structure.
5. For an historical analysis of eugenics in America and an overview of how the conceptions of heredity have evolved between environmental and genetic extremes, see Carol Rosenberg Smith (1974). For an examination of the relations between heredity and intelligence, see the whole controversy generated by remarks on the genetic versus the environmental nature of intelligence (Dobzhanski 1968; Jensen 1969).
6. For a systematic analysis of the evolving tension between the egalitarian ideology and the patterns of stratification of American society, see Edward Pessen (1971, 1973).
7. For illustrations of this preference, see Joan Huber and William Form (1973). Closer to us, see James Kluegel and Eliot Smith (1986). In contrast, see J. Porter and his analysis of the social stratification operating in Toronto (1965).
8. For an illustration, see M. L. Fellows, R. Simon, and W. Rau (1978) or M. Sussman, J. Cates, and D. Smith (1970).
9. This attitude is expressed by many rich Americans who have been peri-

odically interviewed on their intentions concerning the use of the wealth they have accumulated [see, for example, Kirkland (1986) or Matthews (1991)].

10. For example, Kingsley Davis and Wilbert Moore (1945) argue implicitly that, in contrast to education or occupation, money is value free and does not, therefore, univocally evoke achievement.

11. As social scientists themselves believe in the mythology of social mobility, they feel dispensed from looking at the behaviors and practices of all strata of their society. Since they think they owe their own social status to their creativity, they deny the existence of any other avenue to success except work and self-actualization. As a result, their scientific activities become articles of faith rather than reasoned acts inspired by scientific doubts.

12. It is revealing in this regard to observe that American liberal social scientists have not taken Rawls (1971) to task for making this observation, which undermines many of the institutions they cherish, notably the whole process of schooling.

13. The question of their interrelations remains unsolved. For some ideologies, the road toward progress requires greater liberty. For others, it must be conducive to greater equality.

14. The resolution of conflicts originating from the liability of large economic organizations illustrates the shortcomings of decentralization. It would be less of a nuisance for plaintiffs to plead their case in a federal court and to follow federal guidelines than to sue their giant opponents in a state jurisdiction, as they are often obliged to do for the time being. The outcome is more predictable in the first instance.

15. In the case of the sculptor Louise Nevelson, the conflict was particularly bitter. Her relatives underline the generosity that she displayed toward her assistant during her lifetime. Friends of the assistant retort that the relations between Louise Nevelson and her son were strained, that she wrote pieces warning against the illusions of motherhood and finally, point out that two documents posterior to the will drawn by Nevelson in favor of her son concern the gift of forty seven sculptures to her assistant.

16. It should be noted that Adam Smith's position is not always valid. In certain socioeconomic environments, it is more efficient to appoint beneficiaries to a variety of income-producing or power-yielding organizations.

17. Interestingly enough, the notion of "heir" remains alive. It is used to describe successors to a position of authority, regardless of the contribution to the selection process by the person who has stepped down.

18. The unfolding of the feud opposing one of the wealthiest Manhattan landowners to his twin sons represents a graphic illustration of the difficulties of a smooth transition (Scardino 1989).

19. The expression "pursuit of happiness" is an element of the American dream since it is often a euphemism for the pursuit of wealth.

20. Of course, detractors of the welfate state retort that the impersonal style of interaction that prevails in public institutions not only lowers the quality of the services rendered, but also undermines existing familial loyalties.

21. For example, when decedents make their bequests contingent on the provision that some of their relatives be appointed to the executive board of the agencies they sponsor, they affirm their preeminence over the interests of the state. Further, the loose accounting system of foundations enables many of them to escape the control of the state (Barber 1983).

22. I believe in this regard that the profession has not paid sufficient attention to the pleas of Cicourel (1974) and of Gouldner (1976).

Chapter 2

1. As quoted by F. Raison Jourde (1991:705), who shows how, on the one hand, their adherence to the cult of the dead and, on the other, the mix of envy and admiration they have for Westerners symbolizes the tension that the inhabitants of Madagascar experience between the continuity required by identity and the change that accompanies modernization. This tension fascinates Europeans, because they are becoming blind to its consequences.

2. Incidentally, the stress placed on the reproductive functions of educational activities minimizes unduly the autonomy of educational personnel. Why should such personnel do the bidding of the elites? More important, this emphasis is contradicted by the hostility that elites have historically displayed toward educational development.

3. One should note that biotechnics may change both the problems of adoption and of inheritance. The freezing of sperm and ovules may alter the constraints that shape intergenerational bonds.

4. Thus, inheritance may involve the gratuitous transfer of the list of patients or clients.

5. The whole literature on birth order is perplexing in this regard from both a substantive and methodological viewpoint. First, differences between first- and later-born are not stable but vary with both the economic complexity of society at large and the phases of the economic cycle. They seem to be more marked when the economy is in the doldrums. Second, as shown by Polit (1982), differences are more documented for certain psychological areas than others and for certain phases of the life cycle than others. Last, the whole issue may be spurious, as there seems to be a systematic birth order distribution of social scientists involved in the study of birth order.

6. This does not prevent the occurrence of conflicts between the decedent's survivors and third parties. For example, see T. Lewin's summary (1990) of the legal action of a lesbian against the employer of her late companion.

7. Vernier (1989) gives an extraordinary account of the relationship between the name of one's spouse and the name of one's parent of the opposite gender in function of birth order and the size of the family.

8. For an empirical analysis of the forms of symbolic capital transferable across generations, see L. L. Cavalli Sforza, M. W. Feldman, K. H. Chen, and S. M. Dornbusch (1982).

9. Of course, neo-Darwinist writers overemphasize the impact of the processes of genetic selection on the vagaries of economic life. But conversely, such processes are systematically denied by so-called liberal intellectuals.

10. For an example of how sociologists can reduce unduly the concept of reproduction to macrosocial terms, see J. Dickinson and R. Russell (1986).

11. Furthermore, whatever they may transfer is transferred sub rosa without documentation.

12. For a review of the literature on college choices, see C. Manski and D. Wise (1983). However, as this literature pays attention to disparities in the aca-

demic trajectories of children from different families rather than those of siblings, it confirms the arbitrary nature of the individualistic bias present in American sociology. The effects of scarce resources may be as intensely experienced within the same family as across families. For the most part, sociologists act as if parents contribute to shape educational aspirations but do not foot the bill.

13. While popular scientific literature acknowledges the effect of the fear of dying on individual moral judgments, the evidence produced to support the phenomenon is rather strange. For instance, morality is assessed in terms of how much money people are willing to invest on a "principle." Furthermore, one of the principles invoked concerns the obligation to squeal on individuals who have mugged innocent passersby (Goleman 1989). Is informing on somebody really a universal form of virtue?

14. Whereas few American sociologists are concerned with the distributions of marriages between distinct national groups, even fewer seem interested in determining the extent to which the "inheritance rules" of the husband's national group prevail over those of the wife's.

15. The Irish model of inheritance has been initially described by Arensberg and Kimball (1948), even though some authors have since brought in a number of nuances and shades (O'Grada, 1980). The German model is briefly evoked by Mitterauer and Sieder (1982).

16. The differential erosion of national culture among Americans raises two significant methodological problems. First, analyses of the relevant behaviors or attitudes should not seek to assess the relative salience of national origin treated as a synthetic overall variable, in relation to other independent synthetic variables. Instead, these analyses should be comparative: how do these behaviors and attitudes respond differentially to the same stimuli as a function of the specific national origin of respondents? In other words, one should compare how much of the variance of the distributions of the relevant attitudes or behaviors one can explain in the case of the Irish-Americans and the German-Americans. In addition, in view of the symbolic qualities of national origin, it may be wiser to probe practices rather than attitudes. Even though an overwhelming majority of Americans deny that ethnic identity had any impact on their marriage, this does not mean that they ever practiced ethnic exogamy. Nor does it mean that their choice of an "outsider" as a conjugal partner has not been conducive to specific linguistic, residential, or legal compromises.

17. Wherever inheritance is a relatively important event in familial life, there is proportional stress on the role of women as socialization agents (Le Wita 1988).

18. While S. McNamee and R. Miller (1989) allude to the segmentation of labor markets, one can generalize their arguments and posit that differences in the types of capital accumulated foster differences in the logic governing transfers *mortis causa*. As an example, the constraints and opportunities offered by movable, fungible, and real assets differ from one another.

19. This technique of social control has been described in great detail by Leo Kuper in his analyses of the South African mix of class and caste.

20. The arrangement is known as *levirate*. Even though It disturbs the hierarchy of cowives, the details of the arrangement have hardly been explored by anthropologists.

21. For an illustration of the first view, see T. Bottomore (1975). For an illustration of the second view, see N. Chodorow (1977).

Chapter 3

1. A positivist researcher has criticized me for using the full census of an African city, rather than relying on a random sample. The procedure he recommended does not make sense when nobody knows what African urban populations look like. One cannot know what sample should be used in order to obtain a miniature representative of the range of behaviors typical of modern African urban dwellers.
2. This is the source of the fascination exerted by wills on the public imagination. This fascination sometimes pertains to the dating of the relevant documents. President Kennedy, for example, never changed the will he wrote six years before being elected. Other wills attract attention because of the calligraphy of the signatures. But the greatest fascination comes from the provisions of the document. For a recent survey of wills written by famous Americans see H. Nass (1990).
3. Of course, it remains necessary to determine whether this estimate reflects less the poverty of economic statistics of the period than the actual distribution of wealth.
4. For a less recent view of the distribution of American wealth, see Projector and Weiss (1966).
5. To improve this notion of proxy, I could have paired 1920 and 1944 decedents with the same family names. But this would have made the construction of the sample even more difficult.
6. This raises questions about the dates when insurance companies took off. Zelizer (1979) dates this take-off earlier than seems appropriate.
7. Of course, the frequency with which decedents made gifts to churches could have allowed me to infer their religious denomination. This, however, would have introduced another bias in the information used.
8. In Europe itself, the contrast may be more complex than it appears at first glance. In Ireland, the extent to which impartibility means primogeniture seems to depend, inter alia, on the age difference between father and first son. Primogeniture tends apparently to prevail in the case of decedents who married late (O'Grada 1980). Further, as far as Germany is concerned, dominant heirship strategies differ across regions.
9. For the population born in 1944, our choices are somewhat validated by the data concerning their place of birth. Thirteen out of fourteen decedents included in the sample born in Germany were German, and the five born in Ireland were Irish. Yet, it was not true that all decedents classified as German or as Irish were indeed born either in the United States or in the corresponding European country. Thus, one supposedly Irish female decedent was born in Germany. Her case illustrates the methodological and substantive difficulties raised by interethnic marriages. Not only is it difficult to ascertain the national origin of married females, but in addition, the nature of the informal or formal inheritance laws retained by ethnically mixed couples in the United States remains unknown. Further, the fact that one decedent had been born in Wales and another one in Canada raises the problem of determining the incidence of intermediary migrations and its effect on inheritance practices.
10. The use of the manifest of the passengers of this ship was inspired by A. G. Roeber (1987) and by Walker (1964).

11. The reason for not using the word *capitalist* suggests amusing changes in the meaning of the word. In both the 1920 and 1944 samples, the word means investor, revealing that the pursuit of wealth per se may be a full-time occupation.

12. In this sense, the situation is less structured than in sub-Saharan Africa and other traditional societies, where interethnic marriages are governed by a body of complex rules specifying the conditions under which the legal traditions from which husbands and wives originate apply to their interactions.

13. The absence of a reliable code has prevented the use of matrimonial status to form the sample.

14. Even though the gap has gotten smaller over the years, the German-Americans seem to have been more successful than the Irish-Americans in the pursuit of wealth.

15. The figures indicated here come from an inspection of the listing provided by IRS and on which the ultimate selection of my sample is based.

16. For another analysis of the attrition caused by the type of analysis suggested here, see Tomes (1988).

17. While some economists are inclined to do so, they are not followed by sociologists.

18. see M. L. Fellows, R. Simon, and W. Rau (1978). One wonders why the authors of the study have not preferred to assemble a stratified sample of wills throughout the individual states or at least through the nation's subsystems and ascertain the actual rank ordering of heirs established by testators. This solution would have enabled them to assess the limits within which wills depart from the model of succession elaborated by state authorities and hence to determine whether the dispositions of wills are written, with or without reference to the immediate context.

19. I use the word *qualitative* in the same sense as C. Ragin (1987). I differ from that author insofar as I think that the choice of a qualitative method has as much to do with what the observer knows as with the character of the object of the study. The qualitative method is necessary whenever theories are mute or inadequate to inspire new modes of analysis.

20. These data come from the "Bulletin on the Statistics of Income" of the Treasury Department.

21. These data originate from the "Census Reports" for the appropriate years.

22. The first data come from Leonore Weitzman (1985:Table C-4). The second originate in C. Shammas, M. Salmon, and M. Dahlin (1987).

Chapter 4

1. In this regard, one can only deplore the ill-conceived applications of neoclassical economy typical of so many social scientists who prefer bad measurements to no measurements. Indeed, Bourdieu (1970) has reminded us that various forms of capital are not evaluated on objective grounds. In education, it is therefore preferable to refer to cultural capital rather than to human capital.

2. This explains why changes in the value assigned to esthetic artifacts do not follow linear patterns but are more likely to reflect cycles whose duration varies over historical time (Reitlinger 1961; Moulin 1976).

3. See Richard Easterlin (1980).

4. In the case of the two cohorts, the amount of debt incurred by individual estates is uniformly low. About one-fourth of estates have no debts and another fourth have debts less than $1,000.

5. Inspection of the estate tax files in the sample suggests that borrowers were often members of the same ethnic group as the decedent, especially in the case of the German-Americans.

6. This represents a particular form of passive ownership evoked by Alexander (1991).

7. American geographic mobility is partially explained by the desire *not* to continue paying "school taxes" after one's children have all graduated from high school.

8. Although IRS returns do not provide a systematic recording of individual decedents' occupations, the fact remains that these decisions are also influenced by the selective information that people in various occupations acquire about the opportunities and constraints of distinct markets. The IRS files enabled me to distinguish, albeit not on a systematic basis, between farmers, self-employed businessmen, and executives. To be sure, the occupational titles used by IRS agents are sometimes puzzling. For example, some decedents are recorded as capitalists. Especially during the 1920s, the title was not derogatory. Instead, it referred to the desire to mobilize capital. Developer or investment banker would be the corresponding title in current parlance. In the following equations, I do not always use the same occupation, since the link between occupations and the assets owned is likely to vary.

9. For 1944, since the file includes the matrimonial status of respondents, this particular variable is added in order to determine the differential responses of widowers and widows in relation to those who leave a surviving partner.

10. As suggested by Rossi and Rossi (1990), decisions concerning familial investments are also influenced by whether the group is intact, and hence by histories of deaths or of divorces.

11. As the file includes information about birthplaces, it is possible to compare individuals who passed away in the state where they were born and those who moved during their lifetime.

12. The use of nonstandardized regression coefficients does not facilitate comparisons across independent variables that cover distinct range of values. On the other hand, the use of such coefficients facilitates the comparisons of the same independent variables across equations.

13. It would have been appropriate to run factorial analyses to ascertain the actual clusters of assets accumulated by decedents in the two subsamples. Unfortunately, there was no program to do this analysis with the computer available.

14. It should be noted that for the 1920 cohort, the presence of both sons and daughters caused an increase in the value of the real estate owned by decedents.

15. The fact that in 1944 male investments in realty were higher than those of women reflects the fact that men also owned a larger number of lots. These two relationships help to underline the continuing role played by realty in the *production* of income.

16. The lack of mobility includes both individuals who were born in the same state where they died and individuals who migrated directly from their country of origin.

17. When one substitutes the number of secondary stocks for the number of high-quality titles in the relevant equation, the total amount of variance accounted for drops from .591 to .445 for 1920, and from .189 to .136 for 1944. Further, for 1920, the contribution of estate size increases from .511 to .533. Similarly, the contribution of occupation (executives), which was not significant, becomes significant at the .01 level with a raw coefficient of 76.080. The only change for 1944 concerns a sharp increase in the contribution of estate size from .177 to .299.

18. Results of the survey undertaken by A. and P. Rossi more recently (1990:467–68) suggest that the presence of life insurance policies peaks during the middle years for married men and women. The incidence of policy owners declines with age, because the declining importance of their obligations induces them to make other investments.

19. I do not report here data concerning the state bond markets. Not only do the markets involve a relatively limited segment of the population, but in addition, the choice to participate in such a market seems to be socially randomly distributed.

20. The analysis of the number of title held by decedents in the bond market pertains to both corporate and state bonds.

21. An impressionistic observation of the listings of such investments suggests that German-American decedents tended to loan their monies to borrowers who had the same national origin. One can infer that German-American communities remained more cohesive during that period than their Irish-American counterparts. The importance of daughters evokes also, albeit indirectly, the role of trust in this type of investment. Both the occurrence of promissory notes or mortgages and endogamy are independent indicators of the salience of trust as a determinant of social interaction among neighbors. But it may also be that the second variable acts as a prerequisite to both mortgages and promissory notes. In many societies, individuals agree to lend money by relying on real securities or on simple commitments through the bonds they have woven with the familial groups into which their daughters have married.

22. It is noteworthy that whereas the presence of daughters stimulated an increase in the number of mortgages ($t = 2.70$) held by 1944 decedents, it had no effect on the value of these mortgages. Conversely, the presence of daughters had a negative effect on the value of promissory notes, but not on their numbers. In short, the consequences of spreading risks differ across markets.

23. The salience of automobiles in estate tax returns reflects two distinct phenomena. It may reflect the adoption of a particular life-style (the increase in the number of cars being the result of the diffusion of this particular innovation). But as already noted, the phenomenon may also be imputed to the obligation for automobile owners to record their deeds, which prevents the executors of their estates from disposing of this item sub rosa.

24. This suggests how recent the growth and the rationalization of American art markets might be a phenomenon related to the emergence of New York as a major art center.

25. It is puzzling to note that in some estate tax returns, carpets are estimated at a higher value than rugs. During a period devoted to technical progress, the definition of rugs as handmade places them in a less desirable category than carpets, which are made mechanically and symbolize the triumph of technology.

Chapter 5

1. See in this regard the whole literature on the progress of the culture of narcissism in American culture, notably Lasch (1978). Indeed, narcissism discourages intergenerational solidarity.
2. This point is stressed by L. Thurow (1975), who sees trusts as instruments enabling testators to exert power on heirs rather than as instruments designed to minimize taxes.
3. This finding illustrates the economic relevance of the notion of cultural capital.
4. It should be noted that the influence of widowhood does not seem to be stable, since the results reported by Sussman, Cates, and Smith (1970) and by Rossi and Rossi (1990) do not go in the same direction.
5. This line of reasoning is derived from L. Weitzman (1985). Many observers of the American social scene have observed that prenuptial agreements are more frequent in second than first marriages. Insofar as the purpose of such agreements is to separate the financial bonds of individuals with their successive spouses and their successive issues, this separation makes sense only if its purpose is to maximize the testators' degrees of freedom as to the final destination of the assets accumulated. The results reported by Rossi and Rossi (1990) confirm the validity of such speculations.
6. Such a contrast may reflect changes in the accounting system of IRS authorities, who were not initially concerned with the fiscal incidence of joint tenancy on estate taxes. But the contrast may also reflect changes in either the fiscal behavior of American couples or the actual feelings that spouses have for one another.
7. IRS officials have been convinced for so long that testacy had become a quasi-universal practice of Americans that they dropped questions regarding the use of wills from their files. The question was reintroduced in 1989.
8. The very fact that individuals with large insurance policies have also drawn wills suggests that the differentiation of assets implies a parallel differentiation of their destinations.
9. From that perspective, it is difficult to compare wills that have been written at differing moments of the life cycle. In addition, the destruction of earlier versions of the same wills prevents any assessment of their editing, notably the identification of the heirs added or of the heirs eliminated.
10. Even though the limited number of cases prevents appropriate analyses, it would clearly be important to identify the variety of age limits that testators use as boundaries between distinct types of benefits. For instance, in the case of trusts that allow progressive access to the capital constituting the individual bequest, it would be revealing to ascertain whether variations in the ages at which individual heirs initially acquire partial and then full control over their bequeaths are systematically distributed along national, social class, or cultural lines. For example, to the extent that trusts allow heirs to get 50 percent of the principal when they reach 25 years of age and the remained after their 30th birthday, are these two limits alike for sons and daughters? Does the extent and the direction of gender variations depend on the social class or on the national origin of the testator?
11. A colleague indicated to me that his dying father made him swear that

the family clock would be passed to his grandson rather than his granddaughters. This promise was symbolically important since the names of the successive heirs of the clock are recorded on its back.

12. The limited number of cases involving the transfer of stocks and bonds suggests that they have limited symbolic properties. Yet, as corporate securities have become a major form of asset, it would make sense to ascertain whether their symbolic properties have become more salient or whether heirs get the proceeds of the sale of these securities, without even knowing which titles the testator had acquired.

13. For instance, Canadian testators bequeath a larger part of the estate to members of their family than to nonrelatives, to their offspring or their siblings than to extended kin, to their offspring than to their siblings, and in the case of small estates to their daughters than to their sons (Smith, Kish, and Crawford 1987).

14. The figures obtained do not add up to 100 percent for two reasons. The universes are different (the alternative to the selection of a spouse being any child). In addition, testators may have chosen an executor outside the alternative.

15. Contrasts between early and late wills summarize correlations between the actual date of the will and the choice of an executor treated as a dummy variable (presence/absence). Determinants of the selection of daughters as executors are not presented in Table 5.4.

16. The gains of married women in this regard were not necessarily systematic. They were apparently more marked in the East than in the West (Shammas, Salmon, and Dahlin 1987:201).

17. However limited, the emergence of selective bonds between mothers and daughters reported here is consistent with the findings of Rosenfeld (1979a and b) on more recent patterns of inheritance. Indeed, the greater the solidarity between mothers and daughters, the more discriminating the former are likely to be in the expectations they harbor toward the latter.

18. In her various publications, S. Salamon 1980; Salamon and O'Reilly 1979; Salamon and Lockhart 1980; Salamon and Davis Brown 1988) suggests indirectly that this type of male solidarity is still operating among the farmers of the Midwest who die testate.

19. As the numbers get too small, it is impossible to make hard-nosed statistical analyses. It is not surprising to note that sons-in-law are more likely to receive the income of a trust than daughters-in-law and that the gifts offered to the latter are conditional on the continuation of their current matrimonial status.

20. Bourdieu (1972) puns on the French expression *parent pauvre* (that is, the least successful relative) to suggest that such a *parent pauvre* is also *pauvre en parenté*, that is, that he has few relatives.

21. For a $R^2 = .06$, the raw regression coefficient is .073 for age, .481 for gender, and -1.144 for percentage of the estate invested in life insurance, as far as the 1920 population is concerned. For $R^2 = .03$, the relevant regression coefficients are .018, .484, and $-.477$, as far as the 1944 population is concerned.

Chapter 6

1. Moore (1967) calls these reciprocal services "serial" to evoke their sequential order during the lifetimes of parents and their children. Caldwell (1982) and,

Notes

after him, Levine (1985) call them "intergenerational flows of wealth" to suggest that depending on societal complexity, the direction of the reciprocal services effectively rendered by members of adjacent generations changes.

2. Even though Thernstrom (1964, 1973) eloquently documents ethnic variations in patterns of wealth accumulation, he does not say anything about the impact of the differences of what is transferred and to whom on patterns of social mobility.

3. As we shall see from the present empirical data, equality is difficult to assess. One can evaluate the number of eligible heirs who are totally disinherited, but one can also assess the percentage of estates for which shares are equal or relatively equal. But even so, differing methodologies yield differing results. For example, Tomes (1988) reports that the most extreme favoritism allows the preferred heir to get 73 percent of all available bequests. Yet, for Menchik (1988), the relevant figure is only 55 percent.

4. Personal communication of Ms. McCubbin.

5. The evidence produced by Smith, Kish, and Crawford (1987) remains, however, fraught with ambiguities: first because the period of time during which the sample of wills was collected remains unclear; and second, because it is not clear whether decedents had both sons and daughters.

6. A friendly reader of Salamon (1980) may object that the author never writes about the origin of the differences between the German- and the Irish-Americans. I am not doing any better. Differences can reflect the greater heterogeneity of the communities from which the two ethnic groups originate. They can also reflect the distinctive migratory experiences of these two ethnic groups. But they can also reflect their differential adaptation to the American labor market.

7. I am extending here the argument developed by J. Cole and E. Wolf (1974) in their study of a valley separating Austria from Italy.

8. The findings of Alba (1990) and of Waters (1990) on the declining significance of ethnicity in America raise two questions. As ethnicity is not a global term, the analysis should consist in comparing the structures of attitudes and practices across distinct ethnic groups rather than in assessing the overall contribution of ethnicity to such structures. In addition, the overt ambivalence of Americans toward the cultures of their countries of origin cannot but taint the use of questionnaires. Further, answers to such questionnaires often fail to discriminate between normative expectations and adaptation to the familial context. For an illustration of this distinction, see the contrasting answers of Korean respondents to the questionnaire used by Cheung Moon Cho (1989). Unfortunately, insensitivity to cultural specificity is rather frequent. For an illustration, see Cherlin and Furstenberg (1986).

9. This relatively high percentage may be explained in three complementary ways. First, testators expect their children to take care of the surviving spouse. Second, conjugal obligations may have been defined through prenuptial decrees. Finally, widowers and widows are present in the sample.

10. There is some contrary evidence of this phenomenon. Thus, male decedents who gave a specific share of the estate to their wife were also more likely to have a larger number of beneficiaries. Correlation between the two variables increases from .147 to .302 from 1920 to 1944.

11. Here, I examine the ratio between the entire range of values observed for the particular category of assets under consideration and the value of the entire estate.

12. The percentages that follow are computed on the basis of decedents who drew a will and had at least two children.
13. In Cleveland, Tomes (1988) reports that 11 percent of testators excluded at least one child.
14. The same test could not be made for 1920, since the tape made by IRS does not include the number of children, which can only be surmised from the raw data.
15. This included a nun, who, the testator wrote, had no needs.
16. The evaluation of inequalities is not always easy to do since some categories of assets were evaluated as a whole, which prevents accurate assessments of the individual shares obtained by children.
17. The numbers indicated here do not add up to 100 percent. The remaining figures mirror inequalities that affected both sons and daughters.

Chapter 7

1. But when he failed really to give him the corresponding authority, he allowed his closest associates to stage a rebellion that threatened the survival of the company.
2. The best-known students of nationalities in American sociology (Richard Alba, Andrew Greeley, Stanley Lieberson) pay a lot of attention to the distribution of these phenomena. To my taste, they do not pay a sufficient amount of attention to the consequences of these distributions on the retention of national identity. For example, are mixed couples (Italian-American males and Irish-American females or vice versa) more Irish- or Italian-American in certain key aspects of their familial choices? What are the determinants of the differential salience of their Irishness or their Italianness?
3. I am surprised by the relative frequency with which the children of the individuals included in the sample have run away from their homes.
4. In contrast to American analysts, who are indifferent on the consequences of fiscal incentives on home ownership and the formation of a transferable capital, French authors stress the significance of institutional factors in the formation of estates, notably as far as realty is concerned. For an example, see Capdevielle (1986).

References

Adams, B. 1972. "Birth Order: A Critical Review." *Sociometry* 35:411–39.
Adams, B. and M. Meidam. 1968. "Economics, Family Structure and College Attendance." *American Journal of Sociology* 74:23–39.
Adams, J. 1980. "Personal Wealth Transfers." *Quarterly Journal of Economics* 95:159–79.
Alba, R. 1988. "Cohorts and the Dynamics of Ethnic Change." Pp. 211–28 in *Social Structures and Human Lives*, edited by M. Riley, B. Huber, and B. Hess. Beverly Hill, CA: Sage.
———1990. *Ethnic Identity: The Transformation of White America*. New haven, CT: Yale University Press.
Alexander, G. 1991. "Pensioners in America: The Triumph and Failures of Passive Ownership." Paper presented at the Law and Society International Meetings, Amsterdam.
Alston, L. J. and M. P. Shapiro. 1984. "Inheritance Laws across Colonies: Causes and Consequences." *Journal of Economic History* 44:277–87.
Arensberg, C. and S. Kimball. 1948. *Family and Community in Ireland*. Cambridge, MA: Harvard University Press.
Aries, Philippe. 1981. *The Hour of Our Death*. New York: Pantheon.
Baker, R. 1989. *The Good Times*. New York: Plum Books.
Barber, B. 1983. *The Logic and Limits of Trust*. New Brunswick, NJ: Rutgers University Press.
Becker, G. 1981. *A Treatise on the Family*. Cambridge, MA: Harvard University Press.
Becker, G. and N. Tomes. 1976. "Child Endowments and the Quantity and Quality of Children." *Journal of Political Economy*, 84:143–62.
Becker, G. and N. Tomes. 1986. "Human Capital and the Rise and Fall of Families." *Journal of Labor Economics* 4,3:51–539.
Behrman, J., R. Pollak, and P. Taubman. 1982. "Parental Preferences and Provisions for Progency," *Journal of Political Economy* 90:52–78.
Bellah, R., R. Madsen, W. Sullivan, A. Swidler, and S. Tipton. 1985. *Habits of the Heart: Individualism and Commitment in American Life*. Berkeley: University of California Press.
Berkner, L. K. 1976. "Inheritance, Land Tenure and Peasant Family Structure: A German Regional Comparison." Pp. 71–95 in *Family and Inheritance*, edited

by J. Goody, J. Thiersk, and E. P. Thompson. Cambridge: Cambridge University Press.
Black, H. 1987. "Planning for Co-habitants." *Symposium Abstracts of the Foundation of Thanatology.*
Blau, P. 1964. *Exchange and Power in Social Life.* New York: Wiley.
Blinder, A. 1976. "Inequality and Mobility in the Distribution of Wealth." *Kyklos* 29:607–36.
Blumberg, P. 1980. *Inequality in an Age of Decline.* New York: Oxford University Press.
Bodnar, J., et al. 1982. *Lives of Their Own.* Ithaca, NY: Cornell University Press.
Bottomore, T. 1975. "Structure and History." Pp. 159–71 in *Approaches to the Study of Social Structure,* edited by P. Blau. New York: Free Press.
Boudon, R. 1986. *L'Idéologie: L'Origine des Idées Reçues.* Paris: Fayard Universitaires de France.
Boulding, K. 1975. "The Pursuit of Equality." Pp. 11–28 in *The Personal Distribution of Income and Wealth,* edited by J. Smith. New York: Columbia University Press.
Bourdieu, P. 1972. "Les Stratégies Matrimoniales dans les Stratégies de Reproduction." *Annales ESC* 4–5.
Bourdieu, P. and J. C. Passeron. 1964. *Les Héritiers.* Paris: Editions de Minuit.
———. 1970. *La Reproduction.* Paris: Editions de Minuit.
Bowles, S. and H. Gintis. 1986. *Capitalism and Democracy.* New York: Basic Books.
Brennan, E., A. James, and W. Morrill. 1981. "Inheritance, Demographic Structure and Marriage." *Journal of Family History* 7:289–98.
Brittain, J. 1978. *Inheritance and the Inequality of Material Wealth.* Washington, D.C.: Brookings.
Caldwell, J. 1982. *Theory of Fertility Decline.* New York: Academic Press.
Capdevielle, J. 1986. *Le Fétichisme du Patrimoine.* Paris: Presses de la Fondation Nationale des Sciences Politiques.
Caplow, T., et al. 1982. *Middletown Families.* New York: Bantam Books.
Carrier, J. 1991. "Gifts, Commodities, and Social Relations: A Maussian View of Exchange." *Sociological Forum* 6,1:119–136.
Carroll, E. and S. Salamon. 1988. "Share and Share Alike: Inheritance Patterns in Two Illinois Farm Communities." *Journal of Family History* 13:219–32.
Cavalli-Sforza, L. L., M. S. Feldman, K. H. Chen, and S. M. Dornbusch. 1982. "Theory and Observation in Cultural Transmission." *Science* 218(I, October):19–26.
Cherlin, A. and F. Furstenberg. 1986. *The New American Grandparent: A Place in the Family, A Life Apart.* New York: Basic Books.
Chester, R. 1982. *Inheritance, Wealth and Society.* Bloomington: Indiana University Press.
Cheung Moon Cho. 1989. "The Study Of Inter-generational Material Transfers of Korean Americans." Ph.D dissertation, University of Maryland, College Park.
Chiswick, B. 1978. "The Effects of Americanization on the Earnings of Foreign-born Men." *Journal of Political Economy* 86:897–921.

Chodorow, N. 1977. *The Social Reproduction of Mothering*. Berkeley: University of California Press.
Cicourel, A. 1974. *Theory and Methods in a Study of Fertility in Argentina*. New York: Wiley.
Cohen, D. 1990. "The Fall of the House of Wang." *Business Month* (February):23–37.
Cole, J. and E. Wolf. 1974. *The Hidden Frontier. Ecology and Ethnicity in an Alpine Valley*. New York: Academic Press.
Coleman, J. S. 1990. *Foundations of Sociological Theory*. Cambridge, MA: Harvard University Press.
Collins, R. 1975. *Conflict Sociology*. New York: Academic Press.
Comte, A. 1848. *General View of Positivism*. Stanford, CA: Academic Reprints.
Cornell, L. 1988. "Taking Reproduction Seriously: Marxism and the Modern Family in China and Japan. Pp. 101–14 in *Social Structures and Human Lives*, edited by M. Riley, B. Huber, and B. Hess. Beverley Hills, CA: Sage.
Craig, D. 1979. "Immortality through Kinship: The Vertical Transmission of Substance and Symbolic Estate" *American Anthropologist* 81:94.
Crane, D. 1972. *Invisible Changes*. Chicago: University of Chicago Press.
Csikszentmihalyi, M. and R. Hochberg Halton. 1981. *The Meaning of Things*. New York: Cambridge University Press.
Cuddihy, J. 1974. *The Ordeal of Civility*. New York: Dell.
Curtis, R. 1986. "Household and Family in Theory on Inequality." *American Sociological Review* 51:463–81.
Davis, K. and W. Moore. 1945. "Some Principles of Stratification." *American Sociological Review* 10:242–49.
DePalma, A. 1989. "Small Farms Bloom as New Jerseyans Return to Roots." *New York Times* (July 26).
Dickinson, J. and R. Russell. 1986. *Family, Economy and State*. New York: Saint Martin's.
DiTomaso, N. 1982. "Sociological Reductionism from Parsons to Althusser: Linking Action and Structure in Social Theory." *American Sociological Review* 47:14–25.
Ditz, T. 1986. *Property and Kinship*. Princeton, NJ: Princeton University Press.
Dobzhansky, T. 1968. "On Genetics, Sociology and Politics." *Perspectives in Biological Medicine* 2:544–54.
Donzelot, J. 1979. *Policing the Family*. New York: Pantheon.
Dunham, A. 1963. "The Method, Process and Frequency of Wealth Transmission at Death." *University of Chicago Law Review* 30:241–85.
Dupont, V. and F. Dureau. 1988. "Renouveler l'Approche de la Dynamique Urbaine par l'Analyse des Migrations." *Pratiques Urbaines*. Paris: ORSTOM CNRS.
Durkheim, E. 1957. *Professional Ethics and Civic Morals*. London: Routledge and Kegan Paul.
Easterlin, R. 1980. *Birth and Fortune: The Impact of Numbers on Personal Welfare*. New York: Basic Books.
Ekeh, P. 1974. *Social Exchange Theory*. Cambridge, MA: Harvard University Press.

Elder, G. 1974. *Children of the Great Depression*. Chicago: University of Chicago Press.
Farber, B. 1973. *Family and Kinship in Modern Society*. Glenview, IL: Scott Foresman.
Farnham, A. 1990. "The Windfall Awaiting New Heritors." *Fortune* (May):72–78.
Fellows, M. L., R. Simon, and W. Rau. 1978. "Public Attitudes about Property Distribution at Death and Intestate Succession Laws in the United States." *American Bar Foundation Research Journal* 2:319–91.
Feyerabend, 1975. *Against Methods*. Atlantic Highlands, N.J.: Humanities Press.
Finkelstein, H. 1954. "Composers and Public Interest: The Regulation of Performing Rights Society." *Law and Contemporary Problems* 19:275–93.
Friedman, L. 1966. "The Law of the Living, the Law of the Dead: Property, Succession and Society." *Wisconsin Law Review* 2:340–78.
Gasson, R., et al. 1988. "The Farm as a Family Business." *Journal of Agricultural Economics*:1–42.
Gilligan, C. 1982. *In a Different Voice: Psychological Theory and Women's Development*. Cambridge, MA: Harvard University Press.
Glendon, M. A. 1987. *Abortion and Divorce in Western Law*. Cambridge, MA: Harvard University Press.
Goblot, E. 1980. *La Barrière et le Niveau*. Paris: Presses Universitaires de France.
Goldthorpe, J. 1987. *Family Life in Western Society*. Cambridge: Cambridge University Press.
Goleman, D. 1989. "Fear of Death intensifies Moral Codes, Scientist find." *New York Times* (December 5).
Goode, W. 1963. *World Revolution and Family Patterns*. New York: Free Press.
Goody, J. 1973. "Strategies of Heirship." *Comparative Studies in History and Society* 15:1–19.
———. 1976. "Introduction." Pp. 1–17 in *Family and Inheritance*, edited by J. Goody, J. Thiersk, and E. P. Thompson. Cambridge: Cambridge University Press.
Gotman, A. 1988. *Heriter*. Paris: Presses Universitairs de France.
Gouldner, A. 1960. "The Norm of Reciprocity: A Preliminary Statement." *American Sociological Review* 25:161–78.
———. 1970. *The Coming Crisis in Western Sociology*. New York: Basic Books.
———. 1976. *The Dialectics of Ideology and Technology*. New York: Seabury Press.
Greenhalg, S. 1985. "Sexual Stratification: The Other Side of Growth with Equity in East Asia." *Population and Development Review* 11:265–314.
Green, K. 1973. "Inheritance: Unjustified?" *Journal of Law and Economics* 16:418.
Greenhouse, C. 1989. "Just in Time: Temporality and the Cultural Legitimation of Law." *Yale Law Journal* 98 (8):1631–51.
Gregory, C. A. 1989. *Observing the Economy*. London: Routledge and Kegan Paul.
Greven, P. 1970. *Four Generations: Population, Land and Family in Colonial Andover*. Ithaca, NY: Cornell University Press.
Grossberg, M. 1985. *Governing the Hearth. Law and the Family in Nineteenth Century America*. Chapell Hill: University of North Carolina Press.
Habakkuk, D. 1955. "Family Structure and Economic Change in Nineteenth Century Europe." *Journal of Economic History* 15:1–15.

Halbach, P. 1977. *Death, Taxes, and Family Property*. Saint Paul, MN: West.
Hauser, R. and W. Sewell. 1985. "Birth Order and Educational Attainment in Full Sibships." *American Educational Research Journal* 22:1–23.
Henretta, J. 1979. "Race Difference in Middle Class Life Style: The Role of Home-ownership." *Social Science Research* 8:63–78.
Henretta, J. and R. Campbell. 1978. "Net Worth as an Aspect of Status." *American Journal of Sociology* 83:1204–23.
Hill, R. 1970. *Family Development in Three Generations*. New York: Shenkman.
Hochschild, J. 1981. *What's Fair? American Beliefs About Distributive Justice*. Cambridge, MA: Harvard University Press.
Homans, G. 1961. *Social Behavior: Its Elementary Forms*. New York: Harcourt and Brace.
Horwitz, M. 1977. *The Transformation of American Law*. Cambridge, MA: Harvard University Press.
Huber, J. and W. Form. 1973. *Income and Ideology*. New York: Free Press.
Hyde, L. 1983. *The Gift: Imagination and the Erotic*. New York: Vintage.
Jaher, F. 1982. *The Urban Establishment*. Urbana: University of Illinois Press.
Jencks, C. 1979. *Who Gets Ahead in America? The Determinants of Economic Success in America*. New York: Basic Books.
Jensen, A. 1969. "How Much Can We Boost I.Q. and Scholastic Achievement?" *Harvard Educational Review* 39:1–123.
Kammeyer, K. 1966. "Birth Order and the Female Sex Role among College Women." *American Sociological Review* 31:508–15.
Keim, C. R. 1968. "Primogeniture and Entail in Colonial Virginia." *William and Mary Quarterly* 25 (third series):545–86.
Kessler, D. and A. Masson. 1988a. *Le Patrimoine des Français*. Paris: Hachette.
———. 1988b. "On Five Hot Issues on Wealth Distribution." *European Economic Review* 32:644–53.
———. 1989a. "Bequests and Wealth Accumulation: Are Some Pieces of the Puzzle Missing?" *Journal of Economic Perspectives* 3:141–52.
———. 1989b. "Qui possede quoi et pourquoi?" *Revue d'Economie Financiere* 10:51–71.
Kirkland, R. 1986. "Should You Leave It All to Your Children?" *Fortune* (September 29):18–26.
Kluegel, J. and E. Smith. 1986. *Beliefs About Inequality: Americans' Views of What Is and What Should Be*. New York: Aldine De Gruyter.
Kobrin, F. and C. Goldscheider. 1978. *The Ethnic Factor in Family Structure and Mobility*. Cambridge: Ballinger.
Kolko, Gabriel. 1962. *Wealth and Power*. New York: Praeger.
Kubat, D., M. Porter, and G. Landa. nondated. "Delving into Probated Wills: A Methodological Note." Mimeo, University of Waterloo.
Langbein, J. 1989. *The Twentieth Century Revolution in Family Wealth Transmission*. Occasional paper No. 25 of the University of Chicago Law School.
Lansing, J. and J. Sonquist. 1969. "A Cohort Analysis of Changes in the Distribution of Wealth." Pp. 31–74 in *Six Papers on the Distribution of Wealth and Income*, edited by L. Soltow. New York: Columbia University Press.
Lasch, Christopher. 1978. *The Culture of Narcissism*. New York: Norton.

Laurie, B. 1980. *Working People of Philadelphia 1800–1850*. Philadelphia: Temple University Press.
Levi Strauss, C. 1957. "The Principle of Reciprocity." Pp. 84–94 in *Sociological Theory: A Book Of Readings*, edited by L. Coser and B. Rosenberg. New York: McMillan.
———. 1958. *Anthropologie Structurale*. Paris: Plon.
Levine, D. 1985. "Industrialization and the Proletarian Family in England. *Past and Present* 107:194–206.
Levine, D., E. Mitchell, and R. Havighurst. 1984. *Opportunities for Higher Education in a Metropolitan Area: A Study of High School Seniors in Kansas City*. Bloomington Phi Delta Kappa, Boston: Allyn and Bacon.
Levine, R. A. 1973. *Culture, Personality, and Behavior*. Chicago: Aldine.
Lewin, T. 1990. "Suit over Death Benefits Asks: What Is a Family? *New York Times* (September 21).
Le Wita, B. 1988. *Ni Vue Ni Connue*. Paris: Editions de la Maison des Sciences de l'Homme.
Lichtman, R. 1982. *The Production of Desire*. New York: Free Press,
Lieberson, S. 1980. *A Piece of the Pie*. Berkeley: University of California Press.
Lindert, P. 1977. "Sibling Position and Achievement." *Journal of Human Resources* 12:198–220.
Maine, H. 1954. *Ancient Law*. London: Dent.
Manski, C. and D. Wise. 1983. *College Choice in America*. Cambridge, MA: Harvard University Press.
Marcus, F. 1989. "Does Napoleonic Law Have Future in Louisiana?" *New York Times* (December 1).
Marcus, G. 1980. "Law in the Development of Dynastic Families among American Business Elites: The Domestication of Capital and the Capitalization of the Family." *Law and Society Review* 14:859–902.
———. 1983. *Elites: Ethnographic Issues*. Albuquerque: University of New Mexico Press.
———. 1989. "The Problem of the Unseen World of Wealth for the Rich; Toward an Ethnography of Complex Connections." *Ethos* 17:110–19.
Matthews, A. 1991. "Alma Maters Court Their Daughters." *New York Times Sunday Magazine* (April 7):40.
Mayer, A. 1980. *The Persistence of the Ancient Regime*. New York: Pantheon.
McCubbin, J. and J. Rosenfeld. 1989a. "Introducing an IRS Data Base for Estate Tax Research." *Trust and Estates* 128(3):62–66.
———. 1989b. "Looking Deeper into the New IRS Data." *Trust and Estate* 128(11):52–56.
MacLysaght, E. 1985. *The Surnames of Ireland*. Dublin: Irish University Press.
McNamee, S. and R. Miller. 1989. "Estate Inheritance: A Sociological Lacuna." *Sociological Enquiry* 39:7–29.
Menchik, P. 1980a. "Primogeniture, Equal Sharing and the U.S. Distribution of Wealth." *Quarterly Journal of Economics* 44:299–315.
———. 1980b. "The Importance of Material Inheritance." Pp. 159–86 in *Modeling the Distribution and Inter-Generational Transmission of Wealth*, edited by J. Smith. Chicago: University of Chicago Press.
———. 1988. "Unequal Estate Division: Is It Altruism, Reverse Bequests, or

Simply Noise?" Pp. 128–42 in *Modelling the Accumulation and Distribution of Wealth*, edited by D. Kessler and A. Masson, Oxford: Oxford University Press.

Merton, R. and E. Barber. 1963. "Sociological Ambivalence." Pp. 97–120 in *Sociological Theories, Values and Socio-Cultural Change*, edited by E. Tiryakian. Glencoe, IL: Free Press.

Michelat, G. and M. Simon. 1977. *Classe, Religion, et Comportement Politique*. Paris: Presses de la Fondation Nationale des Sciences Politiques.

———. 1985. "Determinants Socio-Economiques, Organisations Symboliques et Comportement Electoral." *Revue Francaise de Sociologie* 26(1):32–69.

Miller, D. and G. Swanson. 1958. *The Changing American Parent*. New York: Wiley.

———. 1960. *Inner Conflicts and Defenses*. New York: Wiley.

Miller, P. 1965. *The Life of the Mind in America*. New York: Harcourt and Brace.

Mitscherlich, A. 1969. *Society without the Father*. New York: Harcourt and Brace.

Mitterauer, M. and R. Sieder. 1982. *The European Family, from Patriarchy to Partnership from the Middle Age to the Present*. Oxford: Blackwell.

Moore, Wilbert. 1964. "Predicting Discontinuities in Social Change." *American Sociological Review* 29:331–38.

———. 1967. *Order and Change*. New York: Wiley.

Morris, R. B. 1927. "Primogeniture and Entailed Estates in the United States." *Columbia Law Review* 27:24–51.

Moulin, R. 1976. "Les Intermittences Economiques de l'Art." *Traverses* 11:34–48.

Nass, H., 1990. *Wills of the Rich and Famous*. New York: Warner.

Newby, H., C. Bell, D. Rose, and P. Saunders. 1979. *Property, Paternalism, and Power*. Madison: University of Wisconsin Press.

Newell, S. 1980. "Wealth of Testators and Its Distribution." Pp. 95–138 in *Modeling the Distribution and Intergenerational Transmission of Wealth*, edited by J. Smith. Chicago: University of Chicago Press.

Newell, W. 1986. "Inheritance on the Maturing Frontier: Butler County Ohio, 1803–1865." Pp. 261–303 in *Long Term Factors in American Economic Growth*, edited by S. L. Engerman and R. E. Gallman. Chicago: University of Chicago Press, National Bureau of Economic Research.

Odendahl, T. 1990. *Charity Begins At Home: Generosity and Self-Interest among the Philanthropic Elites*. New York: Basic Books.

Ogburn, W. 1955. *Technology and the Changing Family*. Boston: Houghton-Mifflin.

O'Grada, C. 1980. "Primogeniture and Ultimogeniture in Rural Ireland." *Journal of Interdisciplinary History* 10(3):491–97.

Parkin, F. 1979. *Marxism and Class Theory: A Bourgeois Critique*. New York: Columbia University Press.

Pessen, E. 1971. "The Egalitarian Myth and the American Social Reality." *American Historical Review* 76:989–1034.

———. 1973. *Riches, Class, and Power before the Civil War*. Lexington, MA: Heath.

Piaget, J. 1951. "Pensée Egocentrique et Pensée Sociocentrique." *Cahiers Internationaux de Sociologie* 10:34–49.

Polit, D. 1982. *Effects of Family Size*. Washington, D.C.: Department of Commerce.

Porter, J. 1965. *The Vertical Mosaïc*. Toronto: University of Toronto Press.

Price, J. 1975. "Transmission of Wealth at Death in a Community Property Jurisdiction." *Washington Law Review* 50:277–340.

Projector, D. and G. Weiss. 1966. *Survey of Financial Characteristics of Consumers.* Federal Reserve technical papers, August. Washington, D.C.

Prosterman, R. and T. Hanstad. 1990. "Fight the Deficit with Estate Taxes." *Washington Post* (September 5):A-19.

Ragin, C. 1987. *The Comparative Method: Moving beyond Qualitative and Quantitative Strategies.* Berkeley: University of California Press.

Raison Jourde, F. 1991. *Bible et Pouvoir à Madagascar au XIXéme Siècle.* Paris: Karthala.

Rawls, J. 1971. *Theory of Justices.* Cambridge, MA: Harvard University Press.

Reitlinger, G. 1961. *Economics of Taste.* New York: Rhinehart, Holt and Winston.

Roeber, A. G. 1987. "The Origin and Transfer of German-American Concepts of Property and Inheritance." *Perspectives in American History,* 3, 115–171.

Rosen, S. 1988. "Human Capital." Pp. 681–88 in *The New Palgrave, A Dictionary of Economics,* edited by J. Eatwell, M. Milgate, and P. Newman. New York: Stockton.

Rosenberg Smith, C. 1974. "The Better Fruit: Heredity, Disease and Social Thought in XIXth Century America." *Perspectives in American History* 8:189–235.

Rosenblatt, P., et al. 1985. *The Family in Business.* San Francisco: Jossey Bass.

Rosenfeld, J. 1974. "Inheritance: A Sex Related System of Exchange." Pp. 400–11 in *The Family: Its Structures and Functions,* edited by R. Laub Coser. New York: Saint Martin's Press.

———. 1979a. *The Legacy of Aging.* Norwood: Ablex.

———. 1979b. "Old Age, New Beneficiaries: Kinship, Friendship and (Dis)inheritance. *Sociology and Social Research* 64:86–98.

———. 1980. "Social Strain of Probate." *Journal of Marital and Family Therapy.* 327–32.

———. 1982. "Disinheritance and Will Contest." *Marriage and Family Review* 5:75–86.

———. 1991. "The Heir and the Spare: Evasiveness, Role Complexity, and Patterns of Inheritance" in *Social Roles and Social Institutions,* edited by J. Blan and N. Goodman, Boulder, CO: Westview Press.

Rossi, A. 1965. "Naming Children in Middle Class Families." *American Sociological Review* 30:499–513.

Rossi, A. and P. Rossi. 1990. *On the Human Bond.* Hawthorne, NY: Aldine de Gruyter.

Rubinstein, W. 1980. *Wealth and the Wealthy in the Modern World.* New York: St. Martin's Press.

Ryan, A. 1984. *Property and Political Theory.* London: Blackwell.

Ryder, N. 1965. "The Concept of Cohort in the Study of Social Change." *American Sociological Review* 30:840–61.

Sabine, G. 1956. "Justice and Equality." *Ethics* 67:1–11.

Salamon, S. 1980. "Ethnic Differences in Farm Family Land Transfers." *Rural Sociology* 45:290–308.

Salamon, S. and K. Davis Brown. 1988. "Farm Continuity and Female Land Inheritance: A Family Dilemma." Pp. 195–210 in *Women and Farming: Changing Roles, Changing Structures*, edited by W. Haney and J. Knowles. Boulder, CO: Westview Press.

Salamon, S. and V. Lockhart. 1980. "Land Ownership and the Position of Elderly in Farm Families." *Human Organization* 39:324–31.

Salamon, S. and S. O'Reilly. 1979. "Family Land and Developmental Cycles among Illinois Farmers." *Rural Sociology* 44:525–42.

Scardino, A. 1987. "A Real Estate Empire Stirs a Family Feud." *New York Times* (February 23).

Schama, S. 1989. *Citizens: A Chronicle of the French Revolution*. New York: Knopf.

Schlossberg, N. 1983. *Counselling Adults in Transition: Linking Practice with Theory*. New York: Springer.

Schneider, D. 1980. *American Kinship*. Chicago: University of Chicago Press.

Schoenblum, J. 1987. "Wills Contests: An Empirical Study." *Real Property Probate and Trust Journal* 22:607–59.

Shammas, C., M. Salmon, and M. Dahlin. 1987. *Inheritance in America*. New Brunswick, NJ: Rutgers University Press.

Sheehy, G. 1978. *Passages*. New York: Bantam.

Sheshinski, E. and Y. Weiss. 1982. "Inequality within and between Families." *Journal of Political Economy* 90:105–28.

Smith, J. 1975. "White Wealth and Black People: The Distribution of Wealth in Washington D.C. in 1967." Pp. 329–64 in *The Personal Distribution of Income and Wealth*, edited by J. Smith. New York: Columbia University Press.

Smith, M., B. Kish, and C. Crawford. 1987. "Inheritance of Wealth as Human Kin Investment." *Ethology and Sociobiology* 8:171–82.

Solmon, L. 1974. "The Relationship between Schooling and Saving Behaviors." Pp. 253–92 in *Education, Income and Human Behavior*, edited by F. T. Juster. New York: McGraw-Hill.

Soltow, L. 1971. *Patterns of Wealth Holding in Wisconsin Since 1850*. Madison: University of Wisconsin Press.

———. 1975a. *Men and Women in the United States*. New Haven, CT: Yale University Press.

———. 1975b. "Wealth, Income and Social Class." Pp. 233–76 in *The Personal Distribution of Income and Wealth*, edited by J. Smith. New York: Columbia University Press.

Sorokin, P. 1925. "American Millionaires and Multimillionaires." *Social Forces* 5:627–40.

Steelman, L. and B. Powell. 1989. "Acquiring Capital for College." *American Sociological Review* 54:844–56.

Stys, W. 1957. "The Influence of Economic Conditions on the Fertility of Peasant Women." *Population Studies* 11:136–48.

Sussman, M. and S. Steinmetz. 1987. *Handbook of Marriage and the Family*. New York: Plenum Press.

Sussman, M., J. Cates, and D. Smith. 1970. *The Family and Inheritance*. New York: Russell Sage.

Tarver, J. 1952. "Intra-family Farm Succession Practices." *Rural Sociology* 17:250–62.

Teltsch, K. 1990. "Founded by Idealists, Group Thrives on Needs." *New York Times* (January 30).

Terrell, J. 1971. "The Wealth Accumulation of Black and White Families: The Empirical Evidence." *Journal of Finance* 26(3):365–78.

Thernstrom, T. 1964. *Poverty and Progress*. Cambridge, MA: Harvard University Press.

———. 1973. *The Other Bostonians*. Cambridge, MA: Harvard University Press.

Thompson, M. 1979. *Rubbish Theory*. New York: Oxford University Press.

Thurow, L. 1975. *Generating Inequality: Mechanisms of Distribution in the U.S. Economy*. New York: Basic Books.

Tickamyer, A. 1981. "Wealth and Power: A Comparison of Men and Women in the Property Elite." *Social Forces* 60:463–81.

Titus, S., P. Rosenblatt, and R. Anderson. 1979. "Family Conflicts over Inheritance of Property." *The Family Coordinator* 28:337–46.

Tocqueville, A. de. 1969. *Democracy in America*. Garden City, N.Y.: Doubleday Anchor.

Tomes, N. 1988. "Inheritance and Inequality within the Family." Pp. 79–102 in *Modelling the Accumulation and Distribution of Wealth*, edited by D. Kessler and A. Masson. Oxford: Clarendon Press.

Torrey, B. 1990. "A 64,000 Dollars Question: What Are the Aged Doing with Their Assets?" *Population and Development* 23:17–27.

Treas, J. 1988. "Money in the Bank: Transaction Costs and Privatized Marriage." Paper presented at the Annual Meeting of the Population Association of America New Orleans April 20–23.

Tuckman, H. 1973. *The Economics of the Rich*. New York: Random House.

Tumin, M. 1967. *Social Stratification*. Englewoods Cliffs, NJ: Prentice-Hall.

Vernier, B. 1989. "Fetichisme du Nom, Echanges Affectifs intra-Familiaux et Affinites Electives." *Actes de la Recherche en Sciences Sociales* 78:2–17.

Walker, M. 1964. *Germany and the Emigration 1815–1886*. Cambridge, MA: Harvard University Press.

Ward, E. and J. Beuscher. 1950. "The Inheritance Process in Wisconsin." *Wisconsin Law Review* 396–426.

Waters, M. 1990. *Ethnic Options: Choosing Identity*. Berkeley: University of California Press.

Weber, M. 1968. *Economy and Society*. New York: Free Press.

Weitzman, L. 1985. *The Divorce Revolution*. New York: Basic Books.

Whiting, J. and I. Child. 1953. *Child Training and Personality*. New Haven, CT: Yale University Press.

Williamson, James and Peter Lindert. 1980. "Long Term Trends in American Wealth Inequality." Pp. 9–19 in *Modeling the Distribution and Intergenerational Transmission of Wealth*, edited by J. Smith. Chicago: University of Chicago Press.

Winch, R. 1963. *Identification: Its Familial Determinant*. Indianapolis: Bobbs Merrill.

Wolf, D. 1984. "Kin Availability and the Living Arrangements of Older Women." *Social Science Research* 13:72–89.

Wolfson, M. 1980. "Bequest Process and Causes of Inequality in the Distribution of Wealth" Pp. 187–222 in *Modeling the Distribution and Intergenerational Transmission of Wealth*, edited by J. Smith. Chicago: University of Chicago Press.

Woods, E. 1928. *The Sociology of Life Insurance*. New York: Appleton.

Wyatt Brown, B. 1982. *Southern Honor*. New York: Oxford University Press.

Yaganisako, S. 1978. "Variations in American Kinship: Implications for Cultural Analysis." *American Ethnologist* 5:15–29.

Zelizer, V. 1979. *Morals and Markets*. New York: Columbia University Press.

———. 1988. "From Babies' Farms to Baby M." *Society* 25:23–7.

Zidjerveld, A. 1970. *The Abstract Society.* Garden City, NY: Doubleday.

Index

Abstract (Society), 92–94
Adams, J., 155
Adams, B., 160
Age, 3, 6, 28, 35, 40, 71–72, 75, 86–90, 100, 104, 107, 111, 113, 114, 119, 123, 127
   effects on testacy, 130–132, 135, 136, 138, 145, 149, 150, 153, 162, 165, 168, 172, 176–178, 186, 190, 198
   general assessment of, 200–201, 205
Alba, R., 219n, 220n
Alger, Horatio, 1, 42, 66, 189, 206
Alston, L. J., 13
Aries, P., 49
Arizona, 17, 126
Ascriptive equality, 156–157, 161–162
Asset, 4, 17, 21–22, 39–41, 60, 66, 74, 76, 78, 80–82, 86–88, 90, 92–93
   determinants in their composition, 96–102, 104, 106–111, 120–121, 125–126, 128, 130, 133–134, 138–141, 144, 153, 160, 171, 174, 176–177, 184–187
   general assessment of their effects, 195–197
   variability of, 94–96

Barber, B., 23, 158, 163, 210n
Baker, R., 191
Becker, G., 156, 158–159
Behrman, J., 155, 161
Bellah, R., 191
Berkner, 35, 125
Beneficiaries (number of), 151–153
Biological, 7, 21, 35–36

Birth order, 160, 162, 165, 171, 180, 203, 211n
Black, H., 125
Blau, 157
Brown, D., 169
Bonds (federal, state, or corporate), 4, 76, 78–79, 81, 83, 85, 92, 95–96, 99, 102–104, 106
   contribution to individual wealth, 114–115, 120–121, 145, 168, 174, 176, 185–187, 192
Bonds (social), *see* solidarity (forms of)
Bottomore, T., 212n
Bourdieu, P., 31, 54, 98, 152, 214n, 218n
Bowles, S., 2, 39, 53
Brittain, J., 7, 87, 131
Bucks County, 61, 129, 131, 134, 166–167
Businessman, 70, 90, 109, 130, 145, 193–194

Caldwell, J., 163
Campbell, R., 75
Capitalism, 9, 15, 18, 30, 45, 115, 214n
Carrier, J., 157, 192
Carroll, E., 34, 50, 68, 98, 127
Cates, J., 61, 129, 167
Chester, R., 7, 23, 25
Cheung Moon Cho, 76–77, 169
Child rearing, 3, 32, 36–37, 57, 164
Children (illegitimate), 16–17, 37
Children (number of), 94, 101, 107, 114, 126, 136, 145, 147, 151–152, 162, 166, 173, 175, 178, 181, 199, 202

Index

Chiswick, B., 87
Chodorow, N., 212n
Class (social or wealth), 26–27, 35, 40, 42–44, 49–50
  and reproduction, 51–52, 57, 65, 66, 70, 76, 81, 85, 90, 96, 98, 114, 123, 163, 164, 193, 198, 205
Cohen, D., 193
Cole, J., 127
Coleman, J. S., 156
Collins, R., 41, 75
Common law property states, 74, 90, 126, 202–203
Craig, D., 37
Crane, D., 43
Csikezentimihalyi, M., 97
Cultural, 3–6, 24, 26–27, 29–30, 37, 41, 44, 47–50, 52–53, 56, 58, 61, 67, 71, 74, 96–99, 113, 116, 119–120, 126, 128, 138, 151, 153, 156, 163–165, 176, 181, 187, 191–192
Curtis, R., 75

Daughters, 11, 17–18, 26, 32–33, 36, 40, 53–55, 74, 76–77, 101, 107, 112, 114, 116, 119, 126, 134, 136, 141–145, 147, 150, 160, 163, 166–167, 170, 173, 175, 180–185, 187, 192, 196, 198–200, 203, 205
  effects of marriage on, 112, 114, 116, 134, 149, 161, 180, 185–186, 192, 197, 202
  status of daughters-in-laws, 49–50, 143, 151, 192
Deposits (bank), 102, 104, 106, 116–117
DiTomaso, N., 54
Ditz, T., 17, 56, 170
Divorce, 57, 77, 87, 93, 95, 126, 132–133, 162, 167–168, 190, 192–193, 200, 206
Dobzhansky, T., 36, 209n
Durkheim, E., 25, 157
Dynasty, 159

Education, 15, 31, 35, 41–43, 52–53, 55, 62, 70, 76, 83–84, 87–90, 93–95, 98, 127–128, 160–161, 164–165, 169, 180, 194–195
Efficiency, 7, 15–20, 40, 45, 64, 88, 96, 140–142, 157–161, 170
Ekeh, P., 157
Endogamy, 48, 69, 87, 166, 212n, 216n, 220n
Engels, F., 30–31
Equality, 2–3, 10–16, 18, 22, 24, 28, 30–31, 33–34, 36–37, 41–42, 44–45, 56, 63, 68, 74, 77, 80, 136, 183, 192, 197, 199, 201–202, 204
  and the distribution of human capital, 42–43
  and the distribution of travel opportunities, 44, (see also liberty)
  and the distribution of wealth, 41–42
Estate tax, 15, 20, 22–25, 63, 76, 78, 95, 101, 217n
Ethnicity, (see national origin)
Executives, 70, 112, 114, 141, 152, 175
Executor (of wills), 19, 146–151, 161, 173, 184, 192, 196, 199, 200

Farber, B., 13, 17
Farming, 4, 21, 55, 61–62, 68, 70, 90–91, 96, 98, 107, 118, 121, 127, 130, 133, 141, 149, 153, 159, 168, 175, 183, 191, 193, 200
Farnham, M. L., 126, 129, 131, 209n
Federal, 14–15, 22–23, 63–65, 73, 77, 99, 104, 106, 114, 158, 190
Female (see women)
Finkelstein, H., 93
Forms (of solidarity)
  vertical vs. horizontal, 72, 146–147, 171–174
Functionalist, 1–2, 53

Gay (see homosexuals)
Gender, 3, 18, 26, 28, 31, 35, 38, 40, 43, 49–50
  effect on reproduction, 52–54, 66, 68, 70–72, 74–75, 77, 87, 94, 97, 100–101, 109, 119, 123

effect on testacy, 131–132, 136, 141–145, 147, 150, 153, 160, 163, 166–167, 170, 173, 175
  inequality of bequests due to, 180–185, 187, 192, 196
  general assessment of gender, 198–200, 203, 205
Genetic, 35–36, 38, 39
German, 4–5, 27, 34, 45, 48, 50–51, 61–62, 68–70, 73, 97, 107, 111, 113–115, 120, 127, 136, 138, 152, 165, 169, 184, 191, 193, 201, 212n, 216n
Gilligan, C., 199
Gintis, H., 2, 39, 53
Glendon, M.A., 118
Goblot, A., 51
Gouldner, A., 75, 157, 204, 206, 211n
Grandparents, 4, 57, 97, 142, 151, 153, 193
Greenhouse, C., 157
Grossberg, M., 17

Hauser, R., 160
Henretta, J., 75, 98
Heredity, 7, 36, 38, 209n
Heritage, 38, 128
Historical time, 26, 54, 64, 66–67, 206–207
Homans, G., 57
Homeownership, 164–165
Homosexuals, 20, 57, 125, 211n
Horowitz, M., 15, 19
Hyde, L., 156
Human capital (see education

Identification, 46
Illinois, 34, 62, 68, 72, 168
Immigration, 1, 68, 87, 128, 165, 169
Income, 84, 86, 89–91, 93–95, 100, 105–106, 109, 129–130, 143, 151, 159, 160–161, 168, 170–172, 177–179, 186, 193, 199
Individualism, 8, 34, 76, 90, 101, 123–126, 136, 140, 173, 176, 186, 189, 191

Inheritance,
  and cultural stability, 5–6
  and familial bonds, 4–5
  and reciprocity, 162–164
  and social class, 3–4
  and sociology of knowledge, 6–10
Intergenerational, 1–3, 15, 23, 26, 30, 36–37, 41, 51–52, 54, 56, 61, 64, 66, 71, 76, 85, 92, 147, 190, 193, 199, 202
Intestacy, 22, 32, 124
Irish, 4–5, 50–51, 61–62, 68–69, 70, 73, 107, 111, 115–116, 120, 136, 138, 152, 165, 169, 184, 191, 193, 195, 201, 212n, 216n
Isolation, 48–49

Jencks, C., 62, 155, 209n
Jewelry, 78, 83–84, 91, 99, 119, 126, 144, 205
Joint tenancy, 77, 134–135

Kessler, D., 64, 84, 86

Langbein, J., 42, 194
Lansing, J., 86, 89
Legitimacy, 2, 10, 16, 20, 21, 26, 29, 31, 36–37, 44–45, 47, 49–50, 57–58, 64, 66–67, 82, 96, 125, 136, 144, 158, 161, 163, 167, 198, 201, 204, 206
Legitimation (see Legitimacy)
LeWita, B., 52
Liberty (see also equality), 10–13, 16, 18, 25, 28, 34, 45, 210n
Lieberson, S., 52, 220n
Life insurance, 67, 91, 94, 97, 99, 103, 104, 106
  contribution to the estate, 113–114
Lindert, P., 36, 155
Logics, cultural vs. material (see material, symbolic or cultural)
Louisiana, 14, 17, 102, 126

Maine, H., 25, 34, 48, 123, 140, 173
Masson, 64, 84, 86
Material, 1–5, 8, 14, 26, 29, 32, 33,

Index

Material (*continued*)
  38, 40, 46–47, 50–52, 55, 82, 97, 119–121, 125, 134–135, 155, 158–159, 163–164, 174, 176, 192, 194, 200
Matrimonial mobility (*see* divorce)
Mathews, A., 170, 210
Mc Cubbin, J., 72, 219n
McNamee, S., 8, 76, 212n
Menchik, P., 62, 170, 219n
Miller, D., 51–52
Miller, P., 11, 93
Miller, R., 8, 76, 212n
Modernization, 101, 147, 165–169, 171, 174
Mobility, 1, 3–4, 15, 17–18, 39, 41, 65, 78, 97, 101–102, 111, 127, 136, 189, 192–193, 209n, 215
Moore, W., 1, 53, 218n
Mortgage, 89, 92, 99, 102–104, 106
  contribution to estate, 115–116, 120, 164–165, 176, 185, 187
Mothers, 147, 151, 154, 170, 180, 191, 200, 206

National origin, 3, 18, 26–27, 35, 40, 43, 49
  and reproduction, 50–51, 57, 61–62, 66–67
  and sampling, 68–69, 77, 97–97, 101, 113, 116, 119, 126–128, 135–138, 153, 163, 169, 187, 197, 198
  general assessment of national origin, 201–202, 205
Natural, 11, 21, 29, 31, 42, 91, 126
New York, 21, 22, 55, 102
Nonfarm assets, 104, 106
  contribution to the estate, 108–111, 120

Occupation, 3, 36, 43, 46–49, 51, 55, 57, 62
  and sampling, 70, 77, 82, 86–87, 90, 94, 100, 114, 121, 126, 130–132, 141, 149, 169, 197
Odendahl, T., 151, 159

Partibility, 56, 63, 159, 169, 177, 205
Patriarchy, 30, 44, 53, 57, 146–147, 149, 174, 176, 180–181, 196, 201
Personal property, 78, 91, 95, 97, 99, 118–119, 126, 144–145, 160
Pessen, E., 15, 41–42, 55, 209n
Pollak, R., 155, 161
Popularity of assets, 92, 102–104, 113, 115, 117, 119
Primogeniture, 11, 13–14, 43, 55, 56, 68, 127, 143, 160, 170, 204
Property rights, 8–9, 12–13, 18, 20–23, 45, 90, 95–97, 155

Rawls, J., 210n
Reality, 4, 14, 21, 52, 78, 82–83, 85, 91, 95–96, 99, 103
  contribution to the estate, 107–108, 119–121, 128–129, 134, 138–141, 145, 153, 160, 165, 168, 174, 176, 178–179, 193, 196–197, 215n
Reference group, 2, 34, 40, 154
Regression, 46–47
Religion, 1, 27, 35, 40, 49–50, 57, 62, 66, 126, 163, 198
Replication, 33–34
Representative, 6, 10, 11, 27, 59–60, 62, 66, 78, 206
Reproduction, 6, 26–27, 29–58, 65–67, 88, 102, 121, 156, 189, 191–196, 201, 203–206
  interpretive and mechanical forms, 54–56, 121, 193–194
Revolution, 1, 10–13, 34, 41, 47–48, 67, 69, 86, 88, 123
Risks, 82, 87, 88, 90–91, 94–97, 100, 104, 106–107, 111–112, 114, 117, 120, 130, 150, 161, 174, 179, 185, 187, 195–201
Roeber, A. G., 48, 128, 213n
Rosenfeld, J., 53, 61, 72, 170, 204, 218n
Rossi, A., 38, 127–128, 130–131, 133, 161, 168, 170, 197, 200, 215n
Ryan,, A., 156
Ryder, N., 26

Salamon, S., 30, 34, 50, 61, 98, 127, 169, 218n, 219n
Salmon, M., 33, 82, 129, 131, 134, 167, 171
Schama, S., 11
Segmentation (of capital markets), 4, 31, 40, 43, 49, 52, 81–83, 118
Shammas, C., 33, 82, 129, 131, 134, 167, 171
Siblings, 3, 33, 36, 76, 85, 151, 212n, 218n
Sociological time, 66–67
Solmon, L., 76, 87
Soltow, L., 87, 88
Sons, 3, 11, 13, 18, 25, 32–33, 36, 40, 43, 53–55, 57, 68, 77, 101, 107, 125–127, 133, 140, 142–144, 146–147, 149, 160, 162, 164, 166–170, 177, 180–184, 192–193, 196–202, 204
  status of sons-in-law, 17–18, 36, 146, 151, 192
State, 2, 6, 8, 11–14, 17, 20, 22–25, 32, 34, 65, 73–74, 80–81, 90, 93, 95–96, 100–102, 104, 107, 109, 111–115, 118, 120–121, 124, 126, 134, 140–141, 146, 150, 153, 198, 209n
Stocks, 4, 76, 78–79, 81, 83, 85, 93, 98, 111–112
  contribution to the estate, 120–121, 126, 138, 140, 145, 153, 168, 174, 185, 187, 196, 209n
Sussman, M., 61, 129, 167, 189, 205, 209n
Symbolic, 1–3, 8, 24–26, 29, 32–34, 37–38, 44, 46, 49, 51, 54–55, 82, 84, 97, 106, 119, 124, 140–141, 144–145, 152–154, 159, 163, 167, 174, 181, 192, 195

Thernstrom, T., 97, 165, 219n
Thompson, M., 83, 98, 198
Titles (number of), 100, 104–107, 112, 115–118, 195–196
Tocqueville, A de, 32, 55–56, 118, 156, 194
Tomes, N., 62, 155, 214n, 219n, 220n
Trusts, 167–168, 172, 177–179, 181, 184, 187, 192, 199, 217n

Urban, 85, 90–91, 97, 102, 104, 109, 112–113, 117, 119, 120, 136–137, 141, 150, 168, 181, 194, 197

Validity, 59, 61, 71, 75, 79, 203–206

Weber, M., 45, 161
Weitzman, 4, 22, 214n, 217n
Widows, 3, 22, 31, 54, 79, 94, 132, 144, 171–174
Wills (date of), 174, 176, 181, 217n
Winch, R., 46
Wisconsin, 72, 129, 168
Woods, E., 23, 65
Women, 16–18, 27, 30, 49, 53, 70–72, 74, 87, 91, 97, 101, 109, 112, 114, 120, 123, 131–133, 141, 149, 153, 162, 168, 170–171, 177–179, 181, 192, 198, 200
  married women, 18–19, 31, 37, 132
Wyatt, B., 17, 38, 159

Yankees, 34, 61, 98

Zelizer, J., 21, 88, 94